MW01106131

UNITY IN CHRIST AND COUNTRY

UNITY IN CHRIST AND COUNTRY

American Presbyterians in the Revolutionary Era, 1758–1801

WILLIAM HARRISON TAYLOR

THE UNIVERSITY OF ALABAMA PRESS
Tuscaloosa

The University of Alabama Press
Tuscaloosa, Alabama 35487-0380
uapress.ua.edu

Typeface: ACaslon

Manufactured in the United States of America
Cover image: *Covenanters in a Glen* by Alexander Carse, c. 1800, oil on canvas;
courtesy of the University of Edinburgh Fine Art Collection
Cover design: Todd Lape/Lape Designs

Cataloging-in-Publication data is available from the Library of Congress.
ISBN: 978-0-8173-1945-8
E-ISBN: 978-0-8173-9088-4

For Denise, William, Timothy, and Rachel

Contents

Acknowledgments

While working on this project I have been blessed to have many colleagues, family and friends help make this book a reality. First and foremost is my wife, Denise. Not only has she been a source of comfort and encouragement but she has—even from our first date—challenged me to be a better scholar. Times beyond count she has marshaled her skills as a voracious reader and an exceptional writer to help me translate my first drafts into intelligible prose. Without her, you might still be waiting to read this book. I also owe a great deal to Peter C. Messer of Mississippi State University, who helped me give shape to the idea that would become this book. Fortunately, he has been offering encouragement and helpful critiques ever since we met, and I cannot thank him enough for this support and friendship. Thanks are also due to Jason K. Phillips, M. Kathryn Barbier, Richard V. Damms, Gideon Mailer, David Harmon, Gretchen Adams, Michael Markus, Mehdi Estakhr, Ann Mezzell, Elizabeth Peifer, Aaron Horton, Brian McNeil, and Brian O'Mahoney for taking time from their own scholarship to read either all or part of the manuscript and to graciously give their advice; the book is all the better for it. I am also indebted to Lee Gatlin, Michael Howell, and Patrick Curles who, perhaps too quickly, agreed to edit the occasional chapter when Denise had had her fill. Thank you; your efforts have not been forgotten. Neither has the continual support and encouragement I received from my parents, Raymond and Lynda Taylor. Any list I might attempt to write would be a grave disservice to how much you have helped. Thank you.

I would also like to thank Alabama State University for helping contribute funds for my research. I want to acknowledge the kind staff of the Presbyterian Historical Society, the Congregational Library, the University of Kentucky archives, the Mississippi State University Library, and Alabama State University's Levi Watkins Learning Center for their help in my research. I am also appreciative of the wonderful guidance I have received from the editorial staff of the University of Alabama Press, especially Daniel Waterman, Joanna Jacobs, and the anonymous reviewers. I am also grateful to the University of Alabama Press for allowing me to work with the gifted historian and copyeditor S. Scott Rohrer during this process. Finally, I would like to thank the editors and reviewers of the journals that published early versions of my work and helped me hone my study of these Presbyterians pursuing Christian unity. A portion of the first chapter originally appeared as "'Let Every Christian Denomination Cheerfully Unite': The Origins of Presbyterian Interdenominationalism" in the March 2014 issue of the *Journal of Religious History*, and a selection from the fifth chapter appeared as "Unintended Consequences: Southern Presbyterians and Interdenominationalism in the late Eighteenth Century" in the September 2010 issue of the *Journal of Southern Religion*.

UNITY IN CHRIST AND COUNTRY

Introduction

In this book I argue that a self-imposed interdenominational transformation began in the American Presbyterian Church upon its reunion in 1758
and that the church's experience during the American Revolution altered
this process. The resulting interdenominational goals had both spiritual and
national objectives. As the leaders in the Presbyterian Church strove for
unity in Christ and country, I contend that they created fissures in the
church that would one day divide it as well as further the sectional rift that
would lead to the Civil War. The late colonial and early republican Presbyterian Church warrants study not only because of the prestigious positions
Presbyterians held in academia, society, and government but also because
the church is one of the best representations of a colony/nationwide denomination.[1] In this position the church was able to offer its services, largely through the printed word, as a vehicle in which Americans could address
the religious and civil tumults of the late eighteenth century. A study of the
denomination reveals Presbyterians more than mirroring and accommo-
dating the concerns, beliefs, and desires of Americans; it also illustrates that
they were integral in fostering what captivated the American mind: Christendom, the conflict with Great Britain, nationalism, and sectionalism.[2]

The history of religion during the last half of the eighteenth century is,
fortunately, a well-developed and well-researched field. Despite the strides
historians have made, however, little has been written on denominational
attempts at Christian unity or how churches during this period interacted with or affected nationalism or sectionalism. Religious histories writ-

ten about the late colonial period tend to focus on the great multitude of contests—religious, social, and national—that marked the era and how they led to or influenced the American Revolution. Historians such as Carl Bridenbaugh, Arthur Cross, and, more recently, Kenneth Elliott and James B. Bell have argued the central significance of the Anglican/Dissenter conflict over the establishment of a colonial bishopric to the American Revolution.[3] However, by focusing on the bishopric crisis, these historians are only able to present a narrow history of the late colonial period.

While still focusing on conflicts, other historians have attempted to broaden the understanding of religion's influence on the American Revolution. Both Alan Heimert and Patricia Bonomi stressed the importance of the Great Awakening to the origins of the American Revolution, although Heimart emphasized New/Old Light differences and Bonomi stressed the common heritage of challenging authority.[4] Historians such as Nathan Hatch and Ruth Bloch focused on the millennial beliefs of American churchgoers, sparked by the conflicts between Catholic France and Protestant Britain, as motivation for the American Revolution and the foundation of the republic.[5] For Jonathan Clark, the origins of the revolution lay in the religious traditions of the seventeenth century rather than the eighteenth. This last war of religion, as he defined the American Revolution, was fueled by the anxiety of colonial Dissenters, who were ideologically stuck in the seventeenth century, concerning the heterodox and hegemonic eighteenth-century Anglican Church.[6] Although each of these historians provides indispensable insight into the influence of religion in the late colonial and revolutionary periods, their work, which largely focuses on conflict, overlooks processes of unity such as the interdenominational journey begun by the Presbyterian Church, as well as its eventual significance.

Much of the religious history focused on the late eighteenth century forward can be divided into two schools of thought that center on the "social control" hypothesis. Those who support the argument, such as Fred Hood and Jon Butler, argue that this period was marked predominantly by the clergymen trying to retain their control over the common person.[7] Although the social control thesis was *the* historical interpretation for a number of years, recent historians such as Hatch have attempted to counter it by rewriting the history of the Second Great Awakening. As a result, denominations during this period fall into one of two categories: the "religious newcomers" (the Methodists, Baptists, Mormons, African-American Christians and those within the various strains of the Christian movement) and the "Standing Order" (the Congregationalists, Presbyterians, and Anglicans). For these historians, the "religious newcomers," inspired by the democratic impulses of the American Revolution, were the true catalysts for the Second Great Awakening, as their egalitarian principles sparked the Christianization of Americans, the democratization of American Christianity, and the democratization of the United States in general.[8]

Although my work greatly benefited from Hatch and others, these historians have largely overlooked the American Presbyterian Church. As the "religious newcomers" receive fresh examination that illuminates their significance in the early republic, the Presbyterians remain part of a reactionary movement, but the story is more complex than this.[9] It is true that experimentations with egalitarianism did not entice Presbyterians to alter their approach to their faith. However, neither did they desperately struggle to hold onto a glorious past through "social control" as a reactionary force. One Presbyterian goal was to transform the bickering states into the United States. They desired a unified Christian America that would benefit not only future Americans but also the world. The travails of the American Revolution, which Hatch and others argue sparked democratization in the "religious newcomers," also served to transform the interdenominational goals of the Presbyterian Church. The Presbyterian case illustrates how this process inadvertently promoted sectionalism, as the efforts of this denomination to create one Christian nation led it to create at least two.

As this book examines the American Revolution as the transformative event for the interdenominational pursuit of the Presbyterians its author, again, is indebted to other historians. In *The Long Argument*, Stephen Foster addresses how Puritanism in England and America came to an end. Foster argues that in both cases, the catalyst was a seemingly beneficial external force that eventually spawned internal division; for the English it was the Long Parliament and for the Americans it was the Great Awakening.[10] Borrowing from Foster, I contend that the American Revolution proved a similar catalyst for the Presbyterians. Yet, regarding the Presbyterian pursuit of Christian unity, the impact of the revolutionary era is not primarily found in the church's embrace of Real Whig ideology, which, as Gideon Mailer has shown, did not supplant the Presbyterians' reliance on the Westminster Divines as the foundation for their patriotism.[11] Instead, the significance of the revolution lay in the adoption by the Presbyterians, and other Reformed clergy, of Puritan New England's belief that they were God's chosen people. By applying this notion to the various Protestant churches in the colonies, they not only generated support for an armed resistance against Great Britain but also fostered the belief that God had chosen America as an example to the world.[12] As a result of the Presbyterian Church's experience during the American Revolution, their post-independence cooperative goals had both spiritual and national objectives.

Concerning the creation of nationalism in the United States, historians have, for the most part, concluded that religion played only a small role. What credit religion is given has been presented by historians such as Nathan Hatch and Ruth Bloch, who contend that the millennial beliefs of Americans allowed them to accept the momentous political events of the late eighteenth century, including the ratification of the Constitution, as part of God's unfolding providential plan. After redefining their "religious priorities in republican terms," Hatch wrote, and after "following the logic of their own eschatology, clergymen placed the American nation at the center of redemptive history."[13] This perspective, recently affirmed by historians such as Thomas Kidd, effectively limited the role of religion during the late eighteenth century to that of a deferential observer and granted greater responsibility to secular politics.[14] Other historians of nationalism, such as David Waldstreicher, Simon Newman, and Benedict Anderson, have demonstrated the importance of the printed word in the creation of American nationalism. According to these historians, it was through newspapers, magazines, and other published works that national communities were created among both the elite and common people. Yet these communities were political, not religious.[15] Again, in overlooking the Presbyterian Church, historians have limited religion's role in fostering nationalism. The Presbyterian leadership made use of the printed word to disseminate a consistent interdenominational message in order to create a community of Christian Americans.

Most histories examining the origins of sectionalism either point to the institution of slavery or to the economic and political issues of the nineteenth century.[16] Those historians (such as Donald Mathews and Mitchell Snay) who focus on religion argue that after the evangelical Protestant denominations—Presbyterians, Baptists, and Methodists—successfully overthrew the Anglican establishment, they attempted to alter the South. But in the end, it was the South that would alter the churches.[17] When in the nineteenth century the South came under persistent attack for slavery, the southern evangelical churches came to its defense, these historians contend. The transformation was complete, and eventually the evangelical bodies severed ties with their northern brethren. Similar to the position taken by Hatch and Bloch concerning the role of religion during the last half of the eighteenth century, this perspective effectively removes religion as a contributor to the nation's shaping. The churches are left waiting to support the great work of others.

Although they do not emphasize the importance of religion to sectionalism, other historians, such as Joyce Appleby, David Waldstreicher, and Peter Knupfer, believe that the origins of sectionalism were closely tied to those of nationalism. For Appleby, sectionalism stemmed from the ways in which the first generation of Americans in the North and South embraced the democratic impulses loosed by the American Revolution. Diverging paths emerged as southerners increasingly relied on slavery to sustain their economic and political opportunities and northerners did not.[18] Waldstreicher emphasizes how the use of the printed word not only allowed Americans from across the country to celebrate the nation in harmony but also afforded the opportunity for these diverse Americans to celebrate their specific understandings of, and hopes for, the nation. In this way Americans, elite and nonelite, could "practice nationalism and local politics simultaneously."[19] Working toward a similar conclusion, Peter Knupfer discusses what he terms constitutional unionism. He argues that the Federalist creation of the Constitution was itself a compromise and that the framers wanted the Constitution and compromise to serve as an example of proper national spirit.[20] According to these historians, the rhetoric of national unity would eventually wear thin, revealing the sectionalism that had grown in the safe soil of compromise. Following in the footsteps of Waldstreicher, Knupfer, and Appleby, I examine how the leadership of the Presbyterian Church fostered sectionalism by disseminating vague definitions of interdenominational nationalism in order to encourage church-wide acceptance. Also, this study seeks to enrich the current understanding of the origins of sectionalism by showing how the message of compromise the Presbyterian leaders spread to keep peace in their ranks led to the distrust and eventual separation of many members from the national denomination.

In order to discuss any plan or goal of the Presbyterian Church, it is vital to determine who or what directed the course of the denomination. The colonial Presbyterian Church government was made up of three tiers. At its base was the individual church session, which consisted of the minister and popularly elected elders. Every session sent representatives to their local presbytery (the second tier) and to the overarching Synod of New York and Philadelphia (the third tier). It was the synod's responsibility to lead the church as a whole. This structure allowed every congregation to contribute to the church's governing since the synod was made up of representatives (generally the minister) from every session within its bounds. The structure of the government changed in 1789 after the synod realized that it could not effectively govern the church's rapidly expanding boundaries. To remedy the problem, the Presbyterians reorganized with a four-tier government placing a General Assembly above four synods and sixteen presbyteries. Although representation from every church was not required in the General Assembly, it was still charged with the overall direction of the church.

To this end, my work is steeped in the records, letters, and minutes of the Presbyterian governing bodies, as those entities, by the agreement of the individual churches, spoke for the denomination as a whole.

In addition to the writings of the ruling bodies, I have also relied heavily on the published documents of prominent Presbyterians. Among these sources are sermons, lectures, hymnals, poetry, and letters. In and of themselves, these sources prove little other than the thoughts and actions of individual Presbyterians. However, when used in conjunction with the works of the Presbyterian ruling bodies, these documents provide a clearer picture of how individuals in the church, both clergy and lay, responded publicly to the ruling body's vision. For the same purpose, I also use the private correspondence of leading Presbyterians. Yet, as interdenominationalism rests on how the church interacted and hoped to interact with their fellow Americans, I have focused my attention on the documents that allowed the Presbyterians to most directly address the American people, their published work.

Unity in Christ and Country is divided into five chapters that cover 1758 to 1801. Chapter 1 discusses the deep-laid orthodox Reformed foundations of interdenominationalism. In 1758 the colonial Presbyterian Church reunited, ending a nearly twenty-year schism. As a part of the reunion process, the Synod of New York and Philadelphia, relying on the Westminster Divines, called for Presbyterians to work more closely with other Christians in the hope that their efforts would heal divisions and generally strengthen the body of Christ; in short, they were to strive for interdenominationalism. The chapter traces the interdenominational efforts of the Presbyterians from their reunion until 1765, revealing that despite continued struggles, which came largely in the form of old political and religious animosities, the Presbyterians made significant progress toward their stated goals. The pursuit of Christian unity proved more difficult to implement in reality than the hopes of 1758 had anticipated, but persistent efforts of the Synod of New York and Philadelphia alongside individual Presbyterians created a firm foundation on which to build.

The second chapter continues the examination of the Presbyterian Church's interdenominational struggles from 1765 to 1775. Although the denomination's internal conflict persisted, the biggest obstacles to interdenominationalism were the bishopric crisis and the constitutional crisis that developed between the colonies and Great Britain. The trials allowed the denomination to work closely with other churches. The unions formed were, however, couched in the language of addressing immediate needs and not long-term solutions. A result of these unions was the elevation of temporal liberties as a threat to supplant the idyllic interdenominational cooperation that was envisioned in 1758. Still, the spirit remained within the church.

Chapter 3 follows interdenominationalism in the Presbyterian Church from Lexington and Concord in 1775 to the Treaty of Paris in 1783. For much of the period, the church was preoccupied with the trials of war and supporting the war effort. To achieve victory as well as the glory for which God had chosen the country, the Presbyterian ruling body urged its members to put aside old religious and political animosities and cooperate with other denominations. Due to the devastating toll the war took on the Presbyterian Church, leaders looked for unrepentant sin within their midst. Initially focusing on slavery as the sin in question, increasing numbers of Presbyterians challenged the church to fully embrace the 1758 mission to heal the body of Christ. They agreed that their religious motivation for the war was sound, but they also believed that many in their church and in the country had begun to place political concerns above the welfare of Christendom. Their actions revitalized the Presbyterian ruling body's cooperative spirit, and as peace was achieved in Paris, the Presbyterian synod prepared to embark on a new era of interdenominationalism.

Chapter 4 explores the revival and transformation of the ruling body's interdenominational vision as well as that vision's success within the northern Presbyterian churches from 1783 to 1801. When the Presbyterian synod renewed its emphasis on interdenominationalism in the postwar period, it did not advise its members to abandon their national concerns and motivations; however, the ruling body did intend those issues to be of secondary importance to the welfare of Christendom. During the crisis with Great Britain, the Presbyterians had adopted the New England "elect nation" ideology and had applied it to America as a whole. United, America possessed tremendous potential regarding the expansion of Christendom. The result was that the synod encouraged its members to pursue an interdenominational spirit for the welfare of the country and Christendom; in short, its goal was interdenominational nationalism. Having revised its tactics, the ruling body believed its renewed cooperative attempts would meet with divine approval and more success. In general the synod was pleased with the interdenominational nationalism displayed in the North. There was support enough for the new Constitution, the lines of communication were opened with the Dutch Reformed and Associate Reformed churches, and an intimate relationship with the Connecticut Congregationalists was formed. The Presbyterian Church's fellowship with the Congregationalists was the interdenominational showpiece for the ruling body, and the eventual Plan of Union between the churches in 1801 represented the ideal cooperative relationship. The churches planned to work hand in hand for Christ and country.

The fifth chapter examines the course of the governing bodies' interdenominationally nationalist vision in the southern states and territories from 1783 to 1801. In the North, where the denomination was strongest, the ruling bodies were pleased with the interdenominational nationalism displayed, especially the intimate relationship with the Congregationalists. In the South, however, where the denomination was weakest, the Presbyterian governing body met with difficulties. One big problem was that there just were not enough of these Presbyterian ministers to meet the needs of the southern congregations. In this situation, the various southern synods and presbyteries were at a disadvantage trying to implement and sustain the cooperative vision of the church created by the General Assembly. Coupled with a lack of regular Presbyterian leadership, the priorities of localities, such as emancipation, universal salvation, or egalitarian religion, took precedence over the priorities of the General Assembly for many southern Presbyterians. The church's leadership had a problem in the South, but not of the South. When the Presbyterian ruling body failed to rein in its wayward members, this failure awoke a latent distrust within the General Assembly concerning seeking complete intimacy with other denominations. However, these attempts by the ruling body also convinced many Presbyterians that their local interests were not those of the national organization. The result was that many in the church began contemplating separation. These doubts and insecurities were only magnified by the Cane Ridge revivals of 1801 that were shortly followed by the secession of many members who would form the Church of Christ and the Cumberland Presbyterians.

The beginning of the nineteenth century was a watershed for the Presbyterian Church in that the General Assembly's attempts to maintain peace with their open definition of interdenominational nationalism led to secession in some areas and further cooperative measures in others. Even though it had met with bittersweet success, the Presbyterian ruling body established its approach to interdenominational nationalism for the oncoming century. While cooperation for Christ and country remained—which only aided the growth of sectional nationalism—a destructive distrust arose when interdenominational relationships became too intimate.

I

Foundations of Interdenominationalism, 1758–1765

According to the Book of Matthew, following Jesus Christ's resurrection, he met his remaining disciples on a mountain near Galilee and gave them their final instructions. Christ told them, "All power is given unto me in heaven and in earth. Go ye therefore, and teach all nations, baptizing them in the name of the Father, and of the Son, and of the Holy Ghost: Teaching them to observe all things, whatsoever I have commanded you."[1] As Christianity spread and endured, each generation was responsible for this "Great Commission." The eighteenth-century American Presbyterians were no exception. In 1758, in the midst of the French and Indian War, the Presbyterians humbled themselves before a God they believed to be disciplining them for their sin.[2] Their sin, they knew, was the recent schism in their church. This division hindered the progress of Christianity. The universal church was unable to properly attend to Christ's last command. To make amends, the denomination reunited and publicly repented in 1758. The reunion meant more than this, however, as the Presbyterians revealed that their renewed efforts toward the "Great Commission" would be interdenominational in nature.[3] The transition to a more cooperative church, however, did not go smoothly, as various internal and external distractions in subsequent years slowed the denomination's progress toward its interdenominational goals. Both the ideals set forth in 1758 and the trials that immediately followed lay the foundation for the interdenominational quest that brought the Presbyterian Church both blessings and strife for the rest of the century.

This period in the church's history is generally characterized by the religious and political conflict that plagued the Presbyterians. Following the argument in Leonard J. Trinterud's book *The Forming of an American Tradition: A Re-examination of Colonial Presbyterianism*, historians have concluded that these experiences helped to shape the church into an American denomination.[4] These arguments are not confined to just the Presbyterian Church; generally, historians have focused on the multitude of conflicts, both social and religious, that marked the period and preoccupied churchgoers.[5] Historians have written too little on denominational attempts at Christian unity and what those meant for both the individual groups and the collective American Christian experience.[6] Certainly conflicts existed between churches, and this historical perspective is indispensable for any understanding of the eighteenth century. However, the picture is incomplete. Religiously motivated attempts between churches to cooperate, such as the interdenominational journey begun by the Presbyterian Church during the French and Indian War, offer a useful corrective for the general understanding of the period. In the midst of the Americanization process, the Presbyterians crafted a plan and started a journey to strengthen Christendom that would also one day help define what it meant to be an American. Interdenominationalism served as the foundation for this plan, and although the Presbyterians became embroiled in religious and political controversies that diverted their attention, the goal was established and never completely forgotten.

The schism that troubled the Presbyterians in 1758 began in 1741 amid the excitement of the Great Awakening. A three-tiered government oversaw the Presbyterian Church at this time. The uppermost was the Synod of Philadelphia (which met annually), composed of representatives from every church under its care. Directly below the synod were the presbyteries, which also consisted of representatives from all the member churches. Finally there was the individual congregation, overseen by the minister and elected elders. During the Great Awakening, a debate rose concerning the requirement that ministerial candidates show evidence of experimental religion before ordination.[7] The ordination of ministers was the responsibility and privilege of the presbyteries, which, in the 1730s, were largely controlled by Old Lights, who disapproved of such subjective ordination requirements and favored instead the objectivity of a strong academic grounding. Outnumbered and outvoted in the regional presbyteries, the New Light ministers—those favoring evidence of experimental religion and the revivals—petitioned the synod to form a new presbytery. In 1738, this request was granted and the newly formed New Brunswick Presbytery immediately made experimental religion mandatory for future ministers within its bounds.[8] Troubled by this development, the Old Lights mustered their strength in the synod and stamped out this New Light initiative by granting the synod the final say in the ordination of ministers. The New Brunswick Presbytery protested this encroachment on its authority and continued to ordain its own ministers. Rankled by the lack of deference, the synod passed the *Protestation*, which, in its denunciation of the upstart presbytery, questioned rhetorically, "Is not continuance of union absurd with those who would arrogate to themselves a right and power to palm and obtrude members on our Synod, contrary to the minds and judgment of the body?"[9] Neatly and quickly, the Old Light synod drove out the insubordinate New Brunswick churches. The exiled presbytery, however, was not without its friends and supporters. Soon other New Light churches, primarily from the New York Presbytery, joined it, and together they formed the Synod of New York.[10]

Little thought was given to reconciliation until the mid-1750s, when it appeared that God was punishing the churches for their divisive indiscretion. The divine retribution did not come in the form of slacking membership. In fact, in terms of congregational membership, the Presbyterian schism had little adverse effect. Both the Old Light Synod of Philadelphia and the New Light Synod of New York increased their membership during the years of separation, although the New Lights far outgained the Old Lights. No, war was the righteous judgment chosen for the Presbyterians, not deplete or stagnant membership.[11] In 1754, fighting resumed between the British and French in North America and by 1756 the conflict had officially become a war—the French and Indian War. Early in the contest, western Pennsylvania, Virginia and Maryland, largely home to Scots-Irish Presbyterians,[12] were devastated by France's Indian allies, resulting in the death or imprisonment of seven hundred colonists.[13] Confronted with the violence, bloodshed, and loss that accompanied the war, both the Old Light and New Light Presbyterians looked to their recent rift as the cause of their misfortune. Reunion was no longer an unimaginable prospect.

Shortly before the two synods began negotiating the terms for reunion, the Synod of New York, the New Light contingent, issued a pastoral letter to the congregations under its care. On behalf of the synod, Robert Treat wrote that the ruling body saw itself "bound, not only as members of the community, but [also as part of] the whole Church of God" to implore repentance. "We have been warned and chastised," Treat wrote, "first more gently, then more terribly; but not returning to him that smites us, his anger is not turned away, but his hand is stretched out still. Judgment yet proceeds, the prospect becomes darker and darker, and all things respecting us are loudly alarming." The tool, according to the synod, that God had chosen for this was the army of the French and their Native American allies—"a potent, prevailing and cruel enemy."[14] Driven by fear of a wrathful God, the estranged Presbyterians agreed to meet in Philadelphia to negotiate in May 1758. A few days before their efforts came to fruition that May, two ministers—representing the conciliatory groups within the Old Light and New Light camps—spoke to the two ruling bodies assembled.[15] The orations of Francis Alison and David Bostwick reveal more than the desire of the synods to renew the bonds of fellowship; they also illustrate the hopes many Presbyterians had for this reunion in terms of aiding the universal church.

Speaking before the joint meeting of the synods on May 24, Alison recommended "peace and union." However, the peace and unity Alison proposed was not to be limited to his fellow Presbyterians. Summarizing Alison's work, the anonymous author to the preface of the published account wrote that Alison "uses no endeavours to promote favorite systems, and gain proselytes to party-tenets: He has sublimer things in view! Namely, to enforce those opinions that tend to render GOD more beloved and feared, and mankind more in peace and charity."[16] The author also added "that if all mankind were actuated by the same liberal and christian spirit that appears in this discourse, not only the members of the particular church to which the author belongs, but even ALL who name the NAME OF CHRIST, would unite in the most essential parts of their holy profession."[17] Alison's scriptural basis for his sermon, Ephesians 4: 1–7, attests to the truth of the preface's assertion. Utilizing the apostle Paul's encouragement to early Christians "to keep the unity of the spirit in the bond of peace," Alison offered his vision for interdenominational activity within the reunited Church.[18]

"GOD, is the God of PEACE" Alison stated, "Christ Jesus is the prince of PEACE . . . and to follow PEACE, and to love one another, is the distinguishing characteristic of his disciples." Hitherto, Alison lamented, Christians had "so notoriously failed in this main point."[19] He called on his fellow Presbyterians to remedy the situation. "We have all one father," he said, we are of "the same family" and "to bite and devour one another, is indecent and unbecoming." The Christian union Alison promoted was not to be used to stifle the liberty of their brethren. There was to be freedom in "the lesser matters of religion," so that their agreement on the fundamental principles and the subsequent cooperation would "promote the honor of God; the good of mankind, and the pure and holy religion of our lord and master."[20] Alison concluded his address by reminding his audience, "THERE IS ONE BODY AND ONE SPIRIT . . . christians are represented as one august body, whereof CHRIST is the HEAD. And this consideration must be a powerful motive to union, love and concord."[21]

Following Alison's lead, David Bostwick's sermon the following day also promoted a Christian union based on the fundamental principles.[22] Bostwick believed that the primary stumbling block was mankind's innate love of "SELF" and that was what "men live for." As Christians they were to renounce their "Self," but Bostwick assured his listeners that did "not imply a total disregard to our reputation and character among men, for on this, the success of our ministry, and consequently the advancement of the REDEEMER's kingdom, may, in some measure, depend." A proper Christian made "JESUS CHRIST . . . the SUBJECT MATTER" of his life, and it was this fundamental principle that any union needed.[23] "Let us ever remember," Bostwick concluded, "'we are not our own,' and therefore have no business to live to ourselves, or regard our interest or reputation, any further than the honor of CHRIST, and the interest of religion is concerned."[24]

Four days after Alison and Bostwick addressed the ruling bodies with their hopes for the proposed reunion, the Old Lights and New Lights put aside their differences and reunited the church on May 29, 1758. The newly formed Synod of New York and Philadelphia published an account of the reunion with the hopes that the end of the sinful schism would help appease an angry God who had visited them with the French and Indian War, and bolster the spirits of their fellow colonists.[25] Given the stature of Dr. Alison and Reverend Bostwick, the resulting document largely reflected their sentiments and those of the conciliatory parties from both camps. Fittingly, this account was penned by Alexander McDowell, a minister who had taken part in the separation, and who was, therefore, fully aware of the damage done to Christendom through the Presbyterian schism.[26] Through McDowell's hand, the synod explained that it had been convicted of its sin against God and his church by "the present divided State of the *Presbyterian Church* in this Land." The ruling body realized "that the Division of the Church tends to weaken it's [*sic*] Interests, to dishonour Religion, and consequently it's glorious Author," and so they pledged "to endeavor the Healing of that Breach . . . so it's hurtful Consequences may not extend to Posterity."[27] As their sin had such an impact on the universal church, the Presbyterians made their apology a public one. Conscious of how the church was perceived and how that perception affected Christianity, the synod recognized a publicized reunion as necessary to counteract the dishonor it had already caused their "glorious Author." In this penitent act, the Presbyterians were motivated by the welfare of all Christians, living and unborn; it was the "Establishment and Edification of his [God's] People" that compelled them.

This reunion account, however, was more than an act of contrition. The Presbyterian synod also outlined how it intended to "carry on the great

Designs of Religion" through "the Advancement of the Mediator's King-dom."[28] Yet, to fulfill this goal the Presbyterians needed to lay a foundation on which they could craft a framework to overcome the most challenging issues they had yet encountered and one they could rely on to serve the same purpose in future crises. Here the Presbyterians leadership looked no further than the trusted "orthodox and excellent" Westminster Standards to establish peace and rest within the divided church and support them in the years to come.

The Westminster Standards—collectively, the Confession of Faith, the Shorter Catechism, the Longer Catechism, the Directory of Public Worship, and the Form of Church Government—were the statements of faith and practice written by the Westminster Divines between 1643 and 1653. The Long Parliament assembled the Divines to create a new identity and path for the Church of England, and within a decade they had fulfilled their calling. Although the English government's acceptance of their work proved to be short-lived, the Westminster Standards would be embraced by the Presbyterian churches in Scotland and America, which considered them "orthodox and excellent" statements of biblical truths. Yet, despite being deemed invaluable for preserving the purity of the ministry, they were viewed as "subordinate standards" to scripture.[29] Supporting this approach, the Divines themselves explained that "the whole Councell of God concerning all things necessary for his own Glory; mans salvation, Faith and Life, is either expressly set down in Scripture, or by good and necessary consequence may be deduced from Scripture." Clarifying their position, the Divines stressed that that "The Supream Judg by which all Controversies of Religion are to be determined, and all Decrees of Councels, Opinions of Ancient Writers, Doctrines of men and private spirits are to be examined; and in whose sentence we are to rest; can be no other but the Holy Spirit speaking in the Scriptures."[30] Not only did they confirm the supremacy of the Bible in all matters but the Divines also further noted that rest, elusive in the midst of spiritual controversies, should and could only be found in the scriptural pronouncements. Rest was exactly what the American Presbyterians desperately sought in 1758.

Believing themselves firmly grounded, the Presbyterian leadership then explained to the colonial reading world the basic infrastructure of their new union. Among the details of how divided congregations and presbyteries would be brought in to the new Synod of New York and Philadelphia, the necessity of the Westminster Standards, and the rules of order for delegates of the synod, the ruling body discussed the issues that originally divided them. They explained that the physical and spiritual manifestations of experiential religion were only indicators of the "gracious work of God" if they were coupled with "the Scriptural characters of a work of God." Here, as in all matters, scripture was to be the ultimate guide for living their faith, and without satisfying this requirement no ministerial candidate could be ordained by the local presbyteries. An often-overlooked component of the reunion plan was the safeguard established to protect liberty of conscience. The synod noted that "any member or members, for the exoneration of his or their conscience before God, have a right to protest any act or procedure" of the synod and "to require such protestation be recorded in their minutes." To ensure this right, the synod agreed that "no member is liable to prosecution on the account of his protesting." Finally, although the Presbyterian leadership hoped that by adopting this thorough reunion plan its congregations "would love each other with a pure heart fervently," it knew that its past troubles could continue to haunt the church. To this end the leaders bluntly concluded "that all former differences and disputes are laid aside and buried, and that no future inquiry or vote shall be proposed in this Synod concerning these things." If this was not deterrent enough, they added that any attempts to exhume these skeletons would "be deemed a censurable breach of this agreement, and be refused, and he [the instigator] be rebuked accordingly."[31]

For the reunited Presbyterian leadership, the divisive issues of the past had been resolved and, as the divine visitors had instructed Lot upon leaving Sodom, no one was to look back. The ruling body sought more than a fresh start. This demand revealed how destructive the leadership perceived those issues and any like them to be. The poisonous root that connected these concerns was the lure of increasingly hostile and unflagging debate, a result of no clear biblical or confessional answers. There was no equivalent of "you shall not murder" for questions such as which ruling body had ultimate authority to ordain ministers. Engaging such questions might ultimately lead to another sinful schism, perhaps one that could not be repaired. Or worse still, a division that no one wished to mend. Considering this threat, when setting the foundation of the union, the Presbyterian leadership did not rely on their own or their descendants' ability to reason; they set the church firmly on scripture and the Divines.

It was upon these carefully chosen pillars that the reunited synod placed its reason for and ability to fulfill the proposed mission as a Christian church. Specifically, the ruling body promised the colonial world four things: to "*study the Things that make for Peace*"; to "*take heed to ourselves*, that our Hearts be upright, our Discourse edifying, and our Lives exemplary"; to "take heed *to our Doctrine*, that it be not only orthodox, but evangelical and spiritual, tending to awaken the Secure to a suitable Concern for their Salvation and to instruct and encourage sincere Christians"; and to commend "*ourselves to every Man's Conscience in the Sight of God*."[32] It is true that these measures were first to be employed to heal the Old Light/New Light wounds, but this fact should not overshadow the denomination's intentions toward the rest of Christendom. The synod made it clear that the ultimate "Design of our Union is the Advancement of the Mediator's Kingdom." As the Presbyterians promised to "cultivate Peace and Harmony among ourselves," they also vowed to consider themselves and their actions as a part of the body of Christ, as Dr. Alison had reminded them.[33] The Presbyterians were submitting themselves to their fellow believers. As Christians they were equals and dependent on one another for success. This fresh start for the penitent Presbyterians in 1758 set the stage for their interdenominational journey.

As formal cooperation with other churches was largely unexplored territory for the Presbyterians, the Synod of New York and Philadelphia, shortly after its inception in 1758, created a Committee of Correspondence to guide its efforts. Taking this aspect of the reunion seriously, the ruling body charged the committee with the task of opening the lines of communication with like-minded churches "in Britain and Ireland, and in these colonies and elsewhere."[34] Although the scope of the committee's interdenominational efforts appears to have been initially limited to Reformed churches, it was a step toward more inclusive cooperation.[35] Another indication of the importance of interdenominationalism to the Presbyterians were the men called to serve on this committee. Gilbert Tennent, Robert Cross, Richard Treat, and Francis Alison, who were among the best and brightest the church had to offer, took the helm of the committee and did their part to guide the church in these uncharted waters.[36] Furthermore, because the commitee included key individuals from both the Old Light and New Light parties, its members presented a face of unity that the synod wished the public to see. By earnestly approaching the interdenominational aspect of the reunion, the Presbyterians were off to a promising start.

Determined to realize its publicized interdenominational aspirations, the Presbyterian ruling body turned to the Native American mission field as its initial venue for cooperation. In part this allowed Presbyterians to engage the task given to all Christians, evangelization and the extension of the redeemer's kingdom. However, church leaders also saw it as a way to foster direct cooperation among different denominations. Before 1758 the Presbyterian Church's missionary efforts were confined to the North and consisted solely of David Brainerd, who was educated at Yale but ordained and commissioned by the New Light Presbyterian Synod of New York in the 1740s. Upon Brainerd's death, his brother John took up the cause.[37] This one family operation was the only Presbyterian attempt at Native American mission work until the late 1750s when Samuel Davies, the popular Virginian minister, led a movement to create the Society for Managing the Mission and School Society for the Propagation of the Gospel. Representing a fresh spirit of Christian outreach and desire to strengthen the redeemer's kingdom within the denomination, the society fittingly dispatched its first missionary shortly after the reunion of 1758. Handpicked by Davies and trained by him, the recently ordained John Martin set out for the frontier—what would become Tennessee—as a missionary to the Cherokee. Tremendously disliked by the Cherokees, Martin was soon replaced by another of Davies's students, William Richardson, whose efforts among the Cherokee were short-lived, as that nation grew increasingly hostile toward American encroachers. Although these efforts were largely unsuccessful, the Presbyterians were striving for the welfare of Christendom as they had promised in 1758.[38]

Undaunted by their failures, many in the Presbyterian Church hoped that their missionary attempts would bear the first fruits of their reunion efforts. On August 29, 1759, this wish came true when, as a result of Presbyterian and Congregationalist cooperation, the Mohegan Samson Occom was ordained as a Presbyterian minister—the first Native American Presbyterian minister.[39] Occom's Christianity was the result of the invigorated Congregationalist preaching of the Great Awakening. Following his conversion, he wasted little time becoming the protégé of Eleazar Wheelock at his school for Native Americans. Realizing Occom's potential, Wheelock and other Congregationalists trained him for the ministry. He, however, was not destined for a Congregationalist pulpit. Samuel Davies, who had himself made impressive inroads among Virginian freemen and slaves, invited Occom to serve as a missionary to the Cherokee for the recently created Presbyterian mission society. Where John Martin had failed, Davies hoped Occom would succeed.[40] Occom and his Congregationalist teachers agreed, paving the way for his examination by the Long Island Presbytery in 1759. After passing the rigorous trials placed before all Presbyterian ministerial candidates, the Mohegan was ordained as the first Native American Presbyterian minister.[41] Historian William Deloss Love wrote that the ministers who attended the ordination "looked upon it as a new departure in the history of Indian missions."[42] Furthermore, this milestone reflected the continued efforts of the Presbyterian Church as its leadership pursued cooperation in Christ.[43]

In 1761, Samuel Buell, the Presbyterian minister who delivered Samson Occom's ordination sermon, published the address to excite interest in, and perhaps funding for, the Oneida mission to which Occom had recently been assigned. In his account Buell not only embraced Occom as a worthy and talented minister, he also stated that Occom would be helpful in the church's interdenominational mission. Confident in Occom's success, Buell believed that the Native American converts from his ministry would bolster the ranks of Christ's kingdom and entice other churches to join the Presbyterians in this venture. Buell wrote, "We can but hope . . . that we shall see Christians, though in some lesser Matters of differing Opinions, agreeing harmoniously in this truly generous, interesting and important Work, contributing liberally toward promoting the Propagation of the glad Tidings of Salvation among the *Heathen*."[44] In his excitement over the cooperative and missionary possibilities, the reverend ended his letter with a song:

> King Jesus reigns, and spreads his glorious Fame,
> The savage Nations know, and trust his Name;
> Triumph ye Saints! Ye Angels strike the Lyre!
> In everlasting Praise, let all conspire![45]

Buell quickly apologized for his extravagance: "Dear Sir, I forget myself, the pleasing Theme has transported me beyond the Limits I had prescribed to my Mind," but the joy that this Presbyterian felt was obvious.[46] The work of men such as Samuel Davies, John Martin, Samson Occom, Samuel Buell, and the Brainerd brothers illustrates that there was a growing desire among Presbyterians to bring Christianity to the Native Americans.[47] However, this was not the only goal. Intertwined with the evangelical zeal to extend the boundaries of Christendom was the Presbyterians' desire to unite with other denominations in this common cause for Christ.[48] Difficult though it was, the interdenominational spirit shaped by the Synod of New York and Philadelphia had successfully transitioned from rhetoric to reality.

The church's relationships with other Christians, particularly the Anglicans, hindered further progress toward its cooperative goals. Throughout its history the Presbyterian Church had endured a tortured relationship with the Anglican Church. As the established church of the English state, the Church of England strove to assert and maintain an ecclesiastical hegemony throughout the realm. Those who dissented were persecuted. Because the American Presbyterian Church was a composite of English Puritans, Scottish Presbyterians and Irish Presbyterians, its heritage was filled with accounts of Anglican persecution. These were stories that colonial Presbyterians frequently revisited and shared with new generations.[49] The Puritans suffered from laws such as the 1581 Act that levied a 20-pound fine against those who refused to attend the Church of England. This act was coupled with other laws that enforced far worse penalties, including exile and execution.[50] Feeling the wrath of the Anglican establishment, the Irish

Presbyterians endured many injustices—including the Clarendon Code and the Test Act of 1704, which, among other things, barred them from public office, universities, and preaching in towns.[51] The Scottish Presbyterians suffered as well, primarily through the patronage system, which circumvented the Kirk's authority to choose and dismiss ministers.[52]

For the American Presbyterians, Anglican persecution was not only part of the past but also part of the present. They experienced firsthand the Anglican Church's attempts to maintain its ecclesiastical hegemony in the colonies, including the imprisoning of Francis Makemie, the "Father of American Presbyterianism," and the seizure of several church properties.[53] Kindly put, Presbyterian relations with the Anglican Church were an obstacle for the Presbyterians on their interdenominational trek. Nevertheless some Presbyterians had hopes of building a better relationship with the Anglicans.

On May 24, 1760, eighteen New Light Presbyterian ministers, in Philadelphia for the annual synod, sent a letter to the Archbishop of Canterbury. They included the renowned Tennents: Gilbert, William, and Charles, as well as Samuel Davies, who was at that time the president of the College of New Jersey. They wrote to Archbishop Thomas Secker, who was also the president of the Society for the Propagation of the Gospel in Foreign Parts, and respectfully petitioned to have one Reverend William McClennachan settled in Philadelphia as an Episcopal minister. McClennachan had served as the assistant to Dr. Robert Jenny in the city and the Presbyterians thought highly of his doctrinal leanings and wished him to stay. They wrote, "It is our humble Opinion, that his continuing to officiate in Philadelphia, will greatly tend to advance our common Christianity: And therefore, we most earnestly PRAY your Grace would use your utmost Influence to have him INDUCTED and settled in said City."[54] These Presbyterian ministers, although not acting in an official capacity for the synod, demonstrated the earnest motivations of many in the church to work with other denominations, even the Anglicans. However, the events that followed did not introduce a period of cooperation; instead they served as the catalyst for increased uneasiness between the denominations. The controversy that the petition triggered reveals the external interdenominational hurdles the Presbyterians faced as well as the rifts still present in their own ranks.

Immediately after the letter had been sent, the Anglicans of Philadelphia took offense to the Presbyterian petition on behalf of William McClennachan. As the synod convened in 1760, "an address from the clergy of the Church of England belonging to this city was brought in and read; wherein they complain that some members of this Synod have intermeddled in their church affairs to their disliking, and query, whether the paper which they say was signed by the moderator and some other members, was signed as a synodical act."[55] The synod responded quickly to "assure these Reverend Gentlemen that they never signed it as a synodical body, nor heard the paper read in Synod, nor was it as much as made known to many of the members of this body." Treading carefully, the ruling body also stated, "We desire to intermeddle with no affairs that do not belong to us, but as a body can neither prevent the private correspondence of our members, nor oblige them to produce their letters." However, they quickly added, trying not to sound too dismissive, "We heartily desire that the same good understanding which has hitherto happily subsisted between us and the Reverend Gentlemen of the Church of England, may still continue."[56] This tense exchange in the summer of 1760 did not conclude the conversation as the Presbyterians had hoped.

To their chagrin, the controversy escalated and the Anglicans sent another, more blunt letter to the synod "complaining of a number of our body for interfering the settlement of Mr. McClenaghan in the city of Philadelphia, together with a letter wrote to the Archbishop of Canterbury on this subject."[57] With this increased pressure, the ruling body replied that the ministers in question "acted without due consideration and improperly in that affair"—an answer that was slightly more contrite than the one the year before.[58] Eventually the Presbyterians were able to restore their "good understanding" with the Anglicans. However, much can be gleaned from this renewed bout of ill will between the churches, as is evident through the works of pseudonymous writers calling themselves a Layman, an Elder, and a Mechanick.[59]

Sometime between May 1760 and May 1761 the ill-fated petition fell into the hands of "an Old covenanting and true Presbyterian layman" who was very displeased with what he read. Agitated and motivated, he published both the original letter and a biting commentary. Within his observations the Old Covenanter quickly revealed the source of his discomfort, the treacherous intent of eighteen New Light ministers. He wrote, "Certainly nothing less than the Cause of the Lord, which I think is basely betrayed, by these men, in signing a Letter, so repugnant to Presbyterianism . . . would have induced me to attempt opening the Eyes of my dear Fellow-Christians; more especially those Presbyterians who have the Misfortune to live under the Ministration of these Men."[60] To the author this letter suggested that the ministers in question were closet churchmen rather than pious Presbyterians. Among other charges, the eighteen were accused of believing an archbishop had received redemptive grace, stating that the Anglican Church was a Christian church, and praying to the archbishop to forcefully "induct" a minister in Philadelphia. The Old Covenanter lambasted the ministers for sixteen pages and all the while he pleaded with his audience, "Does not this prove them our secret Enemies?"[61]

Yet in the end the author called for more than mere acknowledgment; he challenged "honest and worthy Presbyterians, to shut your Meeting-houses upon them."[62] He saw a complete removal of these offending New Light ministers as the only remedy for this grand betrayal of Presbyterianism and Christianity. However much he railed against the eighteen, their actions were not the root of his problem. No, that lay with one of the cornerstones of the recent reunion. Interdenominational cooperation with the Anglicans was more than he could tolerate, and the fact that the church's new direction emphasized forging such friendships stirred the ire of the Old Covenanter. Not all Presbyterians, it seems, were pleased with the post-reunion path of the church. How this affected the integrity of the Presbyterian Church or its interdenominational mission remains to be seen. As the Old Covenanter illustrates, some in the church were unhappy with the recent reunion with the New Lights or the new direction of the church that aimed to make friends from long-standing Anglican enemies.

The eighteen New Light ministers attacked by the Old Covenanter were not without friends in the public sphere of print. One ally, known only as "an elder of the Presbyterian Church," quickly concluded that the censure from the Old Covenanter was a ruse. He contended that the author "cannot be a Presbyterian at all" because of "his gross abusive Misrepresentations of the known Sentiments of the whole Body of Presbyterians."[63] Having no doubts as to the identity of the author, the Elder claimed that the Old Covenanter was an Anglican, as "his primary Design is to pour Contempt on the whole Body of Presbyterians . . . as an *ignorant, narrow, schismatical* Sect."[64] The Elder said that this was more than possible because Anglican ministers had kept the letter controversy alive and well. "Scarce has there any Thing, said to be wrote by a *Presbyterian*, been so countenanced and propagated by Church of *England* Clergy-men," the Elder commented. After all, he continued, "these were the Gentlemen who shewed the greatest Warmth about the LETTER, first and last."[65]

Still, more than a slighted reputation was in jeopardy. The Elder was convinced that the Anglicans were up to their old tricks by trying to divide the Presbyterians in an attempt to weaken their influence so they might have an easier time claiming ecclesiastical dominion in the colonies. The Old Covenanter was a facade created so that the Anglicans could subtly revive "old Slanders, unworthy of Notice, and rakes up old Differences," the end goal being "by any Means, however low and despicable," to "prevent the good Effects of our late Union." For, the Elder continued, "It is a well-known Maxim with Enemies, *Divide, and then destroy*."[66] Still, these

Anglican tactics were not a surprise, the author reflected; "Remember, our pious Ancestors have suffered These in *Scotland* and *England* in Years past, from the Predecessors of these Men in Spirit and Principle." He continued, "The Men I speak of, are such as are for reviving the persecuting Spirit of their infamous A---h-b---p *Sharp*, and others, in *Scotland*; and their bloody Judge Jefferies, in England."[67] As his reference to Sharp and Jeffries indicated, the Elder worried this new controversy was only the beginning of an Anglican plot to establish themselves in the colonies as they had in England. The religious liberties of the Presbyterians and all Dissenters were again in danger from . . . "restless, ambitious Clergymen."[68]

Echoing the themes found in the Elder's work, a second defender, known as "Mechanick," came to the defense of the eighteen New Light ministers. As thoroughly convinced of the Christian character of the ministers in question as the Elder, the Mechanick was perhaps less sure that the Old Covenanter was an Anglican acting alone. He suggested that perhaps "you are a Presbyterian by Profession . . . and perhaps some Episcopal is joined with you in the Affair."[69] Though varying slightly in theory, both defenders were convinced that, in the end, it was preposterous that the blame should be placed on a *true* Presbyterian. Their agreement in this regard revealed a fear of denominational instability that might rend the church anew. If the threat were internal, the denomination could easily collapse, but if an external source could be found, then the church could actually unite against the threat. To this end the Presbyterians took advantage of their long-time grievances with the Anglicans, and, for the time being, interdenominationalism was largely sacrificed for the sake of continued unity in the Presbyterian Church.

This episode reveals two of the hurdles standing before the church on its journey: The first was that despite the hopes of the Presbyterian leadership, the church was still contending with other denominations such as the Anglicans; and the second was that three years after the reunion, the denomination was still worried about possible internal divisions.

Controversies, such as that concerning the eighteen New Light ministers, strained the hope that the Old Light/New Light conflict had been put to rest in 1758. As if to mock this longing, the annual synod meeting in 1762 was fraught with schismatical opportunity. The synod dealt with two issues of delicate importance: the troublesome theology of Samuel Harker, and the necessity of experimental religion.

Although the 1762 synod was replete with potentially divisive issues, they were not altogether unexpected. For instance, the synod first addressed the problem of the Reverend Harker's views on the covenant of grace at the close of the 1759 meeting when the ruling body created a committee "to converse with Mr. Harker, and labour to convince him of his mistakes."[70] Concerns surrounding the New Jersey minister found their way into the records of the ruling body the year before when the Presbytery of New Brunswick informed the synod of his erroneous doctrine, but the synod had been overwhelmed by the task of reunion.[71] When the matter was officially addressed in 1759, the decision to wait until the following year to hear from the committee indicated in part an acknowledgment of the complexity of the case before synodal members, as well as a desire to carefully examine the situation before issuing a decision. Still, it is doubtful the synod knew the difficulties ahead and that this would become one of their more trying tasks in the post-reunion world.

On May 21, 1760, the committee presented its findings to the synod, and it became clear that this issue was not to be taken lightly. Samuel Harker, a minister in good standing within the New Brunswick Presbytery since 1753, had written a theological work he wished to publish. It was not the synod's standard practice to analyze the writings of its members, but it noted "several members of this body have heard him discourse on these subjects, and . . . think he labours under several mistakes."[72] As the ruling body had deliberately taken on a more public role in the reunion, it was all the more important to quickly address potentially dangerous theology espoused by its members, especially if it was intended for publication. The committee's report only confirmed the necessity of this approach. It considered most, if not all, of Harker's theology troublesome, but he had made two particularly troubling arguments that openly challenged "the opinion of . . . our orthodox divines." In his writing, the minister claimed that contemporary Christians misunderstood what was commonly referred to as the covenant of grace between God and humanity. Harker contended that "God has bound himself, by promise, to bestow saving blessings upon the faith and endeavors of unregenerate men; and that God has predestinated persons to salvation, upon a foresight of their faith and good works, or compliance with the terms of the covenant."[73] Concerning these points, the Westminster Divines had been clear: God chose the saved according to "the secret consell and good pleasure of his Will" and "without any fore sight of Faith, or Good works, or perseverance . . . or any other thing in the creature."[74] To its dismay, what the committee saw, and what the Divines had guarded against, was a revival of the ancient Pelagian heresy. The doctrine Pelagius had taught during the Patristic era had reared its head in the midst of the Reformation, and now visited eighteenth-century Philadelphia. Mankind did not need divine aid to be justified; rather they possessed that ability within themselves, if they only would use it. God then, as both Harker and Pelagius claimed, was bound to reward those who had saved themselves. The teaching had been condemned as heresy by the Council of Carthage (418) and the Second Council of Orange (529). It had likewise been rejected by Luther, Calvin and the Westminster Divines.[75] The Presbyterians in 1760 knew the doctrinal dangers, and they knew the orthodox position. However, they did not immediately act.

The committee hoped that Pelgianism was not Harker's intent, and it noted as much in its report to the synod. Apparently in its discussions with Harker, the committee came to realize that much of what he had written was not what he had explained to them in their conversations. His "real sentiments were . . . not . . . clearly expressed in said paper," and the committee members hoped that what they read was the result of a wayward zeal intended to attract more converts by explaining orthodox views in a manner that made them more popularly appealing rather than an attempt to revive an ancient heresy. After explaining to him the errors in question as well as the orthodox view, the committee "recommended to Mr. Harker great caution in his phraseology" and not "to deviate from the usual modes of expression among orthodox divines." Hoping to finally resolve the issue, the synod ordered that two more groups individually "converse on these points" with Harker before the synod's 1761 meeting. The committees were packed with well-respected ministers from both the Old and New Light positions, including Samuel Finley, Robert Smith, Gilbert Tennent, Richard Treat, John Ewing, and Francis Alison. Faced with the lingering danger of two latent factions within the church body, the synod wished to avoid the establishment of a third by mishandling the Harker situation. For several reasons then, Samuel Harker and his theology would be examined by the best the Presbyterian Church had to offer.[76]

The following year, despite this effort, Harker informed the synod that he intended to publish his now complete work without making any modifications. The ruling body, having been previously unaware that he had continued in his erroneous views or that he had finished his tract concluded that "the whole Synod cannot form a judgment upon his sentiments from the report of a few who may understand them." However, if Harker proceeded to publish his work, the synod "at present declare to the world . . . they do not approve." In spite of these warnings, Harker published a work, *Predestination consistent with general liberty: or The scheme of the covenant of grace.* Concerned for the doctrinal integrity of its church and the blatant disregard for its authority, the synod determined to resolve the matter during its 1762 meeting. However, the ruling body was prevented from deciding Harker's fate due to the time spent settling another explosive issue, the question of experimental religion, and so his case was postponed to 1763.[77] Another balanced committee was formed to examine and write an overture respecting Harker's book. On the ninth day of the conference, May 26, 1763, the committee brought its findings before the synod, and unsurprisingly it revealed the same issues that had been noted by the previous committees. Harker's principles were "of a hurtful and a dangerous tendency." Still the minister's fate rested in his own hands, as the ruling body decided to give him an opportunity the next day to either defend his position or recant.

The synod found his fresh defense unconvincing, and as he was still unwilling to recant his Pelagian views, the Presbyterian leadership publicly declared his theology "contrary to the word of God and our approved standards of doctrine" and removed him from the church. To be clear, both the ruling body and Harker wanted the same thing, further progress extending Christ's kingdom. But the temptation to court heterodoxy, even if only in this instance, to accomplish this goal went further than the synod would go, and it was beyond what the ruling body would tolerate within its bounds. It defended this action by recounting the multiple failed attempts during the past five years "to reclaim him from his erroneous notions," which had proven too "seducing" for many "unwary and unstable" believers. It was this threat, the synod claimed, that forced it to move beyond toleration to excommunication.[78] As difficult as it was, this decision helps provide a model for understanding the synod's judicial process in the post-reunion world. Presbyterians were willing to act decisively to keep Christendom from harm if their position was clearly supported by scripture and the Divines.

Another equally revealing challenge to the church came with the revived contest over experimental religion. When the issue first resurfaced during the 1761 synod meeting, many believed the three-year-old union was in jeopardy. A dejected Francis Alison confided to his Congregationalist friend Ezra Stiles, "Our Synod are like to be divided" over this "experimental acquaintance of Religion."[79] Sensing the same danger, the synod postponed a final decision and spent the next year scrambling for a definitive answer to one of the questions that had splintered the church decades earlier. As had been the case then, both the Old Light and New Light remnants appeared to hold to their respective positions, and tensions were high as the ruling body convened in May 1762 at the First Presbyterian Church in Philadelphia. For five days the recommendation that all ministerial candidates satisfactorily illustrate their experiential religion was debated. Finally a vote was taken on May 27, and the overture "was carried in the affirmative."[80] The New Lights had won the day, but it was unclear whether it would be a lasting victory.

Contesting this decision, the Old Light leadership submitted their protests, which led many in the synod "fearing a breach . . . on this question . . .

to be absent." Those remaining created "a committee to attempt an amicable accommodation of the affair."[81] The issue was now in the capable hands of men such as Francis Alison, Samuel Finley, and Richard Treat. These men had helped to bridge the original divide in 1758, and it was hoped they could avoid a similar calamity.[82] Working quickly to defuse the situation, the committee reached a conclusion on behalf of the synod for the 3:00 p.m. session the following day. Its decision was as follows: "The Synod earnestly desiring that all due liberty of conscience be preserved inviolate, and that peace and harmony be maintained and promoted, do agree that, when any person shall offer himself as a candidate for the ministry to any of our Presbyteries, every member of the Presbytery may use that way which he in conscience look upon proper, to obtain a competent satisfaction of the person's experimental acquaintance with religion."[83]

The committee had ingeniously kept the expectation of proof of experimental religion to satisfy most New Lights while also inserting the right of each member of the presbytery to decide for himself how this would be accomplished, which pleased the Old Lights. Yet this was far more than a useful maneuver to satisfy the current whims of their fellow members; the committee also maintained the body's scriptural and confessional integrity as specified in 1758. The solution to this recurring problem, the synod stated, had to address both the presbyteries' directorial charge "to inquire touching the grace of God"[84] in a ministerial candidate's life and the "Liberty of Conscience" protected by the Bible and the Divines. The committee's overture satisfied both requirements while pleasing the parties in their midst. Although it upset the few diehards in both camps, the overture was passed by the synod. Once again, by relying on the scriptures and the Divines the church's leadership had navigated another impasse potentially "destructive to the externall Peace and Order which Christ hath established in the Church."[85]

When considered alongside the controversy of the eighteen New Light ministers and the trouble with Samuel Harker, the renewed crisis over experimental religion illustrates well the internal distractions of the Presbyterian synod in achieving its interdenominational goals. Still, although tested and weary, the Presbyterian leadership saw cause for hope. In 1763 the British and the French agreed to peace and lifted the darkness that had engulfed the colonies. God's displeasure, it seemed, had waned. Elated, the synod stated that a day of celebration should be set aside "for the blessings of . . . peace."[86]

Yet as quickly as the colonists embraced this hope for peace, it was stripped from them as the frontier was clouded by Pontiac's Rebellion. Inspired by the revivalist prophet Neolin's message of resistance, this pan-Indian movement wrestled from the British most of their forts near the Great Lakes and in the Ohio Valley.[87] By the summer of 1763, the Native Americans were attacking and killing from Pennsylvania to Virginia, and the casualty toll neared two thousand colonists. Fear had reclaimed its place amid the colonists and antagonized the already sensitive racial tensions.

In Pennsylvania in the darkness of the early-morning hours on December 14, a group of fifty Scots-Irish Presbyterians from the town of Paxton attacked and burned a Native American village called Conestoga Town. Completely overwhelmed with a desire to destroy all of the Conestoga Indians, the Paxton Boys forced their way into the Lancaster jail and slaughtered the fourteen surviving villagers. Yet the vigilantes were still not satisfied; in early 1764 the group, now numbering five hundred, marched on Philadelphia to kill the one hundred and forty Native American refugees there. At Philadelphia, instead of finding sleeping Indians, the Paxton Boys encountered royal forces, which stopped their bloody spree.[88] Although the physical violence of the Paxton Boys had been thwarted, their troublesome influence would linger a while longer in the political and religious affairs of the colony. The Paxton Boys introduced the Presbyterians to another unseen obstacle on their interdenominational journey, the ability of local colonial politics to undermine their plans.

The Pennsylvania Assembly elections of 1764 reflected the hostile nature of the preceding months as the proprietary party and the Quakers struggled for control. In this contest, the Presbyterians would play a crucial role. Convinced that the Quaker leadership had intentionally refused to aid frontier settlers, who were mostly Presbyterians, against Indian attacks, the Presbyterians sought change and political recognition by siding with the proprietary party. As the tension between the parties mounted, a pamphlet war started that only intensified the situation. The Paxton Boys' actions were among the central issues of this debate, and it soon became clear that they stirred both political and religious animosity between Presbyterians and Quakers.[89]

The Quaker party struck at the Presbyterians when they published what they titled a "dialogue" between "Mr. Positive" and "Mr. Zealot" concerning "the late declaration and remonstrance, of the back-inhabitants of the province of Pennsylvania."[90] As the two men talked about the recent uprising, Mr. Positive stated, "Oh Zealot! tell me not of Cassius, Brutus, Ceasar, Pompey, or even Alexander the Great! We! Paxton Boys have done more than all, or any of them! We have, and it gives me Pleasure to think on't, Slaughter'd, kill'd and cut off a whole Tribe! a Nation at once!"[91] The conversation was soon interrupted by one "Mr. Lovell," who chastised the men for their support of the Paxton Boys. Lovell stated that the Presbyterians were "Party men; warm Bigots . . . an aspiring People, who, when they have attain'd their Aim, or gotten the Reins of Government in their Fists, have grasp'd it hard, and . . . like that conceited giddy-headed Fellow who thought himself sufficient to guide the Chariot of the Sun . . . set the World on Fire."[92]

Adding further sting to this "dialogue," was the accompanying letter written by a Presbyterian admonishing his church. In defense of the Quaker position, the author wrote, "Why are the Quakers, your good Neighbours, so falsely and slanderously abus'd by you?"[93] He then chided the denomination for its support of the Paxton Boys and concluded his correspondence with a scriptural warning: "*Be careful lest you be found Fighters against GOD, calling Light Darkness and Darkness Light, putting Good for Evil and Evil for Good.*"[94] Not only were the political leanings of the Presbyterians being criticized externally and internally, but their Christian spirit and discernment was also being called into question.[95]

The pamphlet war continued, mostly through the work of David James Dove and those of the Quaker party who accepted his lyrical challenges. Although Presbyterians were lambasted in these exchanges, they too were guilty of belligerent publications.[96] On March 30, 1764, Gilbert Tennent, Francis Alison, and John Ewing—representing both a union between New Lights and Old Lights as well as hindrance to interdenominationalism with the Quakers—published a circular letter protesting the unjust treatment of their church in the Paxton affair and warning against the Quaker proposal to place Pennsylvania under royal governance. For Tennent, Alison and Ewing, the two were intimately connected. They reasoned that because "the Presbyterians here" were not inclined to support the recent Quaker party proposition, believing it "not *safe* to do Things of such Importance rashly," their characters and church were being assaulted in print.[97] "This Affair," the trio wrote, "is in all Probability, a *Trap* laid to ensnare the unwary, and then to cast an Odium on the *Presbyterians* for ruining or attempting to ruin the Province." The three ministers believed that the Quakers intended to paint all Presbyterians as villains in order to taint them publicly and distract attention from the Quakers' controversial proposition. Tennent, Alison, and Ewing called upon all Pennsylvanians "whether of our Denomination or others" to be wary of the conniving Quakers and "lose no Time in advising all under your Influence . . . from signing any such Petition."[98] Regardless of whether such measures were justified, politics and not Christendom had become the focal point for many Pennsylvanian Presbyterians. Engaging in this civic debate stirred religious and political animosities and effectively muffled the call for Christian unity that had rung clearly in the church in 1758.

Finally the election came, and the results were bittersweet for the proprietary party as their biggest opponents, Benjamin Franklin and Joseph Galloway, were defeated, but the Quakers maintained their majority in the Assembly. Further to the party's chagrin, the Quaker Assembly found a new use for Franklin and sent him to England to secure their hope that the colony would come under the control of the crown. The election did not provide a solution for the political turmoil in Pennsylvania; instead, it appears to have intensified it.[99] The string of events from the Peace of 1763 to the election of 1764 resulted in a Pennsylvania quagmire that seriously damaged the Presbyterians' goal to strengthen Christendom as their fragile relations with the Quakers quickly deteriorated. However, despite the ideological faltering by many Pennsylvanian Presbyterians, hope remained for the goals of 1758 and it came from the South.

Although the Presbyterians' path to Christian unity was littered with distractions and obstacles, they pressed on and to this end, Virginian Presbyterians were invaluable. In Virginia, the mid-eighteenth century Presbyterians secured an interdenominational victory for the church through the leadership of men such as Samuel Davies and "One-Eyed" William Robinson. These men worked with the Anglican establishment, making themselves a necessity for the colony's leadership. Historian Robert M. Calhoon writes that for the Anglicans the "Presbyterians . . . functioned as a interface between dissent and orthodoxy." The Virginia officials relied on the Presbyterians in this manner so they could emphasize to the increasingly diverse Dissenters "the importance of maintaining order."[100] While serving this function the Presbyterians pressed the establishment for the recognition of Dissenters as valid churches in the colony. It was largely through the relentless efforts of Samuel Davies, who argued that the 1689 Act of Toleration passed by Parliament extended to the colonies, that finally "the Presbyterians . . . won toleration for themselves, and for other denominations willing to secure a license for their ministers and meetinghouses."[101] Exemplifying an interdenominational spirit, the Presbyterians did not hoard the fruit of their labors; instead they fought to secure tolerance for all Dissenters in Virginia. Through these struggles Presbyterians campaigned, as Davies wrote, for "Brotherly Love":

1. Descend, Thou mild, pacific Dove!
Thine Image on our Hearts impress;
Transform our Passions all to Love,
And sooth our Discords into Peace.

2. In Arms of warm Benevolence,

Teach us t'embrace all Human Kind;
And like the Sun, around dispense
The Wishes of a gen'rous Mind.

3. We are but Parts of one great Whole,
And may our Hearts, enlarg'd, exult
To scatter Bliss from Pole to Pole,
And still the Gen'ral Good consult![102]

Davies saw great potential for evangelical outreach in Virginia, and to that end he called other Presbyterians to the colony.[103] The first to respond was the Irish-born John Todd who arrived from the Presbytery of New Brunswick in 1752. The two became close friends, and Todd became a protégé of sorts to Davies. This influence lasted well after Davies left for the College of New Jersey and beyond even his death in 1761. Like his mentor, Todd strove to foster a more cordial relationship between Christian churches and for the general edification of the universal church; and, also like Davies, Todd believed psalmody an invaluable tool to achieve both. In 1763 Todd was called before the Presbytery of Hanover, which consisted of several other disciples of Samuel Davies such as John Wright, William Richardson, Robert Henry, James Hunt, and Henry Patillo, to discuss whether songs other than those found in traditional psalmbooks were fit for Christian worship. Following his presentation, the presbytery encouraged him to publish his work and as he was "desirous to serve the best interest of mankind," he sent "it abroad into to the world."[104]

From the start Todd made it clear that although this discourse was born in a Presbyterian setting, he wanted it to benefit the whole Christian church. He repeatedly challenged "the gospel church" or the "church of Christ" or "Christians anywhere" to consider his argument in favor of using updated psalmodies, such as that penned by Isaac Watts, "to introduce more of the spirit of the gospel into christian worship." Also like Davies before him, when engaging the public sphere, he emphasized general Christian principles, such as the redeeming work of Christ, and not the particular tenets of the Presbyterian Church. Knowing how contentious this issue was for many Christians, the minister recommended the exercise of "that tenderness, forbearance and charity, that is the ornament of the christian character; and to use no other than the gentle arts of reason and persuasion, till with the most cordial union of hearts and voices, we all join in songs to the *Lamb*, that washed us from our sins in his blood."[105] As psalmody was not a problem exclusive to Presbyterians, Todd was careful to discuss the traditional psalmbooks favored throughout British Christianity, including

"*Rouse's* commonly called the *Scotch version*, the *New-England*, or *Sternhold and Hopkins*."[106] With his broad audience in mind, he applauded the merits of these translations, but concluded that even the best would ultimately be "a bright copy of the devotions of the *jewish king*; but it would never make the fittest *psalm-book* for christians at this day." Todd explained that "the psalms of David were suited exactly to the *jewish* day, and this is one of their great excellencies; and a very plain reason why they do not suit us under the gospel." And, he continued, if "*David* should arise from the dead . . . to join the songs of the gospel church on earth . . . . would he not introduce the *Lord Jesus*, as *crucified for us*, and sing his *dying love* upon a cross . . . . would he not mention the *Lamb that was slain from the foundation of the world*, and sing the glories and triumphs of the redeemer over the powers of the earth and hell?"[107]

What death prevented David from writing, Todd argued, men such as Isaac Watts had finished. Watts, the English theologian who won renown for his psalms, in particular, had written "a most agreeable imitation" of the *Psalms* giving "them an evangelical turn, and as far as possible . . . the sense of them in gospel language and sentiments." He reminded his audience that Christ must be in a Christian's songs as he was in their prayers and sermons. How else would they meet St. Paul's command to "*Let the word of Christ dwell in you richly, in all wisdom; teaching and admonishing one another, in psalms, and hymns, and spiritual songs, singing with grace in your hearts to the Lord.*"[108] However, Todd was quick to note that singing Christ-centered songs was not the result of contemporary "*innovations.*" "When it was death to call upon the *name* of the *Lord Jesus*," the minister added, "the primitive christians woud rise before day, to sing a hymn of praise to *Christ* as *God*." They were not alone; this practice was held and supported, Todd claimed, by Christian fathers such as Tertullian, Origen, Dionysius, and Spanheim.[109]

However, not only were such songs orthodox. They also held the potential to unite diverse Christian groups. On this point the minister excitedly added that when one "*Paulus Samosatenus*, a heretical bishop of *Antioch* rose up, and abolished these *psalms*, that were wont to be sung to the honor of the *Lord Jesus Christ*; and appointed women to sing his own praise . . . he was accused and condemned by the council of *Antioch*. And it is worth notice, that this was an *aecumenical council*, the only one that was of that sort for the first 300 years after Christ, that I can find, consisting of *bishops*, *presbyters*, and *deputies*, of as many churches as were pleased to come from all parts of the world." Still, Todd warned, although Christ-centered psalms were capable of fostering Christian unity they should never be imposed on anyone. "The truth is," he said, "this is one among many things which

God has left to the wisdom and direction of the churches, to use those psalms that are most agreeable to their circumstances, and most for their edification."[110] "And since," Todd continued, "the education, the prejudices, the circumstances, the very make and dispositions of men, are so vastly different one from another . . . God may be worshiped sincerely in different modes." This, the Presbyterian maintained, was one of the many "rights of Christians," and "there is no synod, assembly, or council on earth, that hath, or ought to have, power to impose any one version of psalms on the christian churches." Psalmody had great potential for both division and unity, and Todd believed the only way to avoid the former and foster the latter was by preserving Christian liberty. He concluded his address by reiterating the reason for singing and unity, which, simply put, was Christ. "I am not ashamed," he wrote, "to declare to you and to the world, that I believe we should sing the praises of God and the Lamb, that washed us from our sins in his own blood."[111]

Addressing both the need for peace within the universal church and in society in general, another Virginian Presbyterian, David Rice, took up his pen in 1764.[112] Already the young Rice had developed a strong reputation for his intellect and his ability to clearly communicate biblical truths within the church, and his anonymously published tract, *The Universal Peace-Maker, or Modern Author's Instructor*, only cemented that impression. Intending to reach as broad a colonial audience as possible, Rice chose one of the most popular publishers in early America's most prolific publishing city—Anthony Armbruster of Philadelphia. Writing under the pseudonym Philanthropos, he introduced British America to his analysis of "the Divisions which of late have prevailed and are still subsisting amongst us." Borrowing from authorities such as the Israelite King Solomon and the Anglican bishop of Sarum (now Salisbury), Rice concluded "that the great cause of all our Divisions is *Pride*. Only by pride (says *Solomon*) comes contention." All were susceptible to pride, including divines, scholars, and magistrates. Among these leaders, Rice wrote, "some fancy themselves invested with all the powers of the *Apostles*. . . . some of them are proud enough to pretend, that both the mansions of bliss, and the flames of vengeance in a future state, are to be assigned to men according to their directions: And others think themselves impowered to determine at least, who shall be in repute, and who shall be under infamy and disgrace, who shall be dignified, and who shall be despised in the present life." Regardless of their station in life, Rice noted, all "men are generally observed to be mighty selfish creatures, and to think nothing of so much importance in itself, or so worthy their regard, as their own interests . . . . They will prefer them to truth, to justice, to peace, to the public welfare, and in a manner to every thing."[113]

According to Rice, the problem with pride lay in its elevation of the individual. Still, he consoled, "could men be persuaded to prefer the public peace and welfare, to their own private advantages," then "how well would it be with us!" A "happy calm" would "spread itself thro' the church of CHRIST, and over the face of the earth." The society that pursued such relationships would not only be free from internal dangers associated with divisions, but external threats also. The Presbyterian observed that "union has been always esteemed a mark of wisdom, as well as a means of power, it raises the character and reputation of a country and makes it appear formidable; at the same time it is beautiful and lovely: In the language of the sacred poet, It is to look fair as the moon, clear as the sun, and, at the same time, terrible as an army with banners." Divine blessings awaited peacemakers, but those individuals or groups contentedly divided would meet another fate. The obstinate, according to Rice, would meet civil wars where "fellow-citizens imbrue their hands in one another's blood, and triumph in one another's ruin." Their governments would subsequently fall, their liberties would be destroyed, and tyranny and slavery would engulf the land.[114] The subduing of pride and the elevation of charity and peace, then, were necessities for both Christians and society at large.

In the same spirit, a posthumous collection of Samuel Davies's sermons was published, and it appeared that even from the grave the minister called upon the Presbyterian Church to maintain its reunion promises. In his *Sermons on the most useful and important subjects*, which spanned three volumes and over a thousand pages, there was a persistent theme of "catholic" Christianity.[115] The theme was clearest in Davies's sermon "The Sacred Import of the Christian Name." Here he stated, "To lay more stress upon the name of a presbyterian or a church-man than on the sacred name of christian . . . to make it the object of my zeal to gain proselytes to some other than the christian name . . . these are the things which deserve universal condemnation from God and man."[116] Lamenting the rise of "bigotry and faction" in Christ's kingdom, Davies commented that they were "directly opposite to the generous catholic spirit of christianity, and subversive of it." With a caution he continued, "My brethren, I would now warn you against this wretched mischievous spirit of party. . . . Let this congregation be that of a christian society, and I little care what other name it wears. Let it be a little Antioch, where the followers of Christ shall be distinguished by their old catholic name, Christians."[117] Once more, and from beyond the veil, Davies pushed for a united Christendom, and it came at a time when Presbyterians needed reminding of their public promises.

In the land of the living, Charles Jeffrey Smith attempted to maintain the toleration won by Presbyterians such as Davies in Virginia. On July 25,

1765, Smith wrote to the Anglicans in Williamsburg pleading that the co-operative efforts between Anglicans and Dissenters continue for the benefit of Christendom. In particular, he hoped to secure approval for a license for a new Presbyterian church. Playing by the rules written by earlier gener-ations of Virginia Presbyterians, Smith attempted to influence the Angli-cans by reminding them of their past in relation to his church. "You are our witnesses," Smith stated, "that we have used no private or publick artifice, to expose the liturgy, or disparage the members of the church of England. Ye can attest, that we have not designedly disseminated the seeds of schism, or blown the coals of discord, and unchristian separation." He continued, "Our aim has not been to make proselytes to this or that denomination, but *real converts* to *Jesus Christ*."[118] Presbyterian interdenominational spirit, it seems, had not yet succumbed to the snares of colonial politics or past ecclesiastical relationships.

Smith reminded the Anglicans that the Presbyterians posed no threats to their establishment; they did not wish to steal members, and they did not want to engage in doctrinal disputes. The Presbyterians, he stated, "have no other design but to promote *virtue* and *religion*: In which important cause, let every christian denomination cheerfully unite, and vigorously engage, but especially *presbyterians* and *churchmen*; for their essential doctrines are materially the same."[119] Perhaps Smith did not fully expect a formal union between the Presbyterians and the Anglicans, but at the very least he pro-posed informal cooperation for the spread of Christianity. The Presbyteri-an ended his petition to the Williamsburg Anglicans by emphasizing the idea that denominations needed to focus on their common Christian bonds and not their differences, especially in public. He wrote, "How much more generous, noble, and christian like is it, to see the *faithful ministers* of *Jesus*, in *every denomination*, overlooking the diversity of sentiment, in smaller matters, and cultivating mutual love and brotherly kindness, cherishing a good harmony and correspondence; jointly endeavouring to promote the great end of their mission, the *glory of God, and good of mankind*."[120] For many Presbytertian leaders, the pursuit of interdenominationalism was not a Presbyterian exclusive; it was hoped that the "generous, noble, and Chris-tian" spirit might infect other churches. Charles Jeffrey Smith represented a continuation of the interdenominational work started by Samuel Davies and other Virginian Presbyterians. In addition, Smith revealed that even though many Presbyterians had been unable to rise above local religious and political animosities to realize the church's reunion promise of cooperation, some within the denomination were still attempting to achieve those goals.

When the Presbyterians reunited in 1758, they declared to the world that they would strive to promote Christian unity both internally and externally.

The edification of Christ's earthly kingdom, so clearly perceived in 1758, had proven difficult to implement. Yet, considering the state of the church before reunion—at odds with various denominations and themselves—the Presbyterians made significant progress toward their interdenominational goals by the early 1760s. Despite the remaining obstacles, their success drove them forward, and so the church pursued this spirit of cooperation during the following decades. Interestingly, as the constitutional crisis—concerning both civic and religious liberties—between Great Britain and her North American colonies escalated, the denomination found it easier to unite internally and to work more closely with other churches. The resulting interchurch cooperation, however, was not what they had originally envisioned.

2

Threats Inside and Out, 1765–1775

If there was hope by 1765 that the Presbyterians would continue to progress on their interdenominational journey, immense clouds of doubt were seen gathering in the distance. On February 6, 1765, British Prime Minister George Grenville introduced the Stamp Act resolutions, helping to spark the American Revolution.[1] The subsequent constitutional debates concerning the civil and religious liberties of the colonists largely preoccupied the energies of the Presbyterians. Leaders within the Presbyterian Church established the denomination as a vessel for the colonists to better understand and address the imperial conflict. Even though, during these years, Presbyterians proposed both denominational and colonial unity, these suggestions introduced new meanings to the original call. The Presbyterians were still hoping to help heal the divisions in Christ's kingdom, but they also looked to unions for the protection of American liberties, both religious and civil. Still, these unions had religious objectives, and they were firmly rooted in ecclesiastical traditions of resistance that dated back to the Protestant Reformation.[2] These amendments to the interdenominational goals of 1758, however, introduced new concerns that worked in tandem with the intermittent Old/New Light conflicts, and proved a distraction for many churchgoers, but the long sought-for unity of Christendom was never forgotten. Throughout the period, leading Presbyterians continued to push for true eternal cooperation among churches and Christians.

In 1765, the year after his death, a series of sermons by Gilbert Tennent was published. They were originally given before the Synod of New York and Philadelphia in May 1759, but their publication in 1765 served as a timely reminder of the church's reunion goals.[3] As was his tendency, Tennent wasted little time calling his fellow Presbyterians to wholeheartedly take up the title of "*Peacemakers*." This would be difficult, he acknowledged, as human nature strove against such activity and "persons of narrow minds and divisive practices, are applauded." Nevertheless, "in the judgment of our Lord, the *Peacemakers* are blessed, for they shall be called the children of God." The reoccurring Old Light/New Light issues were certainly on the minister's mind, but he did not limit his discussion to the denomination. The divine charge "doubtless extends to all the connections of mankind, in families, church and state;" and, Tennent continued, "*peacemakers* therefore are such who are themselves quiet and peaceable, who sincerely love peace and earnestly endeavor in obedience to God, and regard to man to promote it, wherever their influence reaches, thro' the general series of their behavior, by the use of all lawful means."[4]

There were many obstacles between Christians and peacemaking, Tennent noted, such as "rash-judging" and "unscriptural terms of communion," but there was one that appeared to bother him most, "uncharitable divisions." Reminiscent of the plan of reunion, Tennent cried, "Alas! what multitudes are prejudiced against christianity altogether, by the numerous schisms of the church of CHRIST, and their carnal contentions." Instead of a reflection of Christ's own perfect example or the realization of his prayer "that *his people may be one as he and the father are one*" the world was treated to Christians who "labour to ruin one another's reputations, provoke mutually not to love, but wrath, and practically confine christianity to their several parties, as tho' CHRIST was divided or had many bodies!"[5] At the heart of Christendom's divisive tendencies was the problem of pride, Tennent argued, and it was pride that "blows up peace in families, church and state; it sets men on striving who shall be greatest." To counteract this, he called his audience to "*love* our *brethren with a pure heart fervently*; this will incline us to cover their infirmities, and to live at peace with them; *love endureth all things*: if we love our brethren more, we shall be willing to bear more with them; and to provoke them less."[6]

Although Tennent hoped for such a unity among Christians, he did not believe it would or should come at the cost of what "the Apostle *Paul*" called "christian liberty." As Christians, he stated, it was necessary that "we . . . believe and love lesser points of truth, without imposing them upon others." Here denominations played a useful role, but such associations could be abused and encourage more rifts within the universal church. As the body of Christ, churches served varying roles, "and tho' the body mystical hath some parts which are reckoned less honorable, yet there should be no schism in it."[7] Believers, then, had to embrace the difficult mandate that "*we must buy the truth and not sell it*," and "we must *follow peace with all men*." "But," Tennent observed, "there is a wide difference between our love to it [lesser points of truth] and our imposing of it as a term of communion upon others; the former is our duty, and the latter our sin."[8] Too often, that sin assumed the shape of persecution. Yet, the minister noted, "CHRIST never intended to have his religion propagated by fire and sword, or penal laws, or to own bigotry and intemperate zeal as the marks of his disciples; the children of this world love to fish in troubled waters, but the children of GOD are the *peace-makers*, the quiet of the land."[9]

The "principle and practice of *persecution* or indeavours to force uniformity in matters purely religious, by methods of external violence, such as fines, imprisonment, confiscation of goods, banishment, bodily pains and death" were the tools of anti-Christian forces in the world.[10] Tennent pleaded: "LET *Pharisees, Pagans, Arians, Turks, Papists* and other of the same *stamp*, influenced by the same anti-christian spirit, pride themselves in *cruelty* and *blood*; boast of their *zeal* in *knocking people* on the *head for God's sake*, and *cramming* their faith down their *throats*: but let the sincere *followers* of the *meek lamb of God, glory* as the *primitive christians* did, only in the *cross of Christ!*"[11] Unlike the pawns in Satan's kingdom, Christ's kingdom was "not earthly" in that sense, but rather "spiritual" overseeing humanity's "hearts and minds." "Therefore," Tennent argued, it "is to be promoted and propagated by spiritual means only, which are suited to its nature and design." When force was used, the Presbyterian noted, it worked "to CONFOUND the KINGDOM OF CHRIST with the kingdoms of this world, to change its spiritual NATURE, and make it carnal and political."[12] Instead, Tennent stated, Christians were called to use such methods as "divine wisdom has prescribed" and "therefore stand fast in the liberty wherewith Christ has made us free."[13]

To this end, the 1758 Presbyterian reunion was exemplary, and he called his "reverend *fathers* and *brethren*" to "bless God for the *union* we are at present favoured with, as a religious society; and to intreat you to endeavour *pro virili*, to *keep it in the bond of peace*." While the church had not yet betrayed "*foundation* and important *principles*" in its pursuit of peace, the danger was not removed, and Tennent called for the continued and "constant *testimony*, especially against the corrupt and dangerous tenets of the *Socinians, Arians, Armenians, and Antinomians*," found in "an inviolate adherence to the excellent *system* of divine *truths* contained in the *Westminster confession of faith* and *catechism*, which we have adopted as the confession of our faith, and for which we have reason to bless God to our latest breath." In parting, the minister reminded his audience that even in the face of such heresies persecution was never the answer. "Our zeal should awake," he agreed, "but let it be directed by *knowledge*, and tempered with *humility*. *Let us be valiant for the truth*; and to this end, let us *speak in love*, and exercise *mercy* in connection with *fidelity*."[14]

Gilbert Tennent's posthumous *aide-mémoire* came none too soon. When the Presbyterian synod gathered in New York on May 21, 1766, the delicate peace between the Old Lights and the New Lights was tested again and a reminder of the reunion goals was needed. The first trial came in the form of the two presbyteries of Philadelphia. When the Old Light ministers, such as Francis Alison and John Ewing, realized they had lost control of the onetime Old Light stronghold, Philadelphia, a second presbytery of Philadelphia was created. This move allowed them to stave off irrelevance in a New Light-dominated presbytery and continue pursuing the ministry without experimental religion.[15] There were some ministers, such as William Tennent and John Blair, who wished the two presbyteries to be reunited, but their proposal was voted down in the synod. The ministers then submitted their "disapprobation of the Reverend Synod's determination." Fearful of the precedent the Second Presbytery of Philadelphia was setting, they wrote: "It carries in it the obvious appearance of disunion, and seems to indicate a temper of a schismatical tendency, however, it may be suppressed for the present. It will also be likely to perpetuate party distinctions in reference to candidates licensed by the respective Presbyteries."[16] Noting that the discontented were not so opposed as to leave the synod, they did not make a motion in the ruling body to revisit the question, and it appeared as if the fragile peace would continue. However, the meeting had just started, and the synod had no way of knowing the dangers that lay ahead.

At nine in the morning on May 28, the synod met and considered a petition, by John Beard and Joseph Tate, that the members of the Donegal Presbytery, who had been forced to merge with the Presbytery of Carlisle the year before, be reconstituted as the Donegal Presbytery. Beard and Tate were hoping to capitalize on the synod's decision concerning the Second Presbytery of Philadelphia by proposing their own Old Light haven separate from the New Light Carlisle Presbytery. Despite the recent precedent, the synod voted the Old Light proposal down. Not willing to quit just yet, Tate and Beard proposed that the old Presbytery of Donegal be merged with the Second Presbytery of Philadelphia. Again, the synod voted against them. Old Light leaders Francis Alison, John Ewing, Patrick Allison, and Mathew Wilson made use of their reunion liberties and wrote a dissenting statement in opposition to the synod's decision. The ruling body noted their position but held firm to its decision. Thinking that it had once again thwarted a potential schism, the ruling body was no doubt caught off guard

when Tate and Beard, on behalf of the onetime Presbytery of Donegal, re-
signed from the church.[17] The ministers wrote that even though they "much
desire to be in union and friendship with this reverend body," the recent decision of the synod had made that impossible. In what was possibly a final
effort to sway their brethren, they stated they "would not knowingly be the
real authors of any discord in the church of Christ," using the same reasoning the synod had employed many times before when addressing factions
in its midst.[18] Whether or not it was a ploy, the decision of the ruling body
stood, at least for the moment, and the dreaded splintering of the church
had finally occurred.[19]

The synod was not the only place Presbyterian discord could be found
in 1766. In July, Samuel Finley died, leaving vacant the presidency of the
College of New Jersey in Princeton. As *the* Presbyterian College in North
America and one of the few pre-1758 interdenominationally minded projects
of the church, much hinged on the theological and even political leanings
of the new president.[20] Although the school had always been led by a New
Light Board of Trustees and president, the Old Lights nevertheless wished
to take control of the college. The possibility of attaining the presidency
of *the* Presbyterian college in the colonies meant a possible revival of their
thinning ranks. One of the trustees, John Rodgers, described the position
in this way: "The President of the College of New Jersey will not only have
it in his Power to serve the Interests of Christ in the most enlarged & ef-
fectual Manner by training up Youth for the Gospel Ministry in this wide
extended Country; but He will sit revered at the Head of the Presbyterian
Interest already great & dayly growing in these Middle Colonies. And no
Man can have it more in his Power to advance the Cause of Xtian Liberty
by forming the Minds of Youth to proper Sentiment on this most interesting Subject."[21] No doubt the Old Lights were excited by this opportunity to
take control of "the only true intercolonial educational institution."[22] With
its widespread distribution of ministers throughout the colonies, the college
would give them the means to train a new generation of ministers who
could quickly make the Old Light dream of revival a reality.

Making the Old Light position even more desperate, and therefore
making the situation potentially more divisive, was its members' belief that
they were losing control and influence over the College of Philadelphia,
which had long been their source for ministers (despite the Anglican origins of the school). For years, the Old Light Presbyterians had dominated
the faculty, led by Vice Provost Francis Alison. The Old Light situation had
improved when the Anglican provost, William Smith, spent most of the
1760s in England trying in vain to recruit Anglicans to teach at the school.
In his absence an interim provost, John Ewing, who was a pupil of Ali-

son, was chosen. However, despite this initial good fortune, the Old Lights found it increasingly difficult to attract candidates for the Presbyterian ministry. The primary obstacles were the wary Anglican Board of Trustees and the comparable openings for relatively cushy Anglican pulpits. By 1766 the Old Lights were especially forlorn.[23] In an October 1766 letter to his Congregationalist confidant, Ezra Stiles, Francis Alison revealed this despair: "I am ready to resign my place in the College, and retire to the country merely thro chagrine. The College is artfully got into ye hands of Episcopal Trustees. Young men educated here get a taste for high life and many of them do not like to bear ye poverty and dependence of our ministers. Those that pass Tryals for ye ministry meet with hard Treatment from ye Brethren yt favor Jersey College, and can hardly find settlements, and under that discouragement they are flattrd and enticed by their Episcopal acquaintances to leave such bigots and to go to London for orders."[24] By 1766 the Old Light Presbyterians were driven by more than want of the College of New Jersey; they were driven by need.

According to the College of New Jersey's charter, the trustees had to wait for four months before they could choose another president. Thus a decision could not be made until November 1766 at the earliest, and both Old and New Lights eagerly awaited the approaching day. During these four months the Old Lights developed a scheme they hoped would garner control of the college. A letter from one of Alison's well-connected members, Samuel Purviance Jr., to Erza Stiles provided an outline of the plan. Purviance stated that the Old Lights were going to send a committee to meet with the trustees of New Jersey College when they met in November in order to choose the next president. The committee would propose "to have the Institution put on a new Plan, to have 4 able Professors appointed and Dr. Alison at their Head, and even to offer . . . to give up Mr. Ewing if judg'd necessary for ye publick Good." Knowing that the college was perpetually underfunded, the committee was to sweeten the proposition and "offer to make up by an Annual Subscription whatever their Funds fall short of supporting the proposed number of Professors, and to join all our Influence in Raising Funds sufficient to support the College and in general to throw our whole force into that one Channell."[25] As Purviance noted, the Old Lights needed for this to work, so more still was planned. There was also to be a show of support from various leading citizens, some of whom attended with speeches in hand and others through letters. However, Purviance warned this would only work if the New Lights remained unaware of the scheme, so he begged Stiles to be discrete. "So sensible are we of the narrow Biggotry of our Brethren ye New Lights," he wrote, "that we dare not disclose these our benevolent and generous Views for fear of defeating our Intentions; by apprising them beforehand we know Schemes [would]. Be laid to oppose us . . . we hope to take our Friends off their Guard."[26] The Old Lights were right to worry about the success of their plans.

Despite their best efforts to conceal their scheming, the Board of Trustees discovered the Old Lights' intentions and struck first. The trustees met a day before the scheduled meeting and decided to offer the presidency to the Scot, John Witherspoon. To the chagrin of the Old Lights, when the committee arrived, they were met with the news. Shocked, they protested but the board held to its decision.[27] In the aftermath, Alison took up his pen again and wrote to Stiles, lamenting the lost opportunity. Still, Alison was not without hope. He wrote that the trustees had elected Witherspoon, "a keen satirical writer, but they know nothing of his academic abilities, nor whether he will accept their offer."[28] Even if he did accept and therefore thwart a renewed attempt by the Old Lights for revival, Alison was optimistic: "Should he accept their invitation & undertake this Province, this would be a likely way to unite us, but in the mean time the College is sinking in its reputation for want of a head."[29] Alison wished for Presbyterians to work together, even if he wished for a greater influence for the Old Lights. As he concluded his letter, Alison revealed the reason he strove for unity—"our enemies gain ground by our foolish animosities."[30]

However, as Alison suspected, Witherspoon was not a sure thing, and he refused the board's first offer in 1766 because his wife did not wish to leave Scotland. This turn of events rekindled hope among the Old Lights, and once again in 1767, when the trustees met to decide on a president, the Old Light committee brought its proposal. After some negotiation the Old Light plan was accepted—but with a caveat. The trustees were to fill certain positions on the basis of merit. In order to retain some peace, the Old Lights were not completely overlooked when the decisions were made. John Blair, Hugh Williamson, and Jonathan Edwards the Younger were chosen to fill the professorships, and Samuel Blair, who was only twenty-six at the time, was chosen for the presidency. Edwards the Younger and both of the Blairs were firm New Lights, leaving the young Williamson as the only Old Light hired. To be sure, this rankled the committee and the other Old Light schemers. Not only had the professorships been filled mostly by "narrow bigots," but both the revered Alison and Ewing had been rejected in favor of the youthful Samuel Blair.[31]

By most accounts Samuel Blair was an ersatz president meant to keep Alison or Ewing out of the presidency while the trustees continued to negotiate with Witherspoon. Benjamin Rush, a College of New Jersey graduate who was attending medical school in Edinburgh, became the primary negotiator and persuaded the Witherspoons to move to America.[32] In one of his last letters to the Scotsman, before he ultimately accepted the position, Rush painted a picture of the principal college in North America in a desperate situation: "how thick & fast its enemies increase, and how much the hearts of its pious founders are trembling for fear the united forces of civil & religious combination will end in the ruin of the College." Rush then asked why Witherspoon, who alone could save the school, would not be "head of an Institution on which the spreading of the Gospel thro' wide extended continent of America now entirely depends?"[33] Witherspoon soon after accepted the presidency, and Samuel Blair willingly stepped down. For the Old Lights some consolation came from the eventual acceptance of Witherspoon, even though he was not their first choice.[34] As Francis Alison had written the year before, Witherspoon was "a likely way to unite us."[35]

The resolution of the College of New Jersey crisis did little to redirect the Presbyterian Church's leadership back to its drive for Christian unity. Divisions within the church remained and, in particular, the wound caused by the secession of the Donegal Presbytery still festered. Trying to persuade them to rejoin the church, the synod pursued the wayward ministers from 1766 to 1768. In 1768, the Old Light ministers, through Joseph Tate, resubmitted their request to form their own presbytery, and once again the synod declined. However, the synod also wrote that they were "still willing to . . . attend to all proposals that may be made to heal differences and promote the Mediator's kingdom."[36] Tate, upon hearing the news of the latest defeat, told the synod that he and the other ministers would be willing to rejoin the denomination if they were able individually to join other presbyteries to their liking. The synod responded that "although they highly disapprove of the conduct of these brethren since their departure from the Synod, yet for the sake of peace they authorize the above mentioned Presbyteries to receive them."[37] The ministers chose to align with Old Light presbyteries even if their churches fell well outside of the presbytery's geographical bounds.[38] In allowing this concession, the synod demonstrated again just how far it was willing to bend to maintain unity. The ruling body hoped, as Gilbert Tennent had insisted, that "as peace is the bond of unity, so is unity of peace." Still, some members, such as George Duffield and John Strain, had their disapproval recorded. They argued the synod's decision established a dangerous precedent whereby fear of schism allowed the corrupted few to rule the many.[39] Nevertheless, the synod held to its decision, and some measure of church unity was restored.

As the perceived dangers to American religious and civil liberties grew, Presbyterian leaders from both the Old and New Light camps hoped that the threat would spark more cooperation within the denomination. For the most part, the conciliatory hopes of the Presbyterian synod were realized. However, a series of events beginning in 1771 threatened to tear at the synod's patchwork unity. As the city of Philadelphia and the number of Scots-Irish immigrants continued to grow in the 1760s and 1770s, the two Presbyterian churches in the city could no longer meet the needs of the laity. In response, the Third Presbyterian Church, under the care of the Second Presbytery of Philadelphia, was formed and called Samuel Eakin as its minister.[40] However, Eakin was soon brought before the synod on charges of "antenuptial fornication; lying with respect to [his] marriage; suborning witnesses; and deserting the work of the ministry, in direct violation of [his] ordination vows."[41] After repenting before the synod, Eakin was removed from the pulpit and suspended from the ministry.

The Third Church then called George Duffield, a rising New Light minister, to fill its pulpit. Although Francis Alison and John Ewing were typically able to restrain their dislike of the New Lights, this encroachment into their city and their presbytery was too much. Philadelphia was the last major stronghold of Old Lights in the colonies; the other major pulpits, such as those in New York and New Jersey, had already fallen to the New Lights.[42] The Second Presbytery of Philadelphia blocked Duffield's appointment. In 1772, the congregation appealed to the synod, where "a large majority" overturned the presbytery's decision.[43]

The Old Lights fumed at being overruled and having the New Lights creep into their territory. Anxious about the divisive spirit growing in Philadelphia, the synod wrote a pastoral letter beseeching its churches to "cultivate that spirit of love and Christian union among one another which is so frequently enjoined by the gospel of our Lord Jesus Christ, that it may appear to the world that you are not only one body, but of one mind."[44] The next year the defeated Old Lights changed their tactics and sent a committee, led by George Bryan, to the synod to charge "Mr. Duffield with sundry high crimes and misdemeanors" with the hope "he might be removed from the pulpit and church in Pine street."[45] Not only was Duffield cleared of the charges, but the synod also approved his church's request to be placed under the care of the First Presbytery of Philadelphia. The string of defeats left the Old Lights bitter, and Francis Alison and John Ewing, who still worked at the College of Philadelphia, continued their fight in the synod and even took the matter to civil court. However, in the end, all their attempts failed, and by 1776, George Duffield had become *the* Presbyterian leader in Pennsylvania.[46]

Despite the fact that some fringe Presbyterians (including Joseph Rhea) were "heartily praying to god" that the recent "ill concerted and ill patched union" might end, the Presbyterian Church made significant strides toward ending its strife.[47] Parties remained and crises continued to arise, but even within the most hostile interactions there was a desire among the leaders to work together, to mend the breach. One way the Presbyterian leadership hoped to foster further collegiality was through interdenominational ventures, and after the Donegal reunion, the Old Lights offered the next opportunity both to unite the church and address a troubling external issue.

New and Old Light leaders alike recognized the Stamp Act as an alarming threat to the colonists' liberties, one that required a united effort to resist successfully. As of May 1766, however, the synod had taken no position. But a plan by Francis Alison eventually allowed the synod to state its position and utilize its healing possibilities. Alison suggested an address, which the synod quickly approved, "to our Sovereign, on the joyful occasion of the repeal of the Stamp Act, and thereby a confirmation of our liberties."[48] On the surface it was a simple measure, but it contained an underlying potential that could unite the Presbyterians and protect their English liberties.

Reiterating these principles of unity and liberty, the ruling body wrote a letter to its member congregations as well. God had blessed them by ending the French and Indian War. But the synod lamented, "We rendered not to God according to the multitude of his tender mercies, for no sooner was the rod removed, and the blessings of peace restored, but we became more vain and dissolute than before." This was the reason, the ruling body said, for the "long suspense, whether we should be deprived of, or restored to the . . . privilege of English liberty" that had "filled every breast with the most painful anxiety."[49] For the synod, it was only God's mercy through the repeal of the Stamp Act that had prevented an escalation of the tension. They concluded that God "has given us to experience the paternal tenderness of the best of kings, and the moderation of the British Parliament. . . . May his unmerited goodness lead us to repentance."[50]

Despite having written two letters establishing the official position of the American Presbyterian Church, the synod had not quite finished. On the afternoon of May 30, the Overtures Committee proposed "to obtain some correspondence between this Synod and the consociated churches in Connecticut."[51] The overture was quickly passed, and a delegation led by Francis Alison was formed to meet with the Connecticut Congregationalists. Although the overture itself has not survived, the reason for this cooperative gesture was the fresh rumor that colonial Anglicans were calling for their own bishop. The threat of a colonial bishopric had waxed and waned for a century, and both the Presbyterians and Congregationalists had, individually, worked to neutralize it.[52] A bishop, it was feared, would only be the first step toward establishing an Anglican hegemony in the colonies. The recent murmurs that coincided with the abrasive and encroaching Stamp Act led the wary Americans to conclude that it was no coincidence.

Along with the delegation, the synod sent a letter, which shed more light on the intentions and hopes of the Presbyterians. In it they invited their Connecticut brethren "to a general consultation about such things as may have a hopeful tendency to promote and defend the common cause of religion against the attacks of its various enemies."[53] The task before them was not to be attempted alone, and although they could not be sure, the Presbyterians had reason to believe that their proposal would be well received. After all, it had been Ezra Stiles's *Discourse on a Christian Union* in 1761 that had both shed light on the Anglican plans and argued for cooperation among colonial Dissenters.[54] The synod wrote, "We are all brethren, embarked in the same interest, perfectly agreed in doctrine and worship, substantially pursuing the same method of discipline and church government, and we trust all animated with the same laudable zeal to advance the kingdom of our common Lord, we cannot but hope for your ready concurrence with our invitation."[55] Stressing to the Congregationalists that the union between the denominations was necessary to combat the threats against their liberties, the synod was also emphasizing the point for its own benefit. A common enemy and a noble cause could strengthen more than the bonds between Presbyterians and other denominations; they could also bridge the Old Light/New Light divide.

As it happened, the Presbyterians would not have to wait long for an answer. On June 17, 1766, the moderator of the Congregationalist General Association, Thomas Ruggles, officially accepted the Presbyterian invitation. Ruggles stated that he, and the other ministers, were excited that the churches were working together and that he hoped "the glorious and blessed time approach when love and union may prevail among all denominations of Christians through the world."[56] In the official response, the Congregationalists agreed to cooperate but on one condition: "The great and general interests of the Redeemer's kingdom would be happily promoted, the common cause of religion and virtue strengthened and defended, whilst mutual benevolence and brotherly love would be cultivated, by a general union, agreement, and correspondence with us, so far, and in such manner as is consistent and in no degree interfering with their and our respective internal state and order of government and discipline."[57] In other words, the Congregationalists were willing to meet as long as it was understood that, as a result of these efforts, neither of the denominations should attempt to engulf the other. Finding no problems with the terms, the Presbyterians arranged the first meeting of the convention for November 1766 in New York City.

After the failed coup at the College of New Jersey that November, Francis Alison no doubt found some comfort when the Presbyterian-Congregationalist convention finally met to discuss the Anglican menace.[58] Meeting in Elizabethtown, New Jersey, because of the smallpox outbreak in New York, the convention delegates quickly agreed to a plan of union. Representatives from both the Presbyterians and Congregationalists maintained that while neither church would relinquish its autonomy, they did wish to unite their efforts. Before they closed the first meeting, the delegates also agreed that a letter of invitation should be written to the Congregational, Presbyterian, and Dutch Reformed churches in Massachusetts, New Hampshire, and Rhode Island. To this end, the delegates wrote and distributed sample letters that could be used as templates by churches or individuals to protest the establishment of bishops in the colonies.[59] Basing the letters on a history of intolerance by the Church of England but also loyalty to king and constitution, the churches offered themselves to the many colonists who made up their congregations as a way to understand the ongoing crisis. Although the letters were a small way in which to shape colonial perceptions, the churches, especially the Presbyterians, would increase their efforts during the 1760s and 1770s. As the Presbyterians concluded the convention, they brought to an end a watershed year. The issues that came to the forefront during this time would preoccupy the Presbyterians for years to come.

In 1767, the year of the Townshend Acts, Thomas Bradbury Chandler published *An Appeal to the Public in Behalf of the Church of England in America*, which was an attempt to persuade the colonists of the neutral and unobtrusive nature of the proposed bishops.[60] In this vein, Chandler promised that if bishops were to come to the colonies they would only hold "*Spiritual and Ecclesiastical*" power. These prelates were to have no civil power, and what religious dominion they had "*shall operate only upon the Clergy of the Church, and not upon the Laiety nor Dissenters of any Denomination.*"[61] Although Chandler's intention was to calm colonial fears, his effort was unsuccessful. Shortly after publication of *An Appeal*, leading Presbyterians, both Old and New Light, took up their pens to preserve their religious liberties from Chandler, Charles Townshend, Parliament, and whoever else might threaten them.[62] In doing so, these church leaders broadened their range of influence by stepping beyond their congregations to both publicly connect the civil and religious threats and offered all colonists "a constitutional blueprint of the empire which they could defend."[63]

The first challenge came from the "American Whig," which initially appeared in the *New York Gazette* and subsequently in the *Boston Gazette* and the *Pennsylvania Journal*. Although William Livingston is thought to be the principal author, he was certainly helped by his friends and fellow Presbyterians John Morin Scott and William Smith Jr. who had previously helped him create the weekly journal protesting the Anglican hegemony in New York, the *Independent Reflector*.[64] It is possible that Livingston's list of contributors included other prominent Presbyterian, Congregationalist and Baptist leaders, such as Noah Welles, Charles Chauncey, John Rodgers, Joseph Treat, Archibald Laidlie, and Alexander McDougall.[65]

Like the Presbyterian and Congregationalist annual convention, the "American Whig" was a cooperative venture among various Dissenter churches in order to thwart an Anglican bishopric in the colonies. And like that convention, this project was initiated by Presbyterians. Published on March 14, 1768, the first issue set the tone for the series. Livingston et al. systematically deconstructed Chandler's *Appeal*, "to shew as well the falsity of the facts, as the futility of the reasoning, by which *the appeal* may impose on the weak and credulous." Additionally, the "American Whig" linked the scheming Dr. Chandler with Parliament's attempt to strangle colonial liberties: "Considering the encroachments that have lately been made on our civil liberties; and that we can scarcely obtain redress against one injurious project, but another is forming against us . . . and how peculiarly necessary it is, in these times of common calamity, to be united amongst ourselves; one could scarcely have imagined, that the most ambitious ecclesiastic should be so indifferent about the true interest of his native country, as to sow . . . the seeds of universal discord; and besides the deprivation of our civil liberties, lend his helping hand to involve us in ecclesiastical bondage into the bargain."[66] The writers proposed that colonists should not think of the proposed bishop and the Stamp Act as separate dangers to unconnected freedoms. Together, civil and religious liberty served as "the foundation of public happiness, and the common birth-right of mankind." Therefore, they argued, "it is the duty and interest of every individual, to keep a watchful eye over, and to cherish it with the utmost care and tenderness."[67] Week after week, the authors of the "American Whig" worked to establish themselves as bulwarks for colonial liberties and examples for the colonists.

Ten days after the first issue of the "American Whig," the "Centinel" was published in Philadelphia. Francis Alison, George Bryan, and Jonathan Dickinson authored the articles, with Alison taking the lead. Again, like the convention and the "American Whig," the authors represented at least two denominations, the Presbyterians and the Quakers.[68] Additionally, as with the New York triumvirate, the "Centinel" not only attacked Chandler but also connected the civil and religious when demonstrating the threats to colonial liberties.[69] In short, the "Centinel" argued that "it is readily granted that the Colonies are dependent States, united under one Head; and with the other British Dominions, form one entire Empire. It is also admitted, that the Parliament of Great-Britain, as the supreme legislative Power, has a superintending Authority to regulate and preserve the Connection between the several parts and Members of the Empire. But this does not imply, either a Power for disposing of the Property of the Subjects in the several inferior legislative Jurisdictions; nor of making Laws, for their internal Government. Both of these, by the constitution and Charters of the several Colonies, are lodged, where Nature and Reason and Justice point out that they ought to be lodged; with the Representatives of the People."[70] However, the recent encroachments on both colonial religious and civil liberties were enacted by a Parliament with no American representatives, and the acts were therefore unconstitutional.

Although it was clear how they could preserve their constitutional rights, the "Centinels" noted it was more difficult to identify their enemies. They stated that the Episcopal plot was not the work of all Anglicans; it was not even the work of most.[71] Many colonial churchmen were "the Friends of the Colonies," they declared, and they wished to persuade them to overtly oppose a colonial bishopric, "which is in itself an open acknowledgement of the Claims which the Enemies of America have lately set up, and which are totally subversive of our Rights and Liberties."[72] After all, the "Centinel" claimed, Thomas Bradbury Chandler only spoke for "a few Missionaries . . . of New-York and New-Jersey." "The People were never consulted on the Measure, nor were they ever heard to complain," the "Centinels" wrote. Yet, more than this, the authors argued, such usurping actions by the northern "missionaries" were as unconstitutional as they were indicative of future decision made by the proposed bishop. The "Centinels" stated that in the British constitution, the "Care of Religion" in "his Majesty's extensive Dominions" was given "to the Genius and Persuasion of the People."[73] In the end, the authors argued that the liberties of colonial Anglicans, like the Dissenters, would suffer from the establishment of a colonial bishopric.

Both the "American Whig" and the "Centinel" lasted less than a year in order to avoid alienating friendly Anglicans by constantly assaulting their church. In October 1768, the next stage of opposition began when the Presbyterians and Congregationalists met in their annual convention. On October 5, the delegates decided that it was in their best interest to look outside the colonies and ask the London Committee of Dissenters for help. As they wrote, they stressed that it was their loyalty to George III and the constitution that drove them to oppose bishops, as "nothing seems to have such a direct tendency to weaken the dependence of the Colonies upon

Great Britain and to separate them from her; an event which would be ruinous and destructive to both, and which we, therefore, pray God long to avert."[74] It was important for the convention to ally itself with the London Dissenters (who held some influence with the government) to avoid accusations it was overly biased toward colonial liberties. Fortunately for the Americans, the London committee was willing to help.[75] This alliance proved essential to the opposition; as Carl Bridenbaugh notes, "In the case of the American episcopate, there is every reason to conclude that it was the London Dissenters acting individually and through their organization who prevented any prelatical, ministerial, or parliamentary action from taking place, action which we have seen was seriously considered."[76]

Securing the invaluable aid of the London Dissenters, the Presbyterians and their allies were able to focus again on awaking their colonial brethren to the various dangers that beset them. In February 1769, in New York City, Livingston and Scott once again took the lead, persuading other denominations to create with them their own "Society of Dissenters."[77] Although the society continued to oppose the colonial bishop, the catalyst for the group was the repeated opposition in the city council to grant church charters to Dissenters. The Presbyterians received the most rejections, but they were not the only denomination denied.[78] The preamble to the society's articles of agreement and the articles themselves were quite revealing. It was imperative that Dissenters "unite together for the preservation of their common and respective civil and religious Rights and Privileges, against all Oppressions and Encroachments by those of any Denomination whatsoever."[79] Continuing, they clarified the present danger: "It is thought proper . . . to form a Society for taking Care of the said common and respective, Civil and Religious Rights and Privileges, of those of their Brethren in the Colony of New York, and the Neighboring Colonies, who do not profess to . . . be in Communion with the Church of England."[80] The articles also revealed that this union shared the earlier noted convention's desire "that no Matters of Doctrine, Church Discipline, or Worship shall ever be the subject either of the Acts or Conversation of the said Society."[81] Although this would prove to be a temporary fixture, they hoped that the New York society would soon become the head of a federation of societies throughout the colonies. Had it been accomplished, the federation would have been a major milestone on the Presbyterian interdenominational journey.

The New York society agreed to establish a Committee of Correspondence to encourage its colonial brethren to join its federation. It is no coincidence that both William Livingston and John Morin Scott were chosen to serve on this committee.[82] The letter the committee crafted, which would later be published in the *New York Gazette*, emphasized, as did the other

Presbyterian unions, a historical precedent of religious and civil persecution by the Church of England. This persecution, the committee said, had no basis in the British constitution. Like diplomats at the outset of a war, the committee made it clear that it was not the aggressor in this conflict: "We do by no means propose to Act Offensively against the Episcopalians, but barely to Counteract them, as far as we shall discover them pursuing designs unfriendly to our General interest." The Dissenters only wanted peace "to enjoy and to transmit to our posterity the right of private Judgment; and of Worshipping God according to the dictates of our own Consciences."[83] This, committee members claimed, is what drove them "to Write to all our brethren on the Continent, to exhort them to form themselves into such Societies, to Correspond with each other on these Interesting concerns; and thereby endeavor the preservation of our Common Liberty." The committee also wrote that it was seeking help from "our Brethren in Scotland and Ireland, and with the Standing Committee of Dissenters in England, to engage them to favour the design."[84] As with the convention, the society wished to validate its protest by enlisting the aid of non-colonial Britons.

Unlike the convention, the New York Society of Dissenters apparently did not survive more than one month. The last recorded meeting took place on March 21, 1769, at the home of David Phillips, who lived in the North Ward. Although the minutes stopped in March, various selections from the group's records, including the letter, were published as late as September 25, 1769, allowing the beliefs of the group to further permeate colonial society.[85] The Society of Dissenters was, in essence, the same as all other Presbyterian unions at this time, in that it wished, "notwithstanding our peculiar religious distinctions," to "heartily unite for our common Safety."[86] These cooperative ventures between churches were formed for the "advancement of the Redeemer's kingdom." But they also sought to protect religious and civil liberties, indicating that the original ideals of 1758 had evolved into something more complex. The Presbyterians, it seems, saw that their spiritual goals could be greatly aided by engaging temporal politics. Still, the healing of divisions within Christendom was the chief concern, and the unions were the tools to achieve that end. However, as such, these unions were also in a position to become a distraction for the Presbyterian ruling body's interdenominational vision.

The bishop's crisis peaked in 1770, but the Presbyterians and their friends nevertheless remained cautious.[87] The occasional Anglican outburst in favor of a colonial bishop in the following decade seemed to justify their continued vigilance in the form of the annual convention, but on the whole the church had shifted its focus.[88] Like a general reinforcing his troops where the danger is greatest, the Presbyterian leadership in the years leading up to the American Revolution emphasized informal unions that would still see Christians cooperating to protect their religious liberties, but would allow the church to offer more directly political assistance in the worsening constitutional crisis.[89]

In 1774, *Considerations on the nature and the extent of the legislative authority of the British Parliament* was published by either John Witherspoon or James Wilson. Although the authorship remains in doubt, the fact that both men were Presbyterians is revealing, as the work illustrates a growing danger of the heavy Presbyterian involvement in the constitutional crisis— political concerns overshadowing the spiritual. The author quickly established that this work was primarily political. He opened by stating that "no question can be more important to Great-Britain and to the Colonies, than this—*Does the legislative authority of the British Parliament extend over them?*"[90] Pursuing his answer, the author stated that the argument in favor of Parliament's authority was that the "supreme power, is, by the Constitution of Great-Britain, vested in the King, Lords, and Commons," and that any act from them was "a binding Force on the American Colonies, they composing a part of the British Empire."[91] However, according to the author, one natural law could not be forgotten, and this law was that "all men are, by nature, equal and free: No one has a right to any authority over another without his consent. . . . This rule is founded on the law of nature: It must control every political maxim: it must regulate the Legislature itself."[92] The next question, the author continued, was whether the colonists had representatives "elected by the people . . . and . . . bound, by the ties of gratitude for the honour and confidence conferred upon them, to consult the interest of their constituents."[93] As the colonists had no such representation, the author asked how Parliament claimed to have control over them. In the end, the author offered his audience a blunt answer to his original question, "The American Colonies are not bound by the Acts of the British Parliament, because they are not represented in it."[94]

For the Presbyterians, the years between 1765 and 1775 were filled with numerous unions. Yet these ventures carried the constant danger that the protection of civil and religious liberties would overshadow the religious mission to establish permanent unity in the body of Christ. In one of his many letters to Ezra Stiles concerning the Presbyterian-Congregationalist convention, Francis Alison confirmed both the desire for unity and the danger of being led astray when he wrote, "I would rejoice to see such a union as would be permanent & cordial among all." For Alison, this ideal union would demonstrate and "love christian liberty and purity of life."[95] The hope was there, however, as Alison noted he had not yet seen evidence to rejoice. The foundation for a permanent union had yet to be laid. The formal unions of the Presbyterians had each specified that they were created to ensure the religious and civil rights the colonists were claiming as Englishmen, which meant they were realistically temporary solutions. Ideally, the unions would continue to exist after the threats had subsided, but nothing was put in place to ensure such a reality. As the constitutional crisis intensified in the early 1770s, it should come as no surprise that the church so perfectly mirrored the rest of colonial society with regard to the growing emphasis on temporal liberties over a united Christendom. Presbyterian leaders after all had spent much of the past decade providing a framework to colonists with which they could understand their rights and their place within the empire. And while these efforts were almost always interdenominational and might prove useful in the future, the framework the Presbyterians had crafted by 1775 appeared to have an expiration date.

Despite this new concern brought about by the church's more nuanced interdenominational vision, the Presbyterians did pursue cooperation beyond the political realm. One example took place on October 14, 1770, when the Reverend James Sproat addressed the Second Presbyterian Church in Philadelphia concerning the recent death of George Whitefield. For Sproat, Whitefield was a good man who "is to be understood an holy man; a man, who is conformed to God in heart and life, by the power of divine Grace."[96] By this goodness, Sproat contended, such men were worthy of imitation. In life Whitefield had been a member of the universal church, relishing the common bond of Christianity that he shared with all denominations. Sproat told his audience, "Some, there may be, who measure their success according to the number of proselytes they gain to this, that, or the other party, or particular denomination of Christians: But, sure I am, that the success of every true minister of Christ will be measured according to the number of souls that are *added to the Lord.*"[97] Whitefield pursued "these principles of catholicism, he was determined not to know any thing among the people, but *Jesus Christ* and him crucified." In this vein, Sproat commented that Whitefield preached "to Jews, infidels, freethinkers, as well as to all denominations of christians without exception."[98] Lamenting the fact Christendom had just lost such an excellent emissary, Sproat cried out, "Let *England, Scotland,* and *Ireland* mourn!" And, he continued, "Let all the *American* colonies join the lamentation" because "who that has any regard for the prosperity of poor *Zion,* can refrain from tears, when we repeat the doleful sound, *Whitefield* is dead?"[99] Finishing his sermon, the minister challenged the congregation, "Let us improve to the valuable purposes of religion, the pious exhortations he hath so frequently pressed upon us; and carefully imitate the holy example, which he hath exhibited; so that our last end may be like his, which, we trust, is peace."[100]

Another exceptional year for interdenominational activity within the Presbyterian Church was 1774. When the synod met in May, the ruling body was presented with an opportunity to reach well beyond its American bounds and strengthen Christendom on a global scale. A delegation of two prominent Congregationalist ministers, Ezra Stiles and Samuel Hopkins, proposed that the two denominations work together to provide missionaries for Africa.[101] Their plan called for sending two native Africans to the College of New Jersey, where they would be prepared for mission work. Upon completion of their training the churches would send them to Africa to propagate the gospel. The Presbyterians quickly agreed, expressing "their readiness to concur with and assist in a mission to the African tribes," which they saw in light of "so many circumstances" as the will of God. They concluded by assuring Stiles and Hopkins that "we are ready to do all that is proper for us in our station for their encouragement and assistance."[102]

This trans-Atlantic project was joined the same year by Samson Occom's *A Choice collection of hymns and spiritual songs; intended for the edification of sincere Christians, of all denominations*. In the preface, Occom explained his motivation: "I have taken no small Pains to collect a Number of choice Hymns, Psalms, and spiritual Songs, from a Number of Authors of different Denominations of Christians, that every Christian may be suited." The Mohegan had observed the "great Engagedness, in these Colonies, to cultivate Psalmody," and he felt compelled to encourage "the Duty of Christians to learn the Songs of Zion." Drawing largely on the writings of the Apostle Paul, the Presbyterian cautioned that simply singing was not enough. Christians had "to sing with the Spirit" or otherwise, beautiful or not, "it is like the Sound of a musical Instrument without Life."[103] When "the Songs of Zion" were properly performed and "sung with the Spirit of the Gospel," Occom preached, they "are very comforting, refreshing, and edifying to the Children of God." Further still, such singing was "pleasing to God, and destructive to the Kingdom of Satan," yet another boon for Christ's kingdom. He concluded his prefatory address with his hope that this collection of "cordial Hymns" would "comfort you in your weary Pilgrimage; I hope they will assist and strengthen you through the various Changes of this Life, till you all safely arrive in the general Assembly Above, and Church the First-Born, where you shall have no more need of these imperfect Hymns; but shall perfectly join the Songs of Moses and the Lamb."[104]

Unsurprisingly, several of the songs that Occom chose for the collection called for Christian unity. For instance, Hymn 89 titled "Lord, When Together Here We Meet" pleads:

And let us all in Christ be one,
Bound with the Cords of Love,
Til we before thy glorious Throne,
Shall joyful meet above.[105]

Similarly, Hymn 4, "Hail Happy Pilgrims, Whence Came Ye," implored Christians to reflect on their previous sinful states as means to encourage cooperation:

Thus were we from our Bondage freed,
And set at Liberty,
Come then, dear Brethren, well agreed.
For thus redeem'd were we.

Come let us then together walk,
Together let us sing:
Be this the subject of our talk,
To praise the Lamb our King.[106]

Finally—and very much in line with Gilbert Tennent's view of denominations as necessary parts of the body of Christ—Hymn 103, "How Sweet and Awful Is the Place," speaks on behalf of the increasingly unified Christendom:

We long to see thy Churches full,
That all the chosen Race
May with one Voice, and Heart, and Soul,
Sing thy redeeming Grace.[107]

Although several Presbyterians had earlier toyed with the idea of creating a psalmody or hymnal for the church, it seems fitting that a product of one the earliest interdenominational ventures, Samson Occom, would craft the first and that it would include the need for unity in Christ's kingdom. Occom's compilation would prove invaluable for the Presbyterian journey as it introduced a new tool at the church's disposal—hymns.

The following year, another Presbyterian missionary composed a work intended to benefit all Christians on their "weary Pilgrimage." In *The moral and religious miscellany; or, Sixty-one aphoretical essays, on some of the most important Christian doctrines and virtues*, Hugh Knox, who was serving the Caribbean island of St. Croix at the time, explored the complexity of Christian life. Styled similarly to a devotional, the author broke "the most important Christian doctrines and virtues" into small segments to better meet the needs of society. As he observed, "Five or six pages of a religious book is as much as we can, in conscience expect, that a modern fine Gentleman or Lady should read at one sitting. The taste of the time is, therefore, purposely consulted in the shortness of these Essays."[108] More than a sermon, Knox's book presented people with a tool they could use on a daily basis. The central theme was Christian life, and Knox spent much of the book emphasizing the necessity of a unity among all Christians. In his essay, "Adoption into the Family of God," he wrote, "If we are indeed GOD's children by adoption, and do supremely love him that begat, we shall also love all them that are begotten of him. We shall love the whole *Christian brotherhood*, so far as they bear the image of their heavenly Father, by whatever names known, into whatever sects or parties split and divided."[109] Like David Rice and Gilbert Tennent before him, Knox saw peace between Christians as integral to the continued growth of the faith. There was "nothing more destructive to religion and virtue than malicious strife; nor any thing more unseemly in a Christian. Those therefore who are the happy instruments of removing this hellish evil from between men, are, in a peculiar manner, considered by the God of peace as *his children*."[110] Knox's thirty-eighth essay, "*The best* Method *of maintaining* Peace, Love, and Unity *among* Christian Brethren," was similarly devoted to encouraging an interdenominational spirit. Here, Knox told his readers to "consider the damage done to Christianity by the schism and divisions among Christian brethren; the pleasure it gives to the devil; the tendency it has to prevent other from uniting themselves to those communities, from which deserters have carried off an evil report."[111] Throughout his work his message was clear: Christian life demanded Christian unity, and everyone was subject to this mandate.

As Knox had hoped, the interdenominational message spread beyond a Presbyterian audience. One of his greatest admirers was the father of the Methodist Church in America, Francis Asbury. In his journal, a decade after *The moral and religious miscellany* was first published, Asbury came across the work and wrote: "I have read two volumes of Sermons written by Mr. Knox, of the West Indies. I am much pleased with his defence of revealed religion; and, indeed, through the whole work there is something sublime and spiritual; so catholic too, and free from peculiar doctrines: I esteem him as one of the best writers amongst the Presbyterians I have yet met with."[112] The Methodist's words are revealing. The period from 1765–75 had not only seen the Presbyterians continue their interdenominational efforts but had also witnessed considerable success in that regard. Largely, the cooperative ventures possessed a potentially troubling political element, but on the whole other denominations were beginning to notice the Presbyterian efforts. Still, the Presbyterian Church came to the cusp of war thoroughly and increasingly embedded in the tumult of the time. The efforts of men like Knox illustrate, though, that despite the growing emphasis on temporal liberties, the church retained the spirit that inspired the interdenominational journey begun in 1758.

3

Groaning "Under the Afflicting Hand of God," 1775–1783

As had happened during the French and Indian War, the war for American independence served as the catalyst for interdenominational change. In 1763, the year of the signing of the Treaty of Paris, the American colonists were proud to be British. By July 1776, however, the colonists declared their intent to be independent. The Presbyterians' role in unifying the colonists aided this transformation, and the denomination continued in this task as the war persisted. Its cause—the protection of their natural rights and liberties—was righteous and justified their rebellion. The Presbyterians' success, on the other hand, depended on their ability to be worthy of such divine blessings. Still, the war took a dreadful toll on the church and, as many colonists reacted to the devastation, the Presbyterians believed unrepentant national sins were hindering the cause. It was only through repentance of these sins that Americans could remove the "afflicting hand of God" and secure their liberties. Among the most prominent sin was America's long and determined relationship with slavery, but as the war progressed, a growing number of Presbyterian leaders, reminiscent of the French and Indian War, began to suspect that the true source of their hardships was their dwindling concern for a united Christendom. The war's conclusion saw the Presbyterians elated with the success of the American cause, but while they rejoiced they reminded themselves that Christ's kingdom came first.

During the constitutional crisis that preceded the war, the Presbyterians assumed a share of the colonial leadership, and they continued to throughout the war. Following the bloodshed of April 19, 1775, the Presbyterian synod, meeting in May, encountered the issues that had risen in the wake of Lexington and Concord with determined resolve. As the conflict with Britain continued, the synod issued a pastoral letter addressing the unfortunate series of events and outlining a proposed course of action.[1] In light of what lay before them, Presbyterian leaders reaffirmed their orthodox belief in the sovereign will of God and that just as his sovereignty was known in times of peace, it was "known by the judgment which he executeth." Also, they reminded Presbyterians, it would be "highly criminal not to look up to him with reverence, to implore his mercy by humble and fervent prayer, and, if possible, to prevent his vengeance by unfeigned repentance." Like so many times before, the letter began with an exhortation to repent in order to avoid the wrath God had laid aside for them. The ruling body continued, "Affliction springeth not out of the dust," and there was a reason that God visited them with hardships. The synod called its congregations to "remember and confess not only your sins in general, but those prevalent national offences."[2] The ruling body quickly noted that this divine punishment and necessary repentance did not preclude the colonists from protecting themselves and their liberties. If "the British ministry shall continue to enforce their claims by violence," it wrote, the Presbyterians should fight, alongside the rest of the colonies.[3]

However, the synod clarified that this decision was not a rejection of Great Britain. They retained a hope for reconciliation and that George III would realize the malicious intentions of his advisers. The synod advised, "Let it appear, that you only desire the preservation and security of those rights which belong to you as freemen and Britons, and that reconciliation upon these terms is your most ardent desire." The governing body also told its members to maintain the colonial unity that had developed because "nothing can be more manifest than that the success of every measure depends on its being inviolably preserved." For clarity's sake, the synod wrote that it expected Presbyterians to support the Continental Congress and "that a spirit of candour, charity, and mutual esteem, be preserved and promoted towards those of different religious denominations."[4] The leadership then addressed as many potential problems as it could, in an attempt to have at least offered some advice if further conflict made it impossible for the ruling body to meet. The synod's pastoral letter made three things clear: that despite the growing emphasis of temporal over the eternal, the current troubles were to be understood within its orthodox notion of God's divine will; that interdenominationalism was to persevere; and that all Presbyterians were to focus their energies and their prayers on the conflict at hand.

On Sunday, June 4, 1775, the Reverend John Carmichael encountered a larger audience than usual at his worship services. The additional numbers that had packed into the Presbyterian Church in Lancaster, Pennsylvania, included a company of colonial militia, under the command of a Captain Ross, who had come to hear Carmichael before they were mobilized. The minister informed the militia and the congregation that after the recent events in Massachusetts, "all the other colonies in North-America, like true children of *a free-born family*, are roused to some just resentment of such insults, on their natural and legal rights."[5] The "common cause" that Massachusetts had suffered for, stated Carmichael, was a holy cause, and colonial resistance was biblically justified. He warned that there would be other sincere Christians, such as the Quakers, who might not help in the colonial cause, but he pleaded "for God and conscience sake, to let them alone, if they will not in these terrible times, draw sword *for* Liberty and their country, surely they will not *against* Liberty and their country; and if we can do with them, we can without them."[6] Colonial unity in civil and religious matters was necessary; he called his audience to "work in love with other denominations and to heartily accord with whatever may be the final determination of all America agreed to in the CONTINENTAL CONGRESS."[7] Carmichael, like the synod, made clear his ultimate desire that "God, will save this country, and . . . the British empire from apparent ruin."[8] Likewise he told his audience, "You must still continue to revere royalty, and observe your allegiance to the King, on the true principles of the constitution."[9] War was a last resort, but there was to be no doubt that it was a valid resort. He ended his message on a rousing note: "Courage then! Courage my brave American soldiers, *if God be for, who can be against you*? . . . Thus go forth in the name of the Lord of hosts; and may he protect you, bless you, and succeed your very laudable and grand undertaking."[10] Carmichael's sermon closely mirrored and ultimately supported the general consensus in the synod concerning the growing crisis.[11]

The Declaration of Independence signaled a transition in the colonial cause, and most Presbyterians supported this change. Before July 1776, the denomination was fully confident in and supportive of the Continental Congress, but still they hoped for reconciliation with Great Britain. After the Declaration of Independence, however, the Presbyterian synod recommended that members support the Continental Congress, and most, like James Caldwell, followed suit.[12] It was reported that when Caldwell—who would earn the moniker the "Fighting Parson" of Elizabethtown, New Jersey—and his regiment received news of the Declaration and heard it read aloud, he toasted, "Harmony, honour, and all prosperity to the Free and Independent United States of America: wise legislators, brave and victorious armies, both by sea and land, to the United States of America."[13] Witnessing this widespread support among Presbyterians, Charles Inglis, Anglican loyalist and rector of Trinity Church in New York City, commented to a friend, "I do not know one of them, nor have I been able, after strict inquiry, to hear of any, who did not, by preaching and every effort in their power, promote all the measures of the Congress, however extravagant."[14] As the synod had hoped, the Presbyterians were not only united in the cause of liberty, but their efforts with regard to unifying the colonists and guiding the process were not overlooked.

Having gained the allegiance of the Presbyterian synod, Congress's Declaration of Independence was promoted by more than the "Fighting Parson." Indicative of this point was Jacob Green, a Presbyterian pastor in Hanover, New Jersey, and his pamphlet titled *Observations, on the Reconciliation of Great-Britain and the Colonies*.[15] Noting uncertainty among Americans concerning independence, Green published an address to answer the question of "whether it is best there should be a reconciliation, or a proper separation, and we in America be independent."[16] As many Presbyterians had done during the constitutional crisis, Green offered his abilities as a writer for what he believed to be the public's benefit. Green intentionally avoided a one-sided argument. He presented both sides of the discussion so his readers could see the validity of his eventual conclusions.

Green began by investigating "Britain's right to American government and dependence." He stated that when the mother country acted "the part of an enemy" by refusing the colonies "the privileges which are ours by constitution, seize our properties, and deprive us of our mutual rights. . . . Every rational person would say, that Britain had forfeited her right to American dependence."[17] Green continued by systematically debunking reasons why independence would prove detrimental to Americans. The author claimed that the American cause enjoyed God's favor, whereas the British did not. If it was true, as Green noted, that others argued that "'the independence of the colonies meant the ruin of Great Britain, then "'tis by her own misconduct, and we cannot help it.—If she is ruined, 'tis because she is ripe for ruin, and God's judgments must come upon her." If this proved to be the situation, the author wrote, it was imperative that Americans remain far removed from this calamity and create their own government that would please God and have his blessing. According to Green, this would be "a government most favourable to religion as well as liberty, and the natural rights of mankind." If Americans continued on their course, he wrote, "God will smile upon and bless us; . . . and prevent the evils that earth or hell may devise against us."[18]

The last half of Green's work focused on arguments for and against independence. The author, whose preference for independence was clear by this point, demonstrated the many benefits separation could bring. Among other boons, Green stated that America would have fewer wars once the tie to a European power was severed; corruption would lessen because elections would replace hereditary authority; and Americans would have more money in their pockets, as they would be freed from imperial taxes and the yoke of a lavish court. Most important, however, Green remarked, "If we are independent, this land of liberty will be glorious on many accounts: Population will abundantly increase, agriculture will be promoted, trade will flourish, religion unrestrained by human laws, will have free course to run and prevail, and America be an asylum for all noble spirits and sons of liberty from all parts of the world."[19] As Green's comments indicate, by 1776 the Presbyterians had adopted the "elect nation" ideology from New England and were applying it to America as a whole.[20] In this way the Presbyterians were helping to shape an independent America worth fighting for, one that, as Green hoped, would take up the fallen mantle of civil and ecclesiastical liberty that Great Britain had let slip.

These themes were echoed on October 20, 1776, by William McKay Tennent, a Presbyterian chaplain from Connecticut, who, while waiting for an expected British attack on Mount Independence, delivered a final sermon to the troops.[21] Using Nehemiah 4:14 as his text, Tennent attempted to allay the fear of the men gathered before him. God was on their side, Tennent reminded his audience, so "be not ye afraid of them: remember the Lord, which is great and terrible, and fight for your brethren, your sons, and your daughters, your wives, and your houses."[22] The soldier, Tennent explained, had to conquer his fears to do the noble deed before him. There was more still at stake than the protection of families, and so again the chaplain exclaimed, "'Be not ye afraid of them' is the voice of Heaven, the voice of the Church, and the voice of all who are dear to you—with respect to the approaching foe." The worthiness of their cause was clear, and the minister stated that "the hour is expected when, with the blessing of Heaven, you will have it in your power to do the most signal, important, and lasting services to your native land." This service, the Presbyterian minister made clear, was the preservation "of our liberty and property," for the enemy hoped "to reduce us to the most abject slavery." Americans had to resist their fears and fight against the British for, as Tennent stated, "they fight in an unrighteous cause."[23] As the Presbyterians had shown during the constitutional crisis, both civil and religious liberties were at stake. The protection of these natural rights was a mandate from heaven, whereas their endangerment was "an unrighteous cause." The sides were clearly drawn, and Presbyterians, such as William McKay Tennent, urged their listeners to heed heaven's call and fight for righteousness.

Alongside their fellow revolutionaries, the Presbyterians wished it understood that the civil and religious liberties they enjoyed as Americans were their greatest achievements. But more than this, those rights were also some of the greatest sources of potential the struggling people possessed. Emphasizing this point, on August 9, 1776, the Continental Congress created a three-man committee "to devise a plan for encouraging the Hessians, and other foreigners, employed by the King of Great Britain, and sent to America for the purpose of subjugating these states, to quit that iniquitous service."[24] Of the three members, two were Presbyterians, Richard Stockton and James Wilson; the third was Thomas Jefferson. Submitting its report to the Congress five days later, the committee recommended that any attempt to sway foreign mercenaries should be based on the lure of American liberties. The committee wrote: "Whereas it has been the wise policy of these states to extend the protection of their laws to all those who should settle among them, of whatever nation or religion they might be, and to admit them to a participation of the benefits of civil and religious freedom; and, the benevolence of this practice, as well as its salutary effects, have rendered it worthy of being continued in future times." The three men believed "that such foreigners, if apprised of the practice of these states, would chuse to accept of lands, liberty, safety and a communion of good laws, and mild government, in a country where many of their friends and relations are already happily settled." Not only did the committee believe they would wish to live in the United States, it also thought that the foreign soldiers would cease fighting "when they reflect, that after they shall have violated every Christian and moral precept, by invading, and attempting to destroy, those who have never injured them or their country."[25] With this recommendation Presbyterians, alongside the likes of Thomas Jefferson, perpetuated more than the ideal of an American nation that was a beacon for civil and religious liberties; they also supported the belief that this ideal was central to the future prosperity of the country.

Despite the holiness of their cause, the Presbyterians suffered significant loss and destruction of property during the war. Although many Americans endured devastating losses, a number of Presbyterians believed that the British were singling them out for special punishment. Writing to his friend, Richard Henry Lee, in January 1777, the renowned Presbyterian physician Benjamin Rush described the destruction of one of the most important Presbyterian assets and a bastion of revolutionary sentiment, the College of New Jersey. Rush wrote, "Princeton is indeed a deserted village. You would think it had been desolated with the plague and an earthquake as well as with the calamities of war. The College and church are heaps of ruin. All the inhabitants have been plundered."[26] Yet, the College of New Jersey was not alone, and additional stories circulated concerning the destruction of Presbyterian property. Following the battle of Long Island at the end of August 1776, the minister of the Presbyterian Church there, Ebenezer Prime, fled for safety. Although Prime escaped capture, his church did not. Much was destroyed, including the minister's library, and the building itself was remade into a depot and barracks. The church cemetery was leveled for a common and the gravestones were used to construct the troops' ovens.[27] Still more awaited the denomination. In August 1779 the *New Hampshire Gazette* published a report that seemed to validate the suspicion by many within the church that British forces were particularly aggressive toward the Presbyterians: "They manifest peculiar malice against the Presbyterian churches, having, during this month, burnt three in New York State, and two in Connecticut. What, Britons! Because we won't worship your idol King, will you prevent us from worshipping the 'King of kings' Heaven forbid!"[28] The more their churches and homes were destroyed, the more the Presbyterians convinced themselves something was amiss.

Although the destruction of property incensed the Presbyterians, what was more upsetting were the reports of attacks on Presbyterian ministers and their families. At the meeting of the 1777 synod, the New Brunswick Presbytery told how "the Rev. Mr. John Rosborough was barbarously murdered by the enemy at Trenton on January second."[29] According to the story, Rosborough was captured by Hessians while he was looking for his horse. Once it was discovered that he was a Presbyterian minister, he was stabbed repeatedly and left to die.[30] Such brutality was not unique, however, and the Presbyterians were to grieve further before the end of the war. Exemplary was the fate of the "Fighting Parson" James Caldwell, who, as the stories circulating within the patriot ranks claimed, was also singled out for particular punishment by the British. Accordingly, the British persecuted him in a series of events that culminated in his death. In January 1780, Caldwell's church in Elizabethtown, New Jersey, was burned by the British. However, when this attempt to intimidate the "Fighting Parson" failed, a new plan was crafted. On June 24, 1780, while the Reverend Caldwell was away from home, his wife was shot dead while praying with their children. The British troops then razed Caldwell's home to the ground. Distraught, James Caldwell continued to support independence and was not silenced until he was assassinated in November the following year while he was under a flag of truce.[31]

However righteous the revolutionary cause was, it did not prevent setbacks from crippling the American war effort or acts of terror from plaguing their communities. The Presbyterian torments, church members persuaded themselves, like those of their revolutionary brethren, were the result of unrepented sin. In this spirit, the 1777 synod pleaded with their "congregations, to spend the last Thursday of every month . . . in fervent prayer to God, that he would be pleased to pour out his Spirit on the inhabitants of our land, and prepare us for deliverance from the chastenings he hath righteously inflicted upon us for our sins."[32] The only solution, the ruling body knew, was a deep introspection to root out the offending transgressions to be followed by general atonement. Repentance and devotion to the law of God were the only safeguards for the proposed nation that the Presbyterians had helped imagine.

The October 5, 1777, sermon by Abraham Keteltas was indicative of this mandated introspection. Keteltas was still very much convinced of the holiness of the American cause, and he reassured his audience by drawing comparisons between the Americans and the Israelites. The former colonists, the Presbyterian minister noted, like the Israelites, were to rely solely on God 'for refuge in time of trouble."[33] Keteltas was quick to note that God always defended his cause, which was "the cause of truth, the cause of religion, the cause of righteousness, the cause of his church and people." "I think we have reason to conclude," Keteltas stated, "that the cause of this American Continent, against the measures of a cruel, bloody, and vindictive ministry, is the cause of God. We are contending for the rights of mankind, for the welfare of millions now living, and for the happiness of millions yet unborn." The Presbyterian noted that this responsibility had once belonged to Great Britain, a nation blessed by God. However, the British had turned away from him and now God moved against them by means of this costly civil war.[34] The example of Great Britain illustrated the potential benefits and dangers that lay in wait for God's people.

Keteltas reminded his audience that, like the British example, unrepented national sins could lead to further hardships. "Go to Charlestown," Keteltas challenged, "go to Norfolk, go to New York, go to Danbury . . . let the smoking ruins of well finished and valuable houses, by their speechless, but flaming oratory, melt you into tears, over your country's ruin." Keteltas continued, "Behold your ministers mocked, insulted, buffeted, mark'd out for destruction, for their attachment to religion and liberty, and their zeal against illegal and oppressive measures."[35] The only way to avoid these continued difficulties, Keteltas stated, was to "cast all your burdens and cares upon the Lord, and he will sustain you—he will never suffer the righteous to be moved." This pursuit of godliness through "continual prayer and supplication" and "repentance and reformation," Keteltas maintained, would render complete the ideal "that America will be a glorious land of freedom, knowledge and religion—an asylum for distressed, oppressed, and persecuted virtue."[36] America still possessed a bright and promising future as liberty's safeguard—a position once held by England—but only if its citizens were deemed worthy by God. For that, contrition was in order.

When the synod convened in 1778 in Bedminster, New Jersey, it renewed its call for a monthly day of prayer by the congregations under its care. As before, the ruling body wrote that this time was to be used "in fervent prayer to God," pleading that he would spare their torment.[37] When the synod mentioned the sins it believed were provoking the wrath of God, this was not a blanket admonishment to promote repentance and general spiritual well-being. Rather, when the Presbyterians mentioned these sins, they had particular transgressions in mind, and slavery was near the top of the list. This was in part due to the attention it had received before the war through the efforts of antislavery advocates such as Benjamin Rush.

Rush, the intermittent Presbyterian, led the assault in 1773 with *An Address to the Inhabitants of the British Settlements in America, upon Slave-Keeping*.[38] Although Rush was the first within the church to publicly take up the cause, he began his plea with an apology because "so much hath been said upon the subject." However, as "that evil still continues," he was compelled to continue.[39] Like the synod, Rush based much of his reasoning on scripture. Although he also called on the guidance of Christian divines, he sampled from a greater range of Christian tradition than just that of the Reformation. Yet, this broader perspective did not run counter to the synodical position. Rather, the various Christian denominations represented in his audience called for such a strategy and was in line with the synod's desire "to instruct and encourage sincere Christians" for "the Advancement of the Mediator's Kingdom." Rush was engaging the general public space, just as the church had with its Native American missions, a space that Presbyterians believed that Christians from all denominations were called to evangelize. With relation to slavery, Christians were called to act because if they did not, Rush reminded his audience, divine justice would result, meaning that "national crimes [would] require national punishments."[40]

To avoid this divine but unspecified calamity, Rush leaned on the scriptures for guidance. However, he acknowledged that the greatest challenges to his position were the biblically based arguments for slavery, and so he confronted each in turn, insisting that the only "infallible Rule of Interpretation of Scripture" as the Westminster Divines wrote, "is the Scripture itself."[41] Among the claims he contested were the beliefs that black skin was evidence of the Curse of Cain; that the ancient Israelites, including Abraham and the patriarchs, owned slaves; and that Paul and the other Apostles supported the practice. Predictably, Rush relied on the Bible to not only refute arguments for slavery but also to provide irrefutable evidence of its sinfulness.

Regarding the extension of Cain's curse to Africans, Rush stated that it had no scriptural basis and was really constructed "from our ideas of Beauty." Furthermore, God refuted this claim through natural evidences. Rush wrote, "That so far from being a curse, it subjects the Negroes to no inconveniences, but on the contrary qualifies them for that part of the Globe in which providence has placed them. The ravages of heat, disease and time, appear less in their faces than in a white one." On the second point, Rush conceded that the Israelites owned slaves, but he argued that God never sanctioned the practice. To claim otherwise would then validate a host of sins, Rush stated, because "we can vindicate telling a lie, because Rahab is not condemned for it in the account which is given of her deceiving the king of Jericho." He continued, "We read that some of the same men indulged themselves in a plurality of wives, without any strictures being made upon their conduct for it; and yet no one will pretend to say, that this is not forbidden in many parts of the Old Testament."[42] Concerning the Apostles, Rush contended that they had to be considered by the light of Christ's teachings, and "Christ commands us to look upon all mankind even our Enemies as our neighbours and brethren, and 'in all things, to do unto them whatever we would wish they should do unto us.'" He acknowledged that Christ never called "upon masters to emancipate their slaves" but "every prohibition of Covetousness—Intemperance—Pride—Uncleanness—Theft—and Murder, which he delivered," and "every lesson of meekness, humility, forbearance, Charity, Self-denial, and brotherly-love, which he taught, are leveled against this evil." For, Rush argued, slavery "includes all the former Vices, necessarily excludes the practice of all the latter Virtues, both from the Master and the Slave." Seen as a whole, "there is scarcely a Parable or a Sermon in the whole history of his life, but what contains the strongest arguments against Slavery."[43]

Rush viewed slavery as an especially dangerous evil in that it was sinful and fostered a multitude of sins. This view provided the weight for his argument against the claim that slavery was justified in a Christian society because the enslaved would be introduced to Christianity. Again asserting the necessity of scriptural evidence, Rush stated that "Christianity will never be propagated by any other methods than those employed by Christ and his Apostles." The physician painted a picture of determined resistance by masters, and argued that even if they did not prohibit their slaves from learning about Christianity, the examples they set of the faith would not incline the slave "in favor of our religion." To this end, Rush briefly described the view of Christianity that slaves witnessed every day, which included "the dissolution of marriage vows, or the entire abolition of matrimony," as well as the daily "shocking violations of chastity, which some of them are obliged to undergo without daring to complain. Husbands have been forced to prostitute their wives, and mothers their daughters, to gratify the brutal lust of a master." Rush fumed and chastised his audience: "Blush—ye impure and hardened monsters," as indifference only aided these horrors. In the end, Rush claimed, this culmination of evil was heaped upon Christianity because "this—all—this is practiced . . . by men who call themselves Christians!"[44]

This sin that nurtured sins and was willingly harbored by Christians represented, for Rush, a cancer destroying Christianity from within, and the sooner it was removed the better. However, as the physician noted, some Christians claimed they understood the Bible to support slavery, and so the question of their revered Christian liberty was raised. In their attacks on slavery, Rush and those who followed in his footsteps revealed the breadth of abilities available to individuals within the Presbyterian Church that were not also available to the ruling bodies. Whereas the self-imposed limitations implemented in 1758 meant the Presbyterian leadership repeatedly erred on the side of forbearance in cases of conscience, individuals such as Benjamin Rush could pursue their cause up to the point of forcing others to submit. If Rush and other individuals ever threatened the peace and unity of the church while pursuing a contested issue of Christian liberty, the synod could act decisively as it had in the past. Rush appeared ready to test the synod's resolve when he called his audience to "let such of our countrymen as engage in the slave trade, be shunned as the greatest enemies to our country, let the vessels which bring the slaves to us, be avoided as if they bore in them the Seeds of that forbidden fruit, whose baneful taste destroyed both the natural and moral world." The author's boldness, however, was limited because his charge, although filled with Christian imagery, applied only to the marketplace and did not extend to excommunication from the body of Christ.[45]

Rush also respected this boundary when he insisted that magistrates use their power "in suppressing this evil" and that legislators craft laws in "the Spirit of Religion—Liberty—and our most excellent English Constitution," but he refrained from demanding that ministers expel the guilty in their congregations.[46] Instead, he recommended, "ye Ministers of the Gospel, whose Dominion over the principles and actions of men is so universally acknowledged and felt . . . let your zeal keep pace with your Opportunities to put a stop to Slavery." While slavery remained, ministers were never to desist because, as he had argued earlier, "slavery is an Hydra sin, and includes in it every violation of the precepts of the Law and the Gospel." If slavery was neglected, Rush warned, "in vain will you command your flocks to offer up the incense of Faith and Charity, while they continue to mingle the Sweat and Blood of Negro slaves with their sacrifices." Christendom's purity, both real and perceived, was at stake, and Rush made it clear that "unless God shall cease to be just or merciful," this evil "cannot pass with impunity."[47]

With the fate of independence far from certain (a fact repeatedly thrust upon them by their suffering during the war), many Presbyterians reflected on these calls for abolition and the problem of slavery drew serious attention for the first time within the denomination.[48] They believed this divine punishment visited them in the form of the war, and as the American colonists engaged the British army and the trials of war tested their resolve, the question of slavery remained firmly fixed in their minds. For the Presbyterians, the horrors they experienced during the war were tied directly to unconfessed sins. But if, as the synod had pleaded repeatedly, Presbyterians sought God's will and turned from their entrenched error "he would be pleased to pour out his Spirit on the inhabitants of our land, and prepare us for deliverance from the chastenings he hath righteously inflicted upon us for our sins."[49]

James F. Armstrong, a Presbyterian chaplain from New Jersey who held similar convictions as Rush, had no doubts concerning which were "the offending transgressions," and slavery held a prominent position. The problem of outstanding national sins lay at the heart of his war sermon "Righteousness Exalteth a Nation." Examining Proverbs 14:34, Armstrong lamented and questioned with his audience why they had been "so soon called forth to change our beauty for ashes, the oil of joy for mourning, and the garment of praise for the spirit of heaviness?" As Christians it was their task, Armstrong maintained, "to expose the causes which call for such universal lamentation and mourning." The American cause, which doubtless first sprang to mind, was not the offense because "history doth not furnish us with a growing revolution founded upon better principles." Americans witnessed "the degenerate politics of Britain," and "we have separated ourselves." But it was not a clean break. Challenging his audience, Armstrong asked: "But are we not still in love with the vices which we have sucked from the impure breast of our mother?"[50] Sin so deeply ingrained would be difficult to abandon, the minister warned, and it "will be like cutting off a right hand or plucking out a right eye." Still, the trials must be accepted because "the catalogue of evils swells too high for enumeration," Armstrong cautioned, and "we must consider our circumstances as we find them."[51] Among the sins he considered were public and military neglect of the Sabbath, profaning the name of God, avarice, and atheism. Dangerous as these sins were, Armstrong was convinced that their strength came from the connection to "foreign commerce."

For Armstrong, "foreign commerce" was an irresistible force. It served to perpetually increase the appetite and demand for "unlimited commerce." This unchecked desire had led to "the ravages of war" that the former colonies were suffering. "Oh, America!" Armstrong cried, "How shall we hail thee happy unless Divine Providence should confine thee within thy own shores?"[52] "Oh, foreign commerce," he continued, "Where is the world undammed by thee? Every evil within the human comprehension is marshalled in thy train, and thy vestiges are marked with slavery in all its dreadful variety of forms." More than a product of commerce, slavery was its ultimate manifestation. Armstrong saw the sin of slavery "in the deep, dark mines of Potosi" and nearby "when the untutored Indian of South America yielded to the more savage hands of a bloody Cortez." The practice had also "bound the galley-slave to the ever-plying oar" and "extended thy tyranny to the burning plains of India." Yet the Presbyterian saved the worst scenario for last because it packed the most emotional punch with Americans: "My affrighted imagination follows thee to Africk's scorching climes, where the bought, captured, or plundered inhabitant is torn from his heavenly inheritance—fair freedom." The slave's freedom was lost and that was sin enough, but Armstrong further argued that evil also was heaped upon the community as the slave was "torn, perhaps, from being the only support of an helpless and aged parent, from the embraces of an affectionate and inconsolable wife, or a much loved child," and "torn from all the inexpressible blessings of friendship." This sin, which had been well taught by the British and skillfully executed by Americans, was far "worse than Egyptian bondage." "The tortured blood of the sons and daughters of Adam" were on their hands, and the minister stated his surprise that war alone was the resulting punishment. Americans deserved immediate destruction, Armstrong lamented: "Good heaven! Where sleepeth the lightning and the thunderbolt?" Still, he reminded his audience that God would relent and forgive if they would "pluck the envenomed aspic from thy bosom; nor . . . let the tyrannous grave be with us the only asylum for the slave of Africk." "National calamites," Armstrong concluded, could only be remedied by popular repentance and "reformation of manners;" or in other words, "the exercise of virtue and religion."[53]

Likewise convinced that slavery was a grievous spiritual matter, the Presbyterian governor of New Jersey, William Livingston, used his office to strike at the sin, revealing in the process another public venue the Presbyterians found helpful in their assault.[54] Despite his position within the government, Livingston encountered difficulties pursuing abolition in New Jersey. Writing to his Quaker friend Samuel Allinson on July 25, 1778, Livingston confided in his friend his past failed attempts to persuade the New Jersey Assembly to abolish slavery.[55] Concerning his most recent effort he wrote, "I sent a Message to the Assembly the very last Sessions, to lay the foundation for their Manumission," but he met a cautious Assembly that thought the timing was bad considering the war. Instead, he wrote, they "desired me in a private way to withdraw the Message." Undeterred, the Presbyterian determined to use his influence to "push the matter till it is effected: being convinced that the practice is utterly inconsistent, both with the principles of Christianity & Humanity." Like Rush and Armstrong, he did not call on a specific instance of biblical condemnation but rather the whole weight of Christian teaching. Livingston also confessed that the hypocrisy of the continued existence of slavery while the colonists fought for independence was "peculiarly odious & disgraceful" coming from "Americans who have almost idolized liberty."[56] For Presbyterians such as Livingston, Americans needed more than a contrite spirit, they required "the exercise of virtue and religion" in the form of abolition.

The evil of slavery was also on the mind of Jacob Green, who had earlier called Americans to consider the vast potential of independence. Green preached his sermon condemning slavery on April 22, 1778, but it was received with such enthusiasm that it was published, which considerably expanded its sphere of influence. Marveling at American audacity, Green stated, "Though our contention with Great Britain is so glorious, yet we have reason to be humbled and abased before God. . . . for the many sins, the many vices that prevail among us." Of the many sins that warranted immediate attention, Green believed that "supporting and encouraging slavery" was one of the most pressing. The minister was frustrated that the Declaration of Independence and the Articles of Confederation did not end slavery. He chastised, "Can it be believed that a people contending for liberty should, at the same time, be promoting and supporting slavery? . . . I cannot but think, and must declare my sentiments, that the encouraging and supporting of negro slavery is a crying sin in our land."[57] The minister stated he agreed with the Apostle Paul who declared that "*men stealers* (which is the sin we are guilty of by the negro slavery)" were as vile as the "*murderers of fathers and murderers of mothers, whore-mongers, defilers of themselves with mankind, liars, perjured persons, &c.*" Green called those in his audience and all Americans who owned slaves to preempt the manumission by state legislators and voluntarily free their slaves. He proposed that "if those masters had a true spirit of freedom; if they abhored the very nature of slavery, they would soon free themselves from such a blot in the character of freemen."[58] If such persons would not act for their own benefit, Green stated, they should do so for the welfare of all Americans, because the minister was "persuaded these united American States must, and will groan under the afflicting hand of God, till we reform in this matter." Still, Green said he had "reason to hope this matter will be considered and remedied and that God will turn to us in mercy and prosper us. We should not be discouraged, but repent and exert ourselves in the cause of liberty, both against Britain and among ourselves."[59]

Similar sentiments were expressed by John Murray in Newburyport, Massachusetts. On November 4, 1779, Murray also lamented America's fumbling of its righteous potential with a sermon entitled *Nehemiah, Or the Struggle for Liberty never in vain, when managed with Virtue and Perseverance*. Murray began by stating that Americans, like Nehemiah and the Israelites, had experienced, "The struggles of an oppressed people . . . recovering the civil and religious privileges by which God had distinguished them from all the rest of the world."[60] Like the Old Testament prophets, the minister assured his audience that the nations and people who strove to please God would find their liberties protected against all who threatened them. Murray stated that "the cause of liberty is the cause of God" and that "the cause he has been wont to plead he will never desert, he will work for it."[61] Still, Murray commented, Americans needed to please God to attain his protection and in this they struggled. This failure had resulted in various trials and tribulations, including the persecution of ardent ministers promoting "the public cause" by the British, who "were not insensible that their faithful testimony put rise in the measures used in its support—and therefore their persons—their names—and religion—and the sacred places where God's worship was fixed—became the principal butt" of their malice.[62]

Murray, like Green and Livingston, believed that slavery's persistence in America was one of the primary sins endangering "the cause of liberty." Bluntly, the minister told his audience that "the nations therefore that support or connive at the practice of enslaving the human species, as an article of commerce, ought to be considered in a state of war against all mankind; since none can be thought willing to wear that public brand of the antichristian beast." Murray hoped that "due attention will . . . be paid by all these rising States: for should a toleration of the slave trade be now mingled with our new Constitutions, that leaven will soon corrupt the whole lump."[63] The minister declared that if Americans continued in "the practice of making or retaining slaves," it would certainly "entail the curse of heaven on all our struggles" because *the honor of divine Government is concerned that national sins meet national punishments.*[64] Like Green, Murray ended his sermon with the optimistic hope that his audience would repent their sins and reclaim "the cause of God" so that "America will be IMMANUEL'S land—the seat of his kingdom till the sun shall fade."[65]

As the loudest voice within the public sphere, the group of Presbyterians who challenged slavery were not ignored in the synod. Interestingly, the question of slavery had only recently gained the synod's attention when in 1774 (the year of the earliest recorded mention) the ruling body had entertained the proposal by the Congregationalist ministers Ezra Stiles and Samuel Hopkins to support "two natives of Africa on a mission to propagate Christianity in their native country." When considering the proposition, the synod reported that "the subject of negro slavery came to be considered, and after much reasoning on the matter Dr. Rodgers, Messrs. John Miller, Caldwell, and Montgomery, were appointed a committee to bring in an overture on this subject." Still, when the committee brought its work to the synod it had only to reach a decision on whether to help Stiles and Hopkins, which they happily agreed to.[66] Although the original extension for the discussion was only for a year, the outbreak of war indefinitely postponed a decision. As the war wound down and the synod was able to resume normal operations, the ruling body began to reconsider all of the issues that had been put aside. George Duffield prompted the synod to review these old matters, and he alongside Jeremiah Halsey and James Latta were enlisted to serve on a review committee the morning of May 18, 1780. That afternoon, the committee reexamined "the enslaving of negroes." Immediately "the synod resumed consideration of that affair, and after debating the same to considerable length" members adjourned for the evening. Unfortunately, the 1780 meeting was scheduled to end the next day, which meant although the ruling body called on Americans "to repentance and reformation," the synod postponed again a decision on slavery.[67]

The synod's silence, however, did not quiet individual calls for repentance. For example, in September 1782 Benjamin Rush wrote to Nathanial Greene: "For God's sake, do not exhibit a new spectacle to the world, of men just emerging from a war in favor of liberty, with their clothes not yet washed from the blood which was shed in copious and willing streams in its defense, fitting out vessels to import their fellow creatures from Africa to reduce them afterwards to slavery."[68] Another came in the midst of celebrations following the winning of independence, when the Reverend George Duffield met his Third Presbyterian Church congregation on December 11, 1783, to deliver a congressionally appointed Thanksgiving sermon.

Inspired by both "the restoration of Peace, and establishment of our Independence," Duffield was happy to oblige. He called on his audience to "hail every friend of liberty, on this auspicious day" and to "rejoice ye, with America, and be glad with her, all ye that love her."[69] Duffield did not preach that day to single out national sins. However, as he noted, the divine blessings would only remain if Americans lived righteous lives in honor of the great gift of freedom. Although sin still plagued Americans, the minister revealed that they now had an opportunity to move beyond them so "that we do justice, love mercy, and walk humbly with our God." Then, and then only, "shall God delight to dwell among us" Duffield told his audience.[70] Of the myriad dangers that threatened to destroy the new United States, Duffield mentioned the neglect of those "whose sufferings might yet still be greatly alleviated, by a due attention; and a sacred regard to justice, and good conscience directing affairs." If Americans continued to ignore the claims of justice or pursue "injustice, oppression and fraud," then the judgments of their righteous God would be "poured out on our land: As he afflicted Israel of old, for unredressed injuries to the Gibeonites among them."[71] Out of the many possibilities to biblically illustrate this point, Duffield chose Israel's relationship with the Gibeonites–an especially revealing decision.

As descendants of the Amorites, the Gibeonites were among those divinely chosen targets given to Joshua and the ancient Israelites as they attempted to reclaim their promised land. At worst the Gibeonites were to be destroyed and at best they were to be driven from the land with no hope of return or of future alliance with Israel. Fearing both, they tricked Joshua and the Israelite leaders into a covenant whereby they became the slaves of the Israelites in exchange for remaining in the land among them. When the deceit was discovered, Joshua, prompted by God, demanded that both the Israelites and the Gibeonites fulfill their oaths. The relationship continued in this way until Saul became king of Israel and reportedly slaughtered many of the unsuspecting Gibeonite slaves. Showing no repentance or concern, Israel was made to suffer during David's rule until the nation addressed the sin. To those paying attention that Thursday in December, or to those who would read the published version, it was no accident that Duffield chose this story to illustrate his point about fighting "injustice, oppression, and fraud." The Presbyterian minister shed light on the evils of an institution that threatened the peace and purpose of the United States while not overwhelming his audience with guilt or detracting from his goal of thanksgiving. Further glory awaited Americans if they embraced a righteous future and left behind their sinful past, including, Duffield suggested, slavery.

Not only do these antislavery publications reveal that many in the church saw slavery as a glaring sin, they also reveal the continued efforts of Presbyterians to Christianize the public sphere. Yet, despite the issue's significance to their Christian mission, the slavery question would have to wait to be addressed by the synod. A matter of greater importance for the church had taken the spotlight as the war came to a close—the current state of its cooperative endeavors. Before even the first shot was fired in the American Revolution, the Presbyterians had been determined to maintain colonial unity throughout the difficulties with Britain. The synod that met in 1775 reiterated its belief that American success rested largely on cooperation among the Americans. As the war waned, however, scattered calls were heard from within the church for a return to the interdenominational goals of 1758. Although the Presbyterians had been working closely with other denominations for a righteous cause since the constitutional crisis, they increasingly believed that these cooperative ventures were becoming too preoccupied with temporal rights and liberties. Presbyterians had not been doing enough to bridge the schisms in Christ's kingdom, and despite the importance of securing their liberties through independence, Christendom was supposed to be their primary concern. As had happened during the French and Indian War, the war for American independence served as the catalyst for an interdenominational call to arms.

Samuel Stanhope Smith—protégé and son-in-law of John Witherspoon—founded the College of Hampden-Sidney based on Witherspoon's model at the College of New Jersey. In March 1779, he wrote to Thomas Jefferson (who would become Virginia's governor in June) concerning the latter's plan for education in Virginia. After applauding the effort, Smith addressed what he believed to be the biggest hindrance to the proposal: "I foresee that the chief obstacle to its execution will arise from the variety of religious sentiments that exist in the state."[72] For Smith, the various churches of Virginia were primarily concerned with securing political power, and not with education or even Christendom. For factious Virginians, Smith observed, the state's institutions of higher learning were of great importance, and "whatever party enjoys the preeminence in these will insensibly gain upon the others, and soon acquire the government of the state." He even conceded the regrettable role that his denomination would play when he wrote that "this contest will chiefly lie betwixt the Presbyterians and the Episcopalians." Smith lamented the fact that the various churches would rather jockey for power within the state than work together. This frustrating Old World approach that Virginians, including his fellow Presbyterians, were taking on this issue would not work with Jefferson's plan. "The partialities of sects," Smith wrote, "ought to have no place in a system of liberal education. They are the disgrace of science and would to Heaven it were possible utterly to banish them from the society of men." The minister continued, "Good God! What suspicions, what animosities divide the principles of a religion whose ruling maxim is charity and love! It is time to heal these divisions, as well for the honour of religion, as in order to promote the noblest literary design to which this or any other country has given birth."[73]

For Smith, Christian unity was more than the answer to Virginia's educational problems. Wistfully, he wrote that only "if they were united under one denomination their efforts, instead of being divided and opposed, would concentrate on one object, and concur in advancing the same important enterprise." In this effort, Smith believed Virginians were poised to realize at least some of the potential an independent America promised, but their success rested on their ability to embrace interdenominationalism and reject their Old World schismatic traditions. Having offered warning, advice, and reason to hope, Smith concluded his letter to Jefferson by emphasizing the hope: "My extreme love of peace, of that benevolence which my religion recommends, and of enlarged and liberal inquiry in matters of science, makes me wish for a union, at least of the two capital sects of christians [in] this state."[74] For Smith, as with other Presbyterian leaders, there was a serious need for Christian unity for Christendom's sake. Granted, other aspects of life, in this case the American educational system, would benefit, but those were pleasing products only attained through the proper Christian life.

This renewed interest in interdenominationalism was also found among the Presbyterians in the North. Again writing to Samuel Allinson in March 1780, Governor William Livingston voiced his support for a more cooperative Christian fellowship. He told Allinson that his decision was based on his observation that "it is the lot of humanity to entertain various opinions. And the Almighty has not thought it proper to delegate to frail & erring Mortals his Prerogative of being the Lord of Conscience." Livingston reasoned that since Christians of various denominations were not the lords of conscience, he was able to take comfort in a general Christianity. "Fully persuaded of this important Truth," he wrote, "I know not that I have any personal Attachment to, or prejudice against, any denomination of Christians, but trust that I can embrace any man who appears to be a conscientious Christian . . . with cordial affection."[75] Despite what Livingston wrote or said, his embrace of interdenominationalism was best demonstrated by the fact that Allinson was a Quaker and an intimate friend. In a July letter, he wrote to Allinson expressing his "hope I shall always follow your generous & christian Example of not limiting my friendship to persons of my own way of thinking."[76] Both William Livingston and Samuel Stanhope Smith reveal, as influential figures in Presbyterian circles, the growing concern within the church that Christians should cooperate and work together toward their common goal of edifying Christendom.

In this spirit, the Reverend John Ewing of Philadelphia—protégé and close friend of Dr. Francis Alison—preached one of his staple sermons, the "State of Spiritual Liberty," on June 17, 1780.[77] He began his sermon by reiterating the well-known Presbyterian support for the cause of liberty. "A well regulated Zeal for civil Liberty is a noble & generous Passion" Ewing told his audience, and "endeavours to promote & establish civil and religious Liberty are very commendable." The minister also noted, "It is to be hoped, that ye Spirit of Freedom, which now prevails under our Constitution will never be suffered to decay." However, Ewing added, "amidst all ye vigorous Efforts for Liberty in ye World . . . how negligent and careless are Men in securing spiritual Liberty." The most important liberty, the minister commented, was the most overlooked, and when "man, let his Civil Liberty be what it will, can [n]ever be accounted free."[78] Noting the political preoccupations of Presbyterians, and Americans in general, Ewing was determined to call attention to the welfare of Christianity, which he believed to be of more importance. While American Christians busied themselves securing their worldly rights, Christendom suffered from neglect because souls were not being won. All Christians, "as Heirs of God & joint-Heirs with Christ," were called to safeguard Christ's Kingdom in this way.[79] The work of Christians whether individually or in concert across denominational lines, was to primarily emphasize "spiritual Liberty" available through Christ. While the denomination maintained its support for the securing of civil and religious freedom, leaders like John Ewing began calling for a renewed emphasis on strengthening the body of Christ.

Following in the footsteps of John Ewing, John Murray penned *Bath-Kol. A voice from the wilderness*. In this work Murray placed the blame for the trials of the war squarely on the shoulders of sinful Americans. Murray wrote, "It has pleased the Holy Sovereign of the Universe, for eight long years to continue on AMERICA the awful judgment of a bloody and destructive war. In this, as in all his other dealings, it cannot be denied that righteousness belongeth to him; and sinful mortals should take all the blame."[80] Like Ewing before him, Murray was frustrated that Americans "contented ourselves with investigating the natural or political springs of our troubles; while the chief, that is, the moral causes have been too frequently quite overlooked."[81] Murray reminded his audience that "the Church of Christ in all its branches is erected, as a city set on a hill, on purpose to repel the attacks of infidelity and vice; and by opening and supporting the whole system of revealed truth, to defend the citizens of Zion."[82] According to the author, American Christians had too long neglected their duty to Zion, and as a result "infidelity and vice" had begun to decay Christendom from within. As Christians, Murray stated, not only were they called to do their part but they were to embrace the challenge as one body. United, Christians could better achieve their ultimate end—"the glory of God, and the salvation of the souls of men."[83]

Heeding the calls for repentance and renewal within the church, the synod met in 1783 and formally addressed the situation. With peace finally within reach, the ruling body took the opportunity not only to encourage repentance but also thanksgiving among the congregations and members under its care. Presbyterians had much to be thankful for, as many members of the synod had made known. In his address shortly after the British surrender at Yorktown in October 1781, Robert Smith declared, "Let every individual, let every family, let every congregation, let every town, let every state, let all our confederate states unite in praising our God, as with one heart and one voice."[84] Similarly, when George Duffield called on his congregation to be thankful, the minister stressed: "Here has our God erected a banner of civil and religious liberty: And prepared an asylum for the poor and oppressed from every part of the earth. . . . Here shall the religion of Jesus; not that, falsely so called, which consists in empty modes and forms; and spends it's unhallowed zeal in party names and distinctions, and traducting and reviling each other; but the pure and undefiled religion of our blessed Redeemer: here shall it reign in triumph, over all opposition."[85] True Christian unity was the key, but it had not yet been attained. This spirit of celebration and hope permeated the synod in 1783, but it likewise knew repentance and renewal were needed before interdenominationalism was fully embraced.

When the ruling body publicly reclaimed the interdenominational goals of 1758, it was in large part—just as it was in 1758—an acknowledgment of the synod's own drifting attentions. Included in this published statement was a formal Presbyterian position on religious freedom, which was intended to dispel rumors that the denomination planned, as the American Anglican Church lay in shambles, to make an Old World power play for a privileged position within the new governments. What many in the Presbyterian Church had begun to fear—that temporal concerns had overwhelmed the eternal goals—was a growing perception outside of the church as well. Their efforts before and during the war to help shape and lead the American cause were now being portrayed as the first stages of a master plan. The synod understood that the fear's truth or falsity was moot, because its existence indicated a failure of the church. Among the promises of 1758 were those to *study the Things that make for Peace*"; to "*take heed to ourselves*, that our Hearts be upright, our Discourse edifying, and our Lives exemplary"; to "take heed *to our Doctrine*, that it be not only orthodox, but evangelical and spiritual, tending to awaken the Secure to a suitable Concern for their Salvation and to instruct and encourage sincere Christians"; and finally to commend "*ourselves to every Man's Conscience in the Sight of God*."[86] With its intentions in question, the 1783 synod wrote, "That they ever have, and still do renounce and abhor the principles of intolerance; and . . . believe that every peaceable member of civil society ought to be protected in the full and free exercise of their religion."[87] With this renewal the Presbyterian leadership laid the foundation for the interdenominational campaign that would take place in the postwar period.

By the end of the conflict with Great Britain, the calls for repentance within the Presbyterian Church had shifted from the sin of slavery to that of spiritual schism. The latter was not forgotten, but the former held precedent and the church reclaimed its interdenominational goals of 1758. Although these pleas made the body of Christ once more the church's priority, they were not tantamount to political abstinence. By the war's end, the groundwork for a transformed interdenominational vision had been prepared; it consisted of Christendom and the new nation. Standing at the threshold of a new world—the image of which it had helped to shape—the Presbyterian Church hoped, as Benjamin Rush wrote to John King, that "among the many advantages which the Revolution will produce . . . the union of the friends to truth and simplicity in worship and church government in every quarter of the world into a great Christian republic will not be the least."[88]

4
For Christ and Country

Interdenominationalism in the North, 1784–1801

The postwar years finished the transformation process for the church's interdenominational vision. Following the official cessation of hostilities after the Treaty of Paris in 1783, the Presbyterians saw themselves standing on the threshold of a new world, facing a new opportunity to realize their interdenominational goals. Prompted as they had been during the French and Indian War, the Presbyterians were determined to address their shortcomings and embrace Christian unity. Many in the church believed that if they prioritized this responsibility, God would relieve their war-related sufferings. In this spirit, the Presbyterians began negotiating terms of union with like-minded denominations, such as the Dutch Reformed Church, the Associate Reformed Church, and the New England Congregationalists. The Presbyterians also believed that if they resumed their duties diligently, God would fulfill America's potential as a vehicle for the expansion of Christ's kingdom. With this revised plan in mind, the Presbyterian ruling body encouraged its members to pursue an interdenominational spirit for the welfare of the country and (ultimately) Christendom. And with its tactics modified, the Presbyterian leadership believed its renewed cooperative attempts would meet with more success. These hopes were largely fulfilled in the northern states with the adoption of the Plan of Union of 1801.[1]

When the Synod of New York and Philadelphia met in 1784, it moved closer toward its interdenominational goals by opening lines of communication with the Low Dutch Reformed Synod of New York and New Jersey. Although the two denominations had some past disagreements, especially regarding the charter of King's College in New York City, the persistent cordial ecclesiastical relationship, fostered by men from both churches, such as Hugh Knox, William Livingston, and Theodore Jacobus Frelinghuysen, had laid the foundation for the cooperative venture proposed in 1784.[2] The Presbyterian Correspondence Committee, which had been created in 1758 to interact with like-minded churches in America and across the Atlantic, was given the task of securing this union by the Presbyterian synod. This was the committee's first assignment since the anti-bishop union with the Congregationalists that had ended in 1775. This new Correspondence Committee, led by John Rodgers and Alexander McWhorter, was to meet with the Dutch in order "to determine a line for their future conduct with regard to each other, and to enter into an amicable correspondence with the Dutch committee upon subjects of general utility and friendship between the churches."[3]

The following year the committee reported that it had met with more success than anticipated. Not only did it have an amicable meeting with the Dutch synod, but it also met with the newly formed Associate Reformed Synod.[4] Both ruling bodies, the committee stated, desired "some kind of union . . . whereby they might be enabled to unite their interests, and combine their efforts, for promoting the great cause of truth and vital religion." Presbyterian synod members responded that they "were happy in finding such a disposition in the brethren of the above Synods, and cheerfully concur with them in thinking that such a measure is both desirable and practicable, and therefore appoint . . . a committee to meet with such committees as may be appointed by the Low Dutch Synod . . . and by the Associate Synod."[5]

On October 5, 1785, the three churches met to craft a plan of cooperation. After the core beliefs of each denomination were presented, reviewed, and found satisfactory, the churches began discussing what form their cooperation would take. Although the Presbyterians suggested a biennial meeting, an annual convention was agreed upon that was intended to "strengthen each other's hands in the great work of the gospel ministry; to give, and to receive, mutual information of the state of religion within their respective churches; to consider of, and adopt, the most prudent means to prevent or remedy any causes of dissension that may happen to arise between our respective congregations . . . and to concert measures for uniting our efforts to defend and promote the principles of the gospel, and oppose the progress of infidelity and error; and to adopt plans for effectually assisting the exercise of discipline in our churches, and encouraging each other in its execution."[6] Despite the promise of this initial meeting, the relationship cooled, as both the Dutch Reformed Church and the Associate Reformed

Synod experienced internal problems that stole their attention.[7] As the new decade dawned the interdenominational hopes that had been stirred were left unfulfilled.

Although the Presbyterians' plans with the Dutch were indefinitely postponed, they were not dissuaded from their course. In 1785, the church began discussing ways in which it could reorganize itself so it could be a more effective instrument for Christendom.[8] Though the synod was in agreement concerning the need for a restructuring, it was divided on how to do so. Some members, such as Samuel Stanhope Smith, favored a strong centralized government along the lines of the Scottish establishment, and others, such as Mathew Wilson, favored a decentralized government where the power resided at the local level.[9] In the end, the synod came to a compromise that gave greater authority to the local presbyteries while preserving the responsibility of the central ruling body (after 1788 known as the General Assembly) for the direction and leadership of the denomination as a whole.[10] Even though, by 1786, a general agreement had been reached concerning the layout of the new government, a formal vote to finalize the plans was postponed for two years due to slacking attendance. After essentially begging its members to participate in such an important event, the Presbyterian synod passed the proposed changes and made them effective the following year.[11]

Although the reorganization proved a massive undertaking in terms of denominational structure, very little changed with regard to the church's reliance on the Westminster Standards as its measure of orthodoxy. In 1788 the departing synod wrote, "That the said Directory and Catechisms be printed and bound up in the same volume with the Confession of Faith and the Form of Government and Discipline, and that the whole be considered as the standard of our doctrine, government, discipline and worship."[12] It was important for the ruling body to clearly establish that, in light of all the other changes, its reliance on the Divines would remain. Yet, despite this consistency, it would be inaccurate to claim that the Westminster Standards had survived the process unaltered, minor as the changes proved to be. As the church leadership reexamined the whole, it noted several passages that did not mesh well with the American Presbyterian experience. The Divines had accomplished invaluable work, but their efforts reflected the time and place in which they were written. For instance, Chapters 20, 23, and 30 discuss the authority of the "civil magistrate" concerning the church. Accordingly, they could both punish wayward Presbyterians who had abused "Christian liberty" and call the ruling bodies to order. The Divines assumed a unified state religion with a civil magistrate in a leadership position, and as this situation in no way reflected the realities of late eighteenth-century America, the passages were removed. With these incompatibilities addressed, the synod embraced the rest of the Westminster Standards as its own with the goal of preserving the traditional understanding of orthodoxy.[13]

This reorganization seemed to have fostered, or at least coincided with, a strong desire among the Presbyterian leadership for a new and stronger federal government to better meet the needs of the American people and fulfill the goals of the American Revolution. This process began during the conflict with Britain, when the Presbyterian Church gained an appreciation for the vast potential of its new nation. Particularly important in this process was John Witherspoon and his College of New Jersey. Not only did Reverend Witherspoon train students from across the country with his Americanist curriculum, but many of his students also founded schools of their own based on his model.[14] Generally then, Presbyterians were Americanists, but this did not necessarily mean they were wholly or even initially in favor of a strong central government, as the debates over their own reorganization testify. As the historian James Smylie has noted, "A few Presbyterians opposed the Constitution . . . as anti-Federalists," but there were others who "voted for it and served under it."[15] More specifically, Stephen Marini has revealed Presbyterians "voting strongly for ratification in New Jersey, strongly against it in North Carolina . . . and dividing into more equal blocs in Pennsylvania, Virginia . . . and South Carolina."[16] As individuals, Presbyterians were some of the most adamant anti-Federalists and Federalists, but upon the ratification of the new Constitution the church's ruling body fully welcomed and supported the new government.[17] Not only would the General Assembly support the federal government, but the ruling body also came to see its success as integral to the success of the Presbyterian mission to strengthen the kingdom of Christ. In this way, the Presbyterian Church helped form the vanguard of the nationalist movement while continuing its interdenominational efforts.

Among these interdenominationally driven nationalists was Robert Davidson, Presbyterian minister and professor of history and *belle lettres* at Dickinson College. Called to speak at Carlisle, Pennsylvania's Fourth of July celebration in 1787, Davidson took the opportunity to support a strong national government. Davidson began by reminding his audience of the many blessings, including that of independence, that God had already bestowed upon America. However, "it is our duty," Davidson said, "to improve the blessings of Heaven." The Lord had provided much, but Americans shared responsibility for "our stability, happiness, and glory, as a nation."[18] Davidson was not speaking generally; he had a specific improvement in mind: the creation of a new and stronger federal government to better meet the needs of the American people. "My fellow-citizens," he pleaded, "let us not leave the great work, which we have begun, unfinished." Too much had been left incomplete, including the protection of "the many civil and religious privileges that we enjoy." To accomplish this task he called on "every true patriot" to embrace "a spirit of union, confidence, and brotherly love," because "our character and consequence, as a people, depend on the firm union of these States, now called United."[19] Davidson assured his audience that "the bonds [of] our union . . . must be drawn much closer; and the machine in a greater measure wound up anew, in order that it may perform its operations with new vigour. And now is the important moment come, for this great work."[20] Whether America fulfilled its obligation to improve the blessings of God depended on "the most enlightened patriots from every state" who had convened "to deliberate on these weighty matters." The stakes were high, and these great men needed prayer and support to do God's will, Davidson concluded. As he ended his speech, Davidson reiterated what the country needed to succeed: "faith, piety, and union."[21]

Benjamin Rush was also among these nationalists. He expressed his hopes in an open letter "To the Ministers of the Gospel of All Denominations," written on June 21, 1788. Rush's particular interpretation of this Presbyterian goal involved a "general convention of Christians, whose business shall be to unite in promoting the general objects of Christianity." In this proposed annual convention, denominational differences were to be left at the door. This Christian body would then be able to "possess an influence over the laws of the United States." However, Rush noted, "This influence will differ from that of most of the ecclesiastical associations that have existed in the world. It will be the influence of reason over the passions of men." It was Rush's belief that Christianity was to serve such a role for society, and so the goals of his proposed convention "will be morals, not principles, and the design will be, not to make men zealous members of any one church, but to make them good neighbors, good husbands, good fathers, good masters, good servants, and of course good rulers and good citizens."[22] It was only after Christians laid a solid foundation for the nation, Rush contended, that the United States could strengthen Christendom. At that point in the nation's development, it could "teach mankind that it is possible for Christians of different denominations to love each other and to unite in the advancement of their common interests." In the end Rush argued, "By the gradual operation of such natural means, the kingdoms of this world are probably to become the kingdoms of the Prince of Righteousness and Peace."[23] In this way both Christ and country would be served.

Once the Constitution was ratified, many Presbyterians joined their fellow Americans in celebration. On July 9, 1788, Benjamin Rush described in great detail to Elias Boudinot the festivities celebrating the Constitution that he witnessed.[24] Forming "a very agreeable part of the procession" was a group of ministers who "marched arm in arm with each other to exemplify the Union." Not only did the clergy manifest "the connection between religion and good government," they also, according to Rush, showed "the influence of a free government in promoting Christian charity" as "pains were taken to connect ministers of the most dissimilar religious principles."[25] For Rush, though, the entire event oozed unity. In particular there was a cotton manufacturing display that "was viewed with astonishment and delight by every spectator." Rush wrote that "on that stage were carried the emblems of the future wealth and independence of our country. . . . Hence will arise a bond of union to the states more powerful than any article of the new Constitution." Despite his lack of clairvoyance, Rush illustrates well the prevalent Presbyterian belief that the Constitution was "as much the work of a Divine Providence as any of the miracles recorded in the Old and New Testament."[26] Mirroring Rush's sentiments, James Wilson gave a speech at the same event Rush described so diligently to Boudinot. Wilson believed the new Constitution would usher in a new world where "peace walks serene and unalarmed over all the unmolested regions—while liberty, virtue, and religion go hand in hand, harmoniously, protecting, enlivening, and exalting all!" "Happy country!" Wilson exclaimed. "May thy happiness be perpetual!"[27] Presbyterians hoped, alongside their countrymen, that the new government would aid in their particular pursuits of happiness.

When the first General Assembly convened in 1789, it issued a pastoral letter addressing "the present state of religion, the new arrangements in church government and discipline, and the state of civil government."[28] In this new era the ruling body stressed unity as the best method to secure "the great ends of religion." Of particular importance was the unity among Presbyterians. The General Assembly wrote, "We ought not to forget how necessary it is, for that great purpose, to preserve our character as a body." "Without . . . concert in our measures," the governing body warned, "our respectability will be diminished; and our efforts for the public good, and for the promotion of religion, will be weakened." Again emphasizing this theme of unity the General Assembly concluded this pastoral letter, "Praying that you may enjoy all peace, union, and prosperity in the Lord, we are, dear brethren, your affectionate fellow labourers in his common vineyard."[29]

That same year the General Assembly also wrote to the recently elected president of the United States, George Washington. In addition to illustrating the support within the Presbyterian Church for interdenominationally driven nationalism, the General Assembly's correspondence shows the ideal qualities of the citizens it hoped would populate the nation. For the ruling body, Washington was the quintessential American, and his election was why it embraced "the earliest opportunity in the power, to testify the lively and unfeigned pleasure which they, with the rest of their fellow-citizens feel, on your appointment to the first office in the nation." Although the pleasure was felt by most, there were Americans, the anti-Federalists, who portrayed Washington and the presidency as nothing more than a new face for an old threat, monarchy. Even among those who fully supported Washington, there was no agreement on what he represented any more than there was agreement on what the nation represented. For the Presbyterian General Assembly, the president was a divine blessing. Presbyterian leaders wrote that they "adore Almighty God, the author of every perfect gift, who hath endued you with such a rare and happy assemblage of talents, as hath rendered you necessary to your country in war and in peace." In part the ruling body was enamored with Washington's self-sacrifice for his country. After all the general had given, "we are happy that God has inclined your heart to give yourself once more to the public." However, the Presbyterians also valued Washington as "a steady, uniform, avowed friend of the Christian religion; who has commenced his administration in rational and exalted sentiments of piety; and who, in his private conduct, adorns the doctrines of the gospel of Christ; and . . . devoutly acknowledges the government of Divine Providence."[30] In choosing George Washington as their ideal American, the Presbyterians provided the core definition for their idea of nationalism. There were only two necessary qualities, that the welfare of the nation supersede that of individuals or groups, and that the only worthy foundation was Christianity.

In the last section of the letter, the Presbyterians pledged to help realize this dream of a Christian nation. To the imitable character of Washington, the Assembly wrote, "We will endeavour to add the wholesome instructions of religion." The ultimate goal of the church was no secret; "we shall consider ourselves doing an acceptable service to God . . . when we contribute to render men sober, honest, and industrious citizens, and the obedient subjects of a lawful government." The ruling body continued, "In these pious labours, we hope to imitate the most worthy of our brethren of other Christian denominations, and to be imitated by them; assured that if we can, by mutual and generous emulation, promote truth and virtue, we shall render a great and important service to the republic; . . . and, above all, meet the approbation of our Divine Master."[31] There was to be no mistaking the church's motivation. The welfare of Christendom drove the Presbyterians' nationalist spirit.

With the new government secured in the seemingly ordained hands of "our WASHINGTON," as the Presbyterian John Woodhull stated in a Thanksgiving sermon in 1789, the Presbyterian Church looked for new opportunities to strengthen the body of Christ.[32] When, in 1788, the General Association of Connecticut approved a new cooperative plan suggested by the Fairfield County Association of Churches, the Presbyterian leadership embraced the chance to renew the bonds of fellowship between its churches and those of the Congregationalists. A committee led by Timothy Dwight was chosen to present the idea to the Presbyterian General Assembly. That Dwight was selected to spearhead this effort revealed its significance to the Congregationalists. Fortunately, this committee was met by an enthusiastic General Assembly. It wrote that it was "peculiarly desirous to renew and strengthen every bond of union between brethren so nearly agreed in doctrine and forms of worship as the members of the Congregational and Presbyterian Churches."[33] With this warm reception, the first steps were taken toward the eventual merging of the churches. In 1792, on behalf of the General Assembly, John Black and Drury Lacey wrote of "the importance of union and harmony in the Christian church, and the duty incumbent on all its pastors and members to assist each other in promoting . . . the general interest of the Redeemer's kingdom."[34] From 1790 to 1792 committees from both ruling bodies were sent to determine the exact terms for the union. In 1793, the two denominations began to send delegates to the meetings of their respective ruling bodies. In 1794 these delegates were given the power to vote in both the General Assembly and in the General Association.[35] For the next seven years the bond between the Presbyterian and Congregationalist churches grew stronger, and the churches increasingly became involved in each other's daily affairs. This aspect of the union was important, because it had hitherto been absent from the Presbyterians' cooperative ventures.

Although friendly interaction between the laity, clergy, and ruling bodies of different denominations was vital to the success of the Presbyterian Church's interdenominationally national hopes, individual ministers and lay Presbyterians also increasingly relied on the printed word to disseminate the vision after the war. This medium gave ministers from both churches the opportunity to strengthen the fellowship between Presbyterians and Congregationalists and also to promote cooperation among all Christians. Taking up this banner in 1792, Samuel Langdon, a Congregationalist minister, published a lecture he had given twice in the past two years titled "A Discourse on the Unity of the Church as a Monumental Pillar of the Truth." During his talks, Langdon took the opportunity to admonish his audiences that "so long as the grand doctrine of salvation only by JESUS

CHRIST is continued . . . all the different parties and denominations of christians constitute but one church of the living GOD."[36] Langdon's plea for Christian unity would not be the last.

In 1791, the Presbyterian David Austin published a project that he hoped would have a great impact on the unity of Christians. Titled *The American preacher*, Austin's work was a compilation of great sermons by eminent ministers "of different denominations in the Christian Church."[37] Included in this four-volume series were sermons by Presbyterians; Dutch Reformed; Massachusetts, Connecticut, and New Hampshire Congregationalists; and Episcopalians. His intent was "to direct the present prevailing disposition to liberality in matters of religion, into a proper channel; and open the door for Christian communion, upon principles ACKNOWLEDGED and UNDERSTOOD." He continued, "To lay a foundation for the universal agreement of the Christian Church" would more than benefit Christendom as "such religious union, and influence as this work labors to accomplish, will add no small DIGNITY and SUPPORT to the POLITICAL IN-TERESTS of our country."[38] Like the General Assembly two years earlier, Austin stressed that his religious goals drove his national interests. Continuing his pursuit of Christian unity, Austin's next venture joined him with two Congregationalist ministers.

When David Austin, Jonathan Edwards the Younger, and Walter King met in 1794, they decided to reclaim the fallen project of the elder Jonathan Edwards to start an "explicit Agreement and visible Union of God's People, in Extraordinary Prayer, for the revival of Religion and advancement of Christ's Kingdom on Earth." For—and here they agreed with the senior Edwards—"how beautiful, and of good tendency, would it be, for multitudes of Christians in various parts of the world, by explicit agreement, to unite in such prayer." They proposed that "on every first Tuesday of the four quarters of the year," a day of common prayer be set aside by churches willing to participate. They would begin, they hoped, at two o'clock in the afternoon on the first Tuesday of January 1795.[39] Realizing the enormity of their plans, the three ministers called on their friends to help spread their message. The Presbyterians of Philadelphia and New York were particularly helpful.[40] Ashbel Green of Second Presbyterian Church in Philadelphia, a son of Jacob Green, replied, "The plan for a Concert has my most cordial approbation; and I shall endeavour, by all means in my power, to carry it into effect." Volunteering to distribute copies of the call to prayer, Green also promised "if my life and health are spared, to lay it before" his local presbytery. Both the Presbytery of New York and the Synod of New York and New Jersey recommended to the congregations under their care that they should embrace this universal call to "prayer, for the general revival of religion, and the advancement of the Redeemer's Kingdom in the world."[41]

In addition to the Congregationalists and Reformed churches, the Presbyterians made a more deliberate effort to interact, albeit outside the bounds of formal unions, with other denominations, such as the Baptists and Methodists. Again, the medium of print served an important purpose for the Presbyterians.[42] As early as April 1789, the Presbyterians began participating in nondenominational Christian magazines.[43] Individual ministers submitted articles, and the ruling bodies often supplied minutes and pastoral letters from their last session to magazines, such as *The Christian's, Scholar's, and Farmer's Magazine* (1789–90), *The Theological Magazine* (1796–99), *The United States Christian Magazine* (1796), *The Religious Monitor* (1798), and the *Connecticut Evangelical Magazine* (1799–1807).[44] Aside from regularly contributing to the various Christian journals, the Presbyterians would start their own in 1804.[45]

Set aside but not forgotten were the interdenominational tools introduced by Samson Occom—psalms and hymns. Occom had emphasized the potential of "the Songs of Zion, when they are sung with the Spirit of the Gospel." According to the minister, not only was such singing "comforting, refreshing, and edifying to the Children of God," it was "pleasing to God, and destructive to the Kingdom of Satan."[46] Singing psalms and hymns, the Mohegan had contended could help heal and unite the kingdom. Following independence the Presbyterian leadership agreed, but only with regards to psalmody. In 1785, in the midst of postwar rebuilding, a motion was passed calling for the synod "to take the assistance of all the versions [of the psalms] in our power, and compose for us a version more suitable to our circumstances and taste than any we yet have."[47] A committee was formed composed of Patrick Allison, Robert Davidson, John Ewing, Samuel Blair, and Timothy Jones. After two years of work by the committee, the synod approved the recommendation that the recently edited and expanded version of Watts's psalms by Joel Barlow become the recommended version to "be sung in the churches and families under their care."[48] The synod clarified that this was a recommendation and not an order. As was mandated by the Westminster Confession, the Christian's liberty of conscience in such matters was not to be oppressed.

Yet this was more than a simple recommendation of a work already in existence. The ruling body tasked George Duffield with editing and publishing a version for the churches under its care. In the preface to the collection of psalms, Duffield, on behalf of the Synod of New York and Philadelphia expressed similar sentiments to those of Occom.[49] Despite the numerous negative examples he could have drawn from to explain the ruling body's venture into psalmody, Duffield instead emphasized the benefits to spirituality the music could foster. It was well-known "by the best judges of the sacred text," he wrote, "that the Book of Psalms, in its original dress is a collection of the most elevated and sublime Compositions that are to be found in any language." Many translations, however, had encountered difficulties in keeping the original "piety, dignity, and poetic excellence" and infusing "the bright discoveries of the Gospel." Duffield reassured that "this has been happily executed by the learned and pious Dr. Watts, and the Psalms which he omitted have been supplied by Mr. Barlow, nearly in the same spirit and stile." More than this, he claimed, the psalms "have been carefully altered, so as to render the Composition better adapted to the circumstances of Christians in every country." According to the Presbyterian leadership, all Christians, not just Presbyterians, would benefit from these psalms as they encouraged "understanding and devotion, and thereby continue the elevation and improvement of the Christian temper."[50]

Upon examination of the songs included, Presbyterians were met with numerous psalms espousing interdenominationalism. When singing about the "characters of a saint, or a citizen of Zion," they admired the Christian who "loves all that fear the Lord."[51] The "Short Metre" version of Psalm 133 likewise praised "the communion of saints":

1. Bless'd are the sons of peace,
Whose hearts and hopes are one,
Whose kind designs to serve and please
Through all their actions run

2. Bless'd is the pious house
Where zeal and friendship meet,
Their songs of praise, their mingled vows,
Make their communion sweet.[52]

The "Common Metre" rendition of the same psalm furthers the point:

1. Lo! what an entertaining sight
Those friendly brethren prove,
Whose cheerful hearts in bands unite
Of harmony and love.

2. Where streams of bless from Christ the spring
Descend to ev'ry soul,

And heav'nly peace with balmy wing
Shades and bedews the whole.[53]

Unions with fellow believers would benefit them individually, denomina-
tionally, and as the body of Christ.

Yet more than this, the pslams revealed the benefits such a united church
would provide for the new nation. Psalm 107 extolled the blessings that
God had bestowed upon America, but it also contained a warning:

5. Thus they are bless'd; but if they sin,
He lets the heathen nations in;
A savage crew invades their lands,
Their princes die by barb'rous hands.

6. Their captive sons, expos'd to scorn,
Wander unpity'd and forlon:
The country lies unfenc'd, untill'd,
And desolation spreads the field.[54]

National repentance was key for the continuation (or return) of the blessings, and it was, in part, for this purpose that united Christians were called.
The forty-eighth psalm was titled, "The Church Is the Honor and Safety
of a Nation." Herein it was explained that God "makes his churches his
abode" and that "these temples of his grace" were "the honors of our native
place, and bulwarks of our land." While the church remained true, all who
opposed the nation would fail:

4. When kings against her join'd,
And saw the Lord was there,
In wild confusion of the mind
They fled with hasty fear.

5. When navies tall and proud
Attempt to spoil our peace,
He sends his tempest roaring loud,
And sinks them in the seas.[55]

A healthy body of Christ had as one of its products the glory of the nation.
Although the national connection was part of the developing interdenominational vision, what the synod presented to its congregations as worthy of
singing in 1787 was based on the same tune it had written in 1758.

Excited by these interdenominational successes within the realm of print, some in the Presbyterian Church wanted to extend the range of interdenominational activity even further. In 1797, the Synod of New York and New Jersey, in tandem with the Synod of Philadelphia, wrote to the General Assembly proposing that the church more intentionally target Christians on the other side of the Atlantic. Specifically, the synods wished to establish relationships with "all the Protestant churches in our own country, those in different countries in Europe, and if it be deemed practicable, even with the Greek Church of Russia, or others that you may judge proper in various regions of the globe."[56] Concerned that the breadth of their cooperative spirit might spark opposition in the General Assembly, the synods stated their purpose was not to cause division or hinder "the servants of Christ"; rather, it was meant to "increase the union and harmony of his body . . . and to promote their vigour and co-operation in advancing the glory of God, and the highest interest of the human race." The General Assembly wrote in response, through a committee led by Patrick Allison and Samuel Porter, that it agreed with the synods' sentiments. However, the ruling body added that "the disorders and convulsions of the European world . . . afford little ground to expect a calm, deliberate attention to any new proposal from a distant region," and so the proposal, at least the European aspect, would have to wait.[57]

"The disorders and convulsions" that hindered the synods' interdenominational plans stemmed from the French Revolution. Although the French Revolution initially had widespread support in the United States, its increasingly volatile and violent nature eroded American backing.[58] When the French abolished Christianity and established in its place the Cult of the Supreme Being, the Presbyterian Church condemned the revolution. Through their work, the Presbyterians revealed more than disgust with atheism and infidelity; they also took the time to reinforce their nationalist message.

From 1797 to 1800 Nathan Strong published three Thanksgiving Day sermons, focusing on the threatening darkness of the French Revolution.[59] Strong argued that Americans should show their appreciation for God's numerous blessings by not emulating the French infidels. Among the many recently bestowed divine graces, Strong encouraged his audiences to "praise God for a good civil constitution—a government of our own choice and administered by men of our own choice—a government which freely indulges all personal, social and religious rights." As such, the Constitution was invaluable. It "is the banner of civil and religious liberty, and those who attempt to injure it are bringing misery on millions."[60] Americans should also be grateful that "God hath given us the means of supporting our national and christian independence," which Strong maintained was only possible because American leaders had employed "the word of God and ordinances of religion."[61] Here the minister emphasized the importance of Christianity for the foundation of the United States. However, as Strong reminded his audience, God's actions were always intended to edify Christendom. He stated, "The whole divine government of men is with reference to his church—to the interests of his kingdom, and the accomplishment of the purposes of his grace."[62] If Americans were able to focus on the welfare of their redeemer's kingdom, then they "may stand and look joyfully upon a heritage both temporal and eternal."[63]

Strong noted that a proper regard for Christendom would lead Americans away from the godless lures of the French Revolution. When the rebellious French gained power, they only seemed interested in leveling society, including the Christian church, and "if a man, who is a christian indeed, in heart as well as in profession, hath any discretionary powers in his hands, he will use them for the good of society and individuals."[64] This civically active Christian "will pity the calamities of all nations—he will seek to be good and be just to all—he will pray for all, and not make himself the instrument of any."[65] But if, Strong warned, Americans chose to proceed in the footsteps of the French atheist and infidel, "if we break up our old institutions of religion, order, and government, the Lord will cause our sorrows to be multiplied, in ways more fearful, more rapid, and more desolating, than we are able to foresee." The patriotic Christian American only need look to the French Revolution to better appreciate his country's blessings of "a firm government, civil and religious liberty, and the christian religion." As he concluded his various addresses, Strong stressed his underlying message: "I shall wish you that hear me to be of the same character in all essential things, and that the world may be filled with such as love and serve God on Christian principles. Then infidelity would tremble, and those, who are corrupting the morality and faith of the world would fly to their secret places."[66]

In the same spirit as Nathan Strong, Jonathan Freeman published his thoughts on the French Revolution. For Freeman, recent murmurings that Christian ministers should refrain from addressing national concerns, such as France's influence, were not only unfounded but dangerous because they stripped ministers of their rights. "Is this liberty? Is it republicanism? Are ministers not equally involved with other citizens in the prosperity or calamities of the nation?" Freeman conceded, in adherence to the interdenominational spirit within the Presbyterian Church, that ministers should not focus primarily on politics from the pulpit. However, there were issues, such as the spread of infidelity from revolutionary France, that warranted a minister's attention. "I cannot reconcile it with religion, republicanism, nor patriotism to be entirely silent at such a solemn crisis," Freeman stated. "I always have been a true friend to my country; and I am independent in spirit."[67] If the United States wished to avoid the calamities that devastated Europe, Freeman suggested, Americans had to "be more zealous for the glory of God and advancement of the redeemer's kingdom."[68] If the charitable message of Christ was the rule by which Americans lived, then both Christendom and the nation would benefit. Freeman challenged his audience to "be as charitable in politics as we ought to be in religion." As Christians, Americans should "bear with one another in your different sentiments on political subjects." In the end, though, it was important for Americans to remember "that you must depend on the merits of Christ alone to give success to your prayers, to all your means for reformation, and for averting the curse which threatens to devour us."[69]

These public sentiments of both Nathan Strong and Jonathan Freeman were reflected in the work of other Presbyterian ministers, including those who assembled as the church's ruling body. In 1798, the General Assembly issued a pastoral letter addressing the "formidable innovations and convulsions in Europe" that threatened to destroy religion. Although the ruling body wished to focus on ecclesiastical concerns, it knew that "when scenes of devastation and bloodshed, unexampled in the history of modern nations, have convulsed the world, and when our own country is threatened with similar calamities, insensibility in us would be stupidity; silence would be criminal." As ministers of Christ and as "watchmen on Zion's walls," they were called to direct their churches' "attention towards that bursting storm, which threatens to sweep before it the religious principles, institutions and morals of our people."[70] Both Christ and country were threatened by the rising influence of infidelity in the United States. As Strong noted, such occurrences bespoke a lack of appreciation for divine blessings. The Assembly wrote, "Our ingratitude to God enhances our dreadful guilt. . . . We have abused his favours, and turned them into engines of opposition against himself." It exhorted members to cling to their interdenominational goals for hope. "Let Christians unite more cordially and openly, in adhering to their Master's cause, and opposing infidelity in all its forms," the Assembly said, adding: "Let us prostrate ourselves before him! Let the deepest humiliation and the sincerest repentance mark our sense of national sins."[71] Perhaps then, the ruling body noted, "God, for the sake of the Lord Jesus Christ, would . . . revive his work, not only amongst our churches, but amongst all denominations of Christians, until the blessed promises and predictions, with regard to the extent of the Redeemer's kingdom, be completely fulfilled."[72] The Presbyterians responded to this exhortation by energetically pursuing unions with other churches that would finally allow them to transcend denominational lines and truly work as the body of Christ.

In 1797, the Presbyterians and their interdenominational goals met unexpected success, when the Low Dutch and Associate Reformed churches called for a meeting. Attempting to put their internal struggles behind them, the Dutch Reformed were anxious to "revive the friendly correspondence" among the Associate Reformed and Presbyterian churches. The Associate Reformed matched the Dutch's enthusiasm, and the three denominations began to shape a "plan for correspondence and friendly intercourse."[73] By May 1800 the Presbyterian General Assembly had approved a plan of formal cooperation, and the other churches did so as well shortly thereafter. The plan extended the interdenominational success of the Presbyterian Church and set the stage for the more intimate union that the denomination would experience the following year with the Congregationalists. The plan's simple title belied the concessions each church made for the edification of Christ's kingdom. Alongside the self-evident agreement to maintain lines of communication between the three ruling bodies, the plan allowed for the laity of each church to receive communion in whichever church they chose, and it opened each governing body to visiting delegations from the other churches. As significant as these concessions were, the most important was the agreement to allow any congregation the freedom to choose which denominational ruling body would serve as its parent organization.[74] Much as they had with the Congregationalists, the Presbyterians were actively pursuing a more intimate, denomination-transcending union with the Dutch and Associate Reformed churches of New York and New Jersey. Still, the Connecticut Congregationalists remained the crown jewel of the Presbyterian cooperative efforts.

With the dawn of nineteenth century, the Presbyterian ruling body began discussing the possibility of furthering their ties to the Connecticut Congregationalists. Church historian Williston Walker wrote that "there is every reason to believe that the originator of the discussion was the younger Jonathan Edwards."[75] By 1800, Edwards, once a Congregationalist minister, was the president of Union College, as well as a delegate from the Presbyterian General Assembly to the Congregationalist General Association. He was interdenominationalism personified. Returning from his trip to the General Association in 1800, Edwards and his fellow delegates brought before the Presbyterian ruling body a new plan of union. After careful deliberation the Presbyterians wholeheartedly agreed to it in June 1801.[76] The plan called for the union of the denominations throughout the United States and its territories, allowing for a more efficient mode of Christianizing the nation.

The liberties bestowed upon the individual congregations by the Plan of Union of 1801 demonstrated that the cooperative spirit of this new union was greater than anything the two denominations had yet experienced. According to the plan, any congregation "in the new settlements," despite any previous connections, could choose between either the Congregationalist or Presbyterian Church government.[77] Additionally, each congregation was given the right either to make disciplinary decisions on its own or to send the case before whichever ruling body they chose, regardless of the church government that had previously been chosen. By granting these liberties, which further made the two denominations interchangeable, the ruling bodies demonstrated their willingness to sacrifice, in a sense, "the particular tenets" of their churches for the expansion of Christianity. To be clear, the doctrinal positions and orthodoxy of the Presbyterian Church, as established by the Westminster Standards, could be maintained, but only if the congregation in question aligned with the General Assembly. The same was true for the Congregationalists. At this time, both churches still relied on the work of the Westminster Divines, but that was not set apart as a prerequisite for their continued union. Both or either could change their views and the reunion would remain intact. Similar to the Christian's journey of sanctification, the Presbyterian journey to become more cooperative meant it had to place the welfare of catholic Christianity before the welfare of the particular denomination, although ideally that welfare was not to be neglected. Through the Plan of Union, the Presbyterian Church had made considerable progress toward this end, and, as the new century dawned, it was poised to take larger interdenominational strides for Christ and country.

The Presbyterian Church entered the postwar period eager to resume its pursuit of Christian unity. The Presbyterian ruling body hoped that the denomination's dedication to these responsibilities would see God bless it through the lifting of its hardships and the realization of America's potential. As the decade progressed, the governing body came to see its attempts to heal the body of Christ and its hopes for the country as intertwined. Presbyterians saw in the new United States the best possibility for aiding Christendom and that the country's potential could be increased with a united populace. Hoping to benefit Christ's kingdom, the Presbyterians supported the creation and maintenance of a truly unified nation. As the General Assembly wrote to George Washington in 1789, "In these pious labours . . . we shall render a great and important service to the republic; . . . and, above all, meet the approbation of our Divine Master.[78] This approach led to two distinct results. The first was that the Presbyterians were able to finally achieve the initial interdenominational union with the like-minded

Connecticut Congregationalists. Using a variety of tools at their disposal they brought to fruition nearly a half century of work. They were able to maintain their prized doctrinal standards and work closely with other churches, largely by not imposing their standards on their new allies. Second, the Presbyterians helped to develop an understanding of nationalism—a reflection of their interdenominational views—that helped Americans heal their divisions on the condition that the nation's welfare came first. Viewed from the North, the Presbyterians had seemingly achieved their cooperative dreams. However, such was not the case in the South.

5
Southern Presbyterians
and Interdenominationalism, 1784–1801

As the General Assembly encouraged its ministers and congregations to be more cooperative for the sake of Christ and country, the responses from their constituents varied. In the northern states, where the denomination was strongest, the ruling body was pleased with the interdenominational nationalism displayed through conventions and formal unions with the Connecticut Congregationalists, the Dutch Reformed Church and the Associate Reformed Synod during the 1780s and 1790s. In the southern states and territories where the denomination was weakest, however, the General Assembly met with a troubling inconsistency that derived largely from the church's inability to provide steady leadership. Although there were Presbyterians in the South whose interdenominational nationalism aligned with the vision of the General Assembly, there were also other Presbyterians whose varied local attempts proved irksome to the ruling body. The church's weakness in the South also meant that the General Assembly was seriously disadvantaged when attempting to address the multitude of local concerns. Still, these were difficulties in the South rather than of the South, meaning that for the most part the southern presbyteries and synods reflected the desires of the General Assembly, even if there were congregations and ministers who did not. When the Presbyterian Church's ruling bodies failed to rein in their wayward members, doubts arose concerning the intimate relationships they were striving to achieve with other churches, including the Congregationalists. More than this, however, the Presbyterian leadership inadvertently fostered sectional sentiments through its willingness to compromise on issues of Christian liberty for the sake of orthodoxy and unity. This encouraged the growth of sectional priorities—as long as they did not threaten the union—and increased the separation of members who lost their faith that the Presbyterian Church, as a national entity, represented their interests.

The published work of several prominent southern Presbyterian leaders demonstrated the desire to promote interdenominational nationalism throughout the country in accordance with the vision of the General Assembly. Exemplary of this spirit was the Reverend George Buist of South Carolina. Buist was the minister of the largest Presbyterian Church in Charleston, an important representative in the General Assembly, and the eventual president of the College of Charleston, which was founded in 1770.[1] He was also the chaplain to the South Carolina Grand Lodge of Masons, and his message to that body on December 27, 1793, illustrated how he maintained the General Assembly's vision.[2] Buist stated, "The royal law of love, which forms the basis of the Christian character, comprehends two great branches, love to God, and love to man."[3] Commenting on the surprising lack of obedience among Christians to the "royal law of love," Buist challenged the Masons to promote the cause. He said that the Christians' love for all mankind "is not . . . a useless and inactive principle; on the contrary, it is the foundation of a virtuous character, and is, in truth, the fulfilling of the law."[4] Christians were also called to work with one another in this labor of love for the benefit of society, "for all who bear the name of Christ have the same common faith."[5] According to the reverend, "Man cannot exist but in society; and society cannot exist without love."[6] The Masons, he said approvingly, already showed signs of working toward this end. Their secret, he argued, "as far as the world is concerned . . . is—Love: —Love, the cement of society and the balm of life."[7] The charge Buist laid before the Masons was clear; they were to continue their obedience to the "royal law of love" while at the same time encouraging others to do so. If they faltered, Buist concluded, Americans would divide, society would crumble, and so, too, would Christ's kingdom.

In October 1795, Buist called for interdenominationalism at an event for a Charleston orphanage. Buist was the sixth person to speak at the annual anniversary celebration, and each of the previous orators had come from various denominations affiliated with the institution. This speaking engagement, like the orphanage itself, had become in a sense a nondenominational, although thoroughly religious, venue. Here, as with the Presbyterian contributions to *The Christian's, Scholar's, and Farmer's Magazine*, *The Theological Magazine*, and *The Religious Monitor*, the Presbyterians joined their Christian brethren in an attempt to show the bonds of fellowship within

Christendom.[8] Buist opened his comments with praises for the work of the administrators, workers, and donors to the orphanage. He urged them to continue their good work. Their efforts had made them "charitable men, enlightened patriots and good Christians," and had afforded the children in their care that same opportunity.[9] Buist hinted at the pride that would be felt "when you . . . behold those whom you now protect . . . filling useful stations in society; adorning and improving their country by their ingenuity and industry, or defending it by their valour; becoming . . . the fathers and mothers of families, and transmitting to their children's children, a portion of that happiness which they have derived from this institution."[10]

Buist's efforts at the orphanage connected him with a broader Presbyterian mission focused on providing a Christian and national education for Americans.[11] He illustrated this aspect of the Presbyterian Church's social mission by emphasizing the importance of a Christian upbringing and education in the raising of citizens who would be the very foundation of the republic. The orphans, Buist stated, would be "the surest foundation of national prosperity."[12] This was a reference to the quality education the children received, but more important, it referred to the fact that they were reared as Christian nationalists. At no point in this speech did Buist mention any particular denomination's brand of education; he always referred to a "Christian" education and family. As he had with the Masons, the Presbyterian minister put forth the idea that cooperative Christianty, which the annual address and orphanage exemplified, was necessary for "national prosperity" and that the resulting interdenominational nationalism edified the kingdom of Christ. "It is comely for brethren to dwell together in unity," he said.[13]

Like his sermon to the Masons, Buist's address at the orphanage reveals how some Presbyterians used public venues to champion their interdenominationally nationalist goals. These men targeted public audiences and events because their mission was the advancement of Christendom and America. The public sphere, accessed through publications and public speaking, supplied diverse audiences of citizens ideally suited to this interdenominational purpose.[14] Making use of such an opportunity, Buist presented the characteristics that the Presbyterian General Assembly hoped to instill among Presbyterians and their neighbors. The Americans who possessed these characteristics were charitable, educated, and unity-driven Christians; they were also fierce patriots with a strong love for their country's republican government. A country consisting of such citizens would have little to fear, Buist commented, because "by this public mode of education, you form a host of patriots and warriors, who know no parent but their country."[15] It was preferable, the minister maintained, that citizens imitate "the patriotic republicans of antiquity" who "displayed their splendor and magnificence in public works." It was because of Americans like those who devoted their energies to the orphans' education that the nation had already harvested the first fruits of their labors to create "the inestimable blessings of civil and religious liberty which we enjoy." Buist concluded his message with a prayer calling on his audience to sustain their efforts for the continued "peace, happiness, and prosperity" of the United States government.[16] Again, Buist maintained the vision of interdenominational nationalism put forward by the General Assembly when he prescribed charity and forbearance among Christian Americans for the continued unity and well-being of the country and Christendom.

The publications of the Reverend Samuel Porter also illustrate the ideals proposed by the ruling bodies of the church. The bulk of Porter's published writings focused on the religious rift that had occurred within the Redstone Presbytery of the Synod of Virginia. This was not an internal dispute, but one between the local Presbyterians and an unspecified denomination. The main culprit, according to Porter, was the mystery denomination's minister, John Jamison. As many of the dates involved in the beginning of the story are not provided, it is difficult to state for certain when the troubles began. According to Porter, he and Jamison had been the epitome of interdenominational cooperation. They were intimate friends and, despite the differences in their religious beliefs, they had worked with one another and their respective congregations for Christendom's benefit. Porter noted this in a letter, which was included in the published account he had written to Jamison. Porter wrote that on more than one occasion, "I have invited your Ministers to preach in my pulpit, I have left my congregation, that my people might have an opportunity of attending on your Sacramental occasions."[17] However, despite their relationship and that of their congregations, the Reverend Jamison took it upon himself, with "no ungenerous, unmanly or unchristian treatment, from any" Presbyterians, to attack that church and its ministers as worse than "Antinomians, Deists, . . . Papists, Arminians and Socians."[18] For Porter, these assaults threatened more than local bonds. The author was convinced that Jamison's actions were inconsistent with Christianity. If characteristics such as those possessed by Jamison were rampant in the young republic, the nation would fall to ruin. These unprovoked vicious attacks on Christian unity by Reverend Jamison were not, in Porter's opinion, the actions of a Christian American.

Whether or not the accusations were true, Porter presented himself as a model of appropriate behavior. He wrote to Jamison, "I . . . looked upon you as my real personal friend, and must say . . . that I discredited many of the reports which were brought to me, concerning your treatment of our Church."[19] Porter here illustrated the hopes of the General Assembly that their ministers would look beyond particular tenets or beliefs of other Christians in an attempt to unify the body of Christ. In this spirit, Porter claimed to have approached Jamison to tell him, "I not only forgave you all, but discredited the reports I heard."[20] However, according to Porter, Jamison was relentless in his attacks. As a result of the continued assaults, Porter felt forced to publicly defend his church and salvage the perception of Christendom. The reverend wrote, "When those who profess, to be the Ministers of the Gospel of the Prince of Peace, not only disagree, but bring up their quarrels on the public Stage, the Consequence is disagreeable, and the Cause of Christ is thereby exposed to reproach."[21] As Porter further revealed, Presbyterians held the "public Stage" in high regard. A proper understanding of this medium was, in part, the basis of their relationship with their communities and the nation as a whole. Christian ministers took great care to portray a unified body of Christ, not only to deter their detractors but also to Christianize by example. According to Porter, Jamison did damage to this perception of Christendom by publicizing and focusing on denominational differences. Wishing to project Christian charity, Porter defended his actions in this controversy and his denomination's devotion to Christendom. In line with the General Assembly's wishes, the Reverend Porter wanted his audience to believe that the Presbyterians would do everything shy of hindering the "Cause of Christ" to work with their Christian brethren. Forbearance was of the utmost importance for both Christ and country.

In addition to regularly scheduled sermons, Presbyterian ministers often spoke on election days, days of thanksgiving, executions, and funerals. These activities represented more opportunities for the unity-minded Christian nationalists to reach large, diverse crowds consisting of many who might not otherwise hear them. In 1793 in Bladenburgh, South Carolina, James Muir addressed a gathering at a funeral service. Doing his best to console those grieving, Muir reminded his audience that "from the grain which dieth in the ground a new crop ariseth: From the old stem new branches shoot forth."[22] Illustrating the importance of youth education to the interdenominational vision of Presbyterian ruling bodies, Muir emphasized that youth should follow the godly examples of their elders so that one day they could take their place. This was an important point to stress, as a godly younger generation was integral to the prosperity of the United States and Christendom. In addition, Muir's metaphor revealed the desire that successive generations remain doctrinally pure by not forsaking "the old stem." Still, despite this pursuit of doctrinal integrity Muir emphasized the necessity for cooperation among Christian Americans. He said that the deceased were "lovers of religion" who had a "happy effect upon . . . [their] domestic circle for many years."[23] Furthermore, they had not been "intoxicated with religious pride; nor soured with prejudice." Instead, Muir happily noted, they had considered themselves "as a branch of the human family; and wherever [they] found mankind, [they] found . . . brethren."[24] By stressing both Christian unity and doctrinal purity, Muir's funeral sermon reveals the General Assembly's hope that their members would preserve the doctrinal heritage of the church while at the same time strive to build fruitful relationships with other denominations that would benefit Christ and country.

It was no coincidence that those southern Presbyterians who best illustrated the General Assembly's cooperative hopes were active leaders in the Presbyterian system. The root of the ruling body's problem in the southern states and territories in the postwar period was that there just were not enough Presbyterian ministers to meet the needs of the congregations. When the denomination was reorganized in 1789, the territory composed of Maryland, Virginia, Kentucky, Tennessee, North Carolina, South Carolina, and Georgia was placed under the watch of the Synods of Virginia and Carolina.[25] They were responsible for a far greater realm than the Synods of New York and New Jersey or Philadelphia. Additionally, according to the General Assembly's records, the two southern synods generally had the fewest ministers settled and the most vacant churches.[26] These factors prevented the various southern ruling bodies from effectively implementing and sustaining the interdenominationally nationalist vision of the General Assembly. The lack of consistent leadership coupled with the seemingly open-ended definition of interdenominational nationalism resulted in, not surprisingly, various interpretations of this vision. The seriousness of this predicament for the Presbyterian ruling body was magnified by the fact that the South was not homogenous; it contained pockets of different religious, political, and social beliefs.[27] In this atmosphere, for many southern Presbyterians, the priorities of localities, such as emancipation, universal salvation, or egalitarian religion, took precedence over the priorities of the General Assembly. The church's leadership had a problem in the South, but not of the South.

As has been noted, forbearance in matters of conscience, both spiritually and civically, played an important part in the General Assembly's interdenominational vision. For the spiritual, the Bible and the Westminster Standards stood as the guides for discerning such issues. As a reflection of the spiritual—not altogether a clear reflection—civic issues were influenced by the threat they posed to national unity. For the ruling body, this meant that as long as local or sectional convictions did not threaten the nation, they were to be tolerated but not forced upon other Americans.[28] After independence, American convictions concerning slavery created perhaps the most complex issue that the Presbyterian leadership had faced since the controversy over experimental religion.

Since 1773 and the publication of Benjamin Rush's initial assault, those Presbyterians who took to the public stage had largely condemned slavery. They contended that Christendom, the nation, and the cooperative spirit necessary for them to thrive should be extended in equal measure to people of all races. However, the growing cries against slavery among the clergy and laity were not the only expressions to be heard among the Presbyterians. Comparably they were whispers, but nevertheless some in the church were not as convinced that efforts should be made to abolish slavery, and others further believed it had God's full approval. Often quoted to illustrate this ambivalent or even proslavery stance among Presbyterians before 1800 was Henry Patillo in his *Plain Planter's Assistant.* Interestingly, Patillo agreed that the slave trade was a "wicked branch of trade," but he appeared in no hurry to see its demise. He applauded what he saw around him as a reformed version of slavery where "unreasonable tasks; inhuman corrections; naked backs, and starved bellies, are known no more." With this in mind, he wrote to the slaves, "I wish them to know, that they are by no means their friends, who put freedom into their heads. This is an event, that all the wisdom of America seems at present unequal to; but which divine providence will accomplish in due time." Until the time that God had appointed, "the slaves of my *Plain Planter*, are among the happiest of human beings. Well clothed, and well fed; a warm cabin, and comfortable bedding; with their hearty thriving children, growing up under their eye."[29] Patillo, then, fell into a category of Presbyterians who recognized the wickedness of slavery but who still cautioned against immediate abolition. Although this often cited source was a far cry from defending a perpetual slavery through the scriptures, it did not indicate that such beliefs did not exist. To be clear, many individual eighteenth-century American Presbyterians, as well as some of their churches, owned slaves. However, the growing and prevailing thought during the 1770s and 1780s among the denomination's leadership was antislavery in nature, and they flocked to presses in order to engage the larger reading world. As scholars have noted, it would take what proslavery proponents there were among the Presbyterians, and among American Christians in general, until the mid-nineteenth century to "fully develop" their published arguments.[30]

During the 1780s, and before reorganization, synodal meetings followed the abbreviated pattern established during the early war years, and it was not until 1785 that a synod meeting lasted more than three days or resembled the the prewar sessions.[31] As a result the fresh attention paid to slavery within the ruling body in 1780 was not renewed in earnest until 1787. Dealing with the war and its aftermath, including the reassessment of the national Presbyterian infrastructure, commanded the attention of the Synod of New York and Philadelphia. Still, the issue of slavery was not forgotten; it had merely been placed to the side. The issue's significance to the synod is evident in part by how quickly the discussion was resumed. As historians have noted, although national opposition to slavery was growing, in the 1780s, it was still in its infancy. This was well illustrated in the actions of the Presbyterian leadership. It considered the issue important, but it was not, the leaders believed, the most important issue they faced. That honor fell to the reorganization of the denomination, which they believed was needed if Presbyterians were to better reach an expanding nation. In 1787, with that task nearing completion, the ruling body took up the question of slavery, and once again the test of orthodoxy—as discerned through scripture and the Westminster Standards—came to bear.[32]

When the Presbyterian leaders met on May 16, 1787, at the Second Presbyterian Church in Philadelphia, they had much to accomplish. Over the next thirteen days the synod addressed multiple crises, such as the dissident Presbytery of Suffolk County, which had expressed its desire to separate from the church; the renewed question of appropriate psalmody and the resulting "disturbances which have taken place in the western parts of the church . . . especially within the bounds of the Presbytery of Abingdon"; the many disagreements over the proper form of the new church government; and, finally, the official position on slavery. Following established procedure, the synod considered and addressed each situation. It answered the charges from the Suffolk County Presbyterians "as brethren with us, believed in the same general system of doctrine, discipline, worship, and church government, as . . . contained in the Westminster Confession of Faith, Catechisms, and Directory." In addition to a published letter, a committee was sent to discuss their continued union more thoroughly. Concerning the psalmody, a committee was created to discuss the matter with "the Abingdon brethren." The delegates contended that acceptable psalmody was a matter of Christian liberty in view of the Bible and confession, and when the feuding parties were likewise convinced they "took each other by the right hand, and they promised forbearance towards each other in those matters wherein they had differed in judgment."[33] As for the new infrastructure of the church, each chapter of the confession, catechisms, and directory were scrutinized both for guidance and to determine their continued viability in the new nation.

Although slavery was the last major issue to be addressed by the synod that year, the committee considering it was the first created, immediately following the selection of the moderator and clerks. This committee, being the 1787 Overture Committee, was formed with the sole purpose of crafting the denomination's official position on slavery. In previous years, overture committees had two distinctive features: They were generally larger than the other committees in order to provide broader presbytery representation, and they typically consisted of a mixture of teaching and ruling elders to address both the concerns of the clergy and the laity.[34] The Overture Committee of 1787 was exceptional, but only because it was the largest committee created during the reunion years.[35] After eleven days of deliberation the committee brought its recommendation regarding slavery before the synod on May 27. Like the other synodal committees, what it suggested was representative of the orthodox view of Christianity and not necessarily current thought. As the growing cry of individuals within the church illustrated, there was a general consensus that slavery was evil and that it must be removed for fear of divine vengeance. Yet, there was no explicit condemnation of temporal slavery in either the Bible or the work of the Divines. Again, the Presbyterian leadership found itself in a position where bypassing the boundaries of orthodoxy would afford the denomination the ability to satisfy a generally perceived need as it had in the Samuel Harker case in 1763. The result in 1787 was the same, and the committee embraced the orthodox standard, recognizing its limitations and respecting the Christian liberty of its members.[36] Still, the committee had more options than it had with the divisive issues of experimental religion or proper psalmody. This time, it could do more than suggest equal support for all positions. Orthodoxy only prohibited excommunication for communicant slave owners. Within this spectrum of options, the committee struck as hard a blow against slavery as it believed it was able.

Confirming what Benjamin Rush, Jacob Green, Joseph F. Armstrong, and others had earlier argued, the committee stated that everyone, slave or free, were "made of one flesh" and part "of the same family." As Christians, Presbyterians were supposed "to consult and promote each other's happiness." Arguments that God made certain groups slaves or consigned them to perpetual slavery were outright dismissed by the committee. Such positions rejected "the obligation of Christianity . . . to extend the blessings of equal freedom to every part of the human race." All Presbyterians were called to action, but ministers and elders, by way of their positions, were only "to use such means as are in their power" to spread freedom. Fully convinced of "these truths," the committee also acknowledged the limitation of its power. Although slavery defied the spirit of Christianity, the lack of unequivocal condemnation meant leaders understood they could only exhort and exemplify, not mandate. In this spirit they overtured, "That the Synod of New York and Philadelphia recommend, in the warmest terms, to every member of their body, and to all the churches and families under their care, to do everything in their power consistent with the rights of civil society, to promote the abolition of slavery, and the instruction of negroes, whether bond or free." As the last business introduced that Saturday afternoon, the synod agreed that "the consideration of the above overture" be "postponed until Monday, the 28th."[37]

Rarely were the Overture Committee's recommendations denied, but they were generally revised after further discussion within the full synod. On behalf of the ruling body, James F. Armstrong wrote that synodal members "highly approve . . . of universal liberty . . . and the interest which many states have taken in promoting the abolition of slavery." He clarified that although abolition was the church's goal, individuals moving "from a servile state to a participation of all the privileges of civil society" needed "proper education" to avoid a situation in which freed slaves would pose a threat to civil society. This emphasis on education had been introduced by the Overture Committee, but it had received too little attention and so it was requested that "all the members belonging to their communion . . . give those persons who are at present held in servitude, such good education as to prepare them for the better enjoyment of freedom." The ruling body believed education should happen "at a moderate rate," Armstrong said, so that the experience "may render them useful citizens." Although immediate abolition was not advised, the synod restated in its conclusion the Overture Committee's key point that "final abolition of slavery in America" was necessary.[38] The language had changed from Saturday to Monday, but not the position.

Aside from acknowledging the need for "final abolition," the synod's language clearly reflected the fear of social upheaval that historians have long noted.[39] The extent to which this fear was racist in nature, however, is less clear. It is also not readily apparent that this decision was a compromise crafted to appease slave-owning Presbyterians. In fact, there is nothing in the records or the language of the synod that indicates the ruling body had a proslavery faction whose opposition might prompt such a compromise. Most notably absent in the records were protests against the 1787 policy. The right to protest and to have that protest recorded was one of the central tenets of the 1758 reunion, and it held a place of equal importance in the reorganized church starting in 1789. For synodal members, protest was a dear freedom, which makes the lack of dissent in 1787 all the more significant.[40] It is equally striking that a proslavery faction strong enough to force compromise on this controversial topic would be content with a resolution that publicly denounced slavery and called for eventual abolition. Viewed alongside the dearth of proslavery Presbyterian publications, there is little evidence to support the traditional views of historians that the synod's 1787 slave policy was "based mainly upon fear and racism."

However, if the decision was not primarily a compromise between the proslavery and antislavery factions within the denomination's leadership, what evidence points to a concern within that body to preserve orthodoxy? For the most part, the answer is found within the established tradition. Since 1758 the denomination had brought before the reading world a clear explanation of what comprised its orthodox beliefs and how it intended to engage its fellow Christians in furthering the kingdom of Christ. Orthodoxy, then, was never out of the synod's view, and all of its decisions were purportedly in adherence to that view. The synod published tracts specifically to prove "*ourselves to every Man's Conscience in the Sight of God.*" At the same time, the answer also lies in the ruling body's mixed denominational audience. Realizing that not all American Christians shared a reverence for the Westminster Divines, the Presbyterian synod resorted to the language of general Christianity when it addressed issues that extended beyond the specific circumstances of its denomination. Surprising clarity, then, is gained when examining this paradoxical slave policy within the cumulative historical context of the late eighteenth-century American Presbyterian Church, and fears of heterodoxy replaced those of racism as the primary motivation.

Although it has been overlooked by scholars, neither the spirit of the 1758 reunion nor the framework on which it relied was forgotten by the Presbyterians in 1787 when the ruling body issued its decision on slavery. The synod repeatedly depended on the dual test of the scriptures and the Westminster Divines to maintain the purity of the church while respecting Christian liberty. The Holy Spirit, as established by the Divines, had not explicitly denounced slavery and, as the "Supream Judg . . . in whose sentence we are to rest," the Presbyterian leaders hesitated to push further and condemn slavery as a sin. Affirming its orthodox view of Christian liberty—individually and collectively—and preserving its heritage, the ruling body denounced slavery while simultaneously resting in the decision of the Holy Spirit to pursue "the Things that make for Peace" when it advocated gradual abolition. The battle for orthodoxy was won and precedent was maintained; however, this middle way would haunt the Presbyterian Church well into the nineteenth century.

With the matter left to be peaceably resolved by individuals, some southern Presbyterians, such as David Rice looked to the political realm for redress. Reverently known as Father Rice, the minister had become the leading voice for both the Presbyterians and those opposing slavery in the Kentucky territory. In 1792 he was chosen to serve as a delegate to Kentucky's constitutional convention and, with this honor, he believed he was on the threshold of realizing his goal of keeping the prospective state free from the evil of slavery. Unfortunately, Rice was not the only delegate bringing a compelling vision for the state. While the Presbyterian had his support, so too had the slave-owning delegates. But unlike Father Rice, they had the federal government on their side. The extension of American slavery into western territories such as Kentucky both challenged the dominance of the thriving Spanish empire in the Mississippi Valley and kept slave-owning frontier citizens loyal to the United States and less inclined to defect to the Spanish territories, where slavery was permitted.[41] Even if Rice was unaware of these geopolitical considerations, slavery's growth in the Kentucky territory was undeniable. By 1790 nearly 12,000 slaves were in Kentucky, and the number continued to grow.[42] The 1792 constitutional convention held in his hometown of Danville, Virginia, was all the more crucial.

In accord with the Presbyterian General Assembly's interdenominational vision, Father Rice gave a carefully crafted address to the convention that took into account the civil considerations of his opponents while offering an uncompromising critique of slavery's evils. He began by noting "the great importance and difficulty of the subject" the convention was considering and praising his opponents as "gentlemen of the greatest abilities." The weight of the moment, however, did not weaken his resolve. Rather, Rice said he was driven "by this wretched situation of my fellow-men, whom without a blush I call my brethren. When I consider their deplorable state, and who are the cause of their misery; the load of misery that lies on them, and the load of guilt on us for imposing it on them; it fills my soul with anguish."[43]

He argued that slavery and the statutes that supported it were not only inconsistent but detrimental to other civil laws and to God's law. Aiming at the root of these inconsistencies, Rice questioned where his opponents received the authority to enslave other human beings. He asked, did "the great King of heaven, the absolute sovereign disposer of all men, give this extraordinary right to white men over black men?" "Where is the charter," he wondered, "in whose hands is it lodged? Let it be produced, and read, that we may know our privilege." Rice noted that "human legislatures should remember, that they act in subordination to the great Ruler of the universe, have no right to take the government out of his hand, nor to enact laws contrary to his," and "the people should know, that legislatures have not this power; and that a thousand laws can never make that innocent, which the divine law has made criminal."[44] By shifting the focus from the temporal to the eternal, Father Rice was not only appealing to Christian principles but was also offering a guilt-free path to abolition.

What temporal concerns could possibly overrule the will of "the great King of heaven?" Rice then addressed the objections to emancipation that he believed most bothered his slaveholding neighbors. The minister pondered aloud whether an individual who legally purchased a slave would be wronged if a law were passed abolishing slavery, and he conceded, "The master, it is true, is wronged, he may suffer and that greatly." However, Rice quickly added, "this is his own fault, and the fault of the enslaving law; and not of the law that does justice to the oppressed." He also addressed the concern that "the abolition of slavery . . . would discourage emigrants from the Eastward," which would hinder "the population of this country, and consequently it opulence and strength." Again, Rice confirmed that this could happen, "but this would be far, very far from being an evil," as those discouraged from coming would be slave owners. Finally, the Presbyterian considered an issue that he in his "own pride remonstrates against it"—the fear that if slaves were freed Americans would short time "all be Mulattoes." "This effect," he again conceded, abolition "would produce." But the evil of slavery could not be tolerated "for fear the features and complexion of our posterity should be spoiled." As a parting shot at his opponents, Rice stated, "With mathematical certainty, this evil is coming upon us in a way much more disgraceful, and unnatural, than intermarriages. Fathers will have their own children for slaves, and leave them as an inheritance to their children. . . . Men will humble their own sisters, or even their aunts to gratify their lust."[45]

Rice did not deny that abolition would bring problems, but "the natural evil effects of emancipation can never be a balance for the moral evils of slavery, or a reason, why we should prefer the latter to the former." Therefore, he proposed that the convention remove this cancer from the proposed state. Unfortunately, Rice lamented, slavery "is a tree that has been long planted, it has been growing many years, it has taken deep root, its trunk is large and its branches extend wide; should it be cut down suddenly, it might crush all that grew near it; should it be violently eradicated, it might tear up the ground in which it grows, and produce fatal effects. It is true, the slaves have a just claim to be freed instantly; but by our bad conduct, we have rendered them incapable of enjoying, and properly using this their birth-right; and therefore a gradual emancipation only can be adviseable." Rice made sure to note that while this plan was being executed, slavery would take on a new life, the life prescribed in the "Mosaic law" where slaves were view as, cared for and educated as family.[46]

Despite these arguments and his support in the convention and territory, Father Rice's effort to strike down the proposed proslavery article was defeated by a vote of 16–26. Having failed in the political arena, Rice turned his attention to the authority he and his fellow ministers held as a presbytery within the newly transformed Presbyterian Church. In 1795 the Presbytery of Transylvania, led by Rice, would be the first to challenge the official position of the church regarding slavery. In particular, the presbytery questioned whether it should allow those who "hold slaves, and tolerate the practice in others," to be members in the congregations.[47] Rice and his Kentucky brethren made it clear that as the leaders of the presbytery, they unanimously opposed the institution and wished to expel slave-owning members.[48] The General Assembly responded by telling the Transylvanians that it has "taken every step which they deemed expedient or wise, to encourage emancipation, and to render the state of those who are in slavery as mild and tolerable as possible." Slaveholders would remain communing members.[49] The ruling body also reminded the presbytery that "forbearance and peace are frequently inculcated in the New Testament," and that accordingly Christians should do nothing "to hazard *the peace and union of the Church*."[50] Concluding this letter to the southerners who challenged the interdenominational vision of the General Assembly, the committee quoted Christ, "Blessed are the peace-makers."[51]

As a presbytery, even a united presbytery, the ministers could not act on their beliefs without threatening the vision of the church. The Transylvanians submitted to this decision, but they were not without recourse. Considering the General Assembly's position, they assumed that the achieving abolition would entail changing the minds of individuals and groups within the political realm. The presbytery stated as much in a decision the following year concerning churches in their bounds. Despite the ruling from above, several of its congregations began to bar slave owners from communion. Addressing all of their churches, the presbytery leaders wrote that although they "are fully convinced of the great evil of slavery yet they view the final remedy as alone belonging to the civil power; and also do not think that they have sufficient authority from the word of God to make it a term of church communion; they therefore leave it to the conscience of the brethren to act as they may think proper, earnestly recommending to the people under their care to emancipate . . . their slaves . . . an event which they contemplate with the greatest pleasure, & which they hope will be accomplished as soon as the nature of things will admit."[52] With this, Father Rice and the Presbytery of Transylvania demonstrated their support for the General Assembly and its vision; however, they also illustrated how individuals and groups, especially in the South, could provide various interpretations of that vision. Forbearance, they agreed, was required within the churches, but they did not simply leave the issue there. Using the framework of the General Assembly, the presbytery provided a clear course of action for those whose conscience called for abolition—pressure the "civil power" as "they may think proper" to see the evil removed from the land.

Still, it must be remembered that the Presbyterian Church generally favored emancipation even if the ruling body preached doctrinal purity and national tranquility first. The extent of this cooperative spirit can be seen in the licensing of the denomination's first black minister, John Chavis. In 1800 the General Assembly wrote that "in order to attain one important object . . .(the instruction of the blacks) Mr. John Chavis, a black man of prudence and piety, who has been educated and licensed to preach by the Presbytery of Lexington, in Virginia," was to be "employed as a Missionary among people of his own colour."[53] With strong southern backing, Chavis became an invaluable part of the church's slave and freedmen missions. He also ministered to predominantly white congregations, which included preaching before the General Assembly. Chavis's position remained firmly within the Assembly's larger views on slavery. He was ordained to help with "the instruction of the blacks," but not explicitly to gain their equality. At the end of the day, Christian and national unity were still priorities for the General Assembly. As long as individual convictions did not threaten either their understanding of orthodoxy or the nation's integrity, the beliefs would be tolerated, including that of slave owning. The Presbyterian leaders hoped that nationalism would be a product of such an approach, and they were not disappointed. However, they also unwittingly fostered the growth of sectionalism.

In addition to the question of slavery, the General Assembly was also increasingly concerned with the close relationship many southern Presbyterians were forging with democratically oriented Methodists and Baptists. Intimacy with the Congregationalists was welcomed because of the churches' shared doctrinal heritage; however, the Methodists and Baptists did not necessarily share Presbyterian beliefs, making these relationships problematic.

The Hampden-Sydney revivals from 1787 to 1789 illustrated the Presbyterian ruling bodies' concerns. The Presbytery of Hanover founded Hampden-Sydney College during the Revolutionary War, and it received its official charter in 1783. Committed to interdenominationalism, the presbytery established Hampden-Sydney "on the most catholic plan." Each student of "every denomination, shall full enjoy his own religious sentiments, and be at liberty to attend that mode of publick worship, that either custom or conscience makes most agreeable to them." Despite the efforts of the presbytery, the school experienced a dearth of religious vitality in the postwar period. This apathy ended abruptly when the first revivals began on campus in 1787.[54]

According to one source, the revivals began, interestingly enough, with a mocking of a revivalist sermon. The story revolves around Cary H. Allen, a student at Hampden-Sydney who was requested by his peers "to burlesque a Methodist sermon." "Mounting the counter, he did this in such a comical and ludicrous manner, that his auditors were convulsed with laughter." Perhaps curious about the quality of the impersonation, the group "sallied forth to attend a Methodist meeting in the neighborhood, promising themselves rare sport." However, instead of continuing in their merriment, Allen and the rest were "among the very first who were seized with pungent convictions of sin." They returned to Hampden-Sydney altered, and soon a regular group was meeting to read the Bible and sing hymns.[55] One of the students, William Hill, who would later become a Presbyterian minister, wrote that the first meetings were unpopular with many of the students. He recalled that once "a noisy mob was raised, which collected in the passage before our door, and begun to thump at the door, and whoop, and swear, and threaten vengeance, if we did not forbear and cease all such exercises in the College for the future." This protest continued until the college president, John Blair Smith, intervened. The mob told the president that Hill and his friends were "singing and praying and carrying on like the Methodists and they were determined to break it up." Struck by this outpouring of religion the president cried, "Is it possible! Some of my students are under religious impressions!–and determined to serve their Saviour!" Not only did Smith then give the revivalists his blessing, but he also offered his guidance at their future meetings.[56] Under the president's leadership, the revival spread into the surrounding communities.

Smith operated the revivals carefully, under the philosophy that "God is not the author of confusion, but of peace in all his churches." When the president led the services, William Hill recollected, he was able to keep his congregations from making "noise or disorder or crying out in the worship of God." However, Smith did not always lead the services at his school, as he was also responsible for other neighboring congregations. In his absence, the revivals were led by itinerant Methodist preachers or the young Presbyterian minister Drury Lacey. In both cases, the crowds were allowed to indulge their emotional whims; the Methodists provided encouragement while Lacey was simply unable to retain order. What began as a controlled Presbyterian exercise slowly transformed into an interdenominational revival largely influenced by the Methodists. According to one estimation, this cooperative venture saw around "225 people, primarily youths, became members at churches that Smith served."[57] Although many Presbyterians, including John Blair Smith, welcomed the effects of the revivals, the recently created Synod of Virginia, which oversaw the affairs of the school, kept its distance.[58] The synod, it seems, agreed with the student mob that had threatened William Hill and his friends; the Presbyterians at Hampden-Sydney were "carrying on like the Methodists."

Several years later, the unpredictable cooperative zeal within some southern churches again garnered criticism from the General Assembly. During the 1792 meeting of the General Assembly, the Presbytery of Orange, of the Synod of Carolina, asked whether "they who publicly profess a belief in the doctrine of the universal and actual salvation of the whole human race, or of the fallen angels, or both, through the mediation of Christ, to be admitted to the sealing ordinances of the gospel?" The General Assembly responded "that such persons should not be admitted."[59] Disappointed but persistent, the presbytery, led by Samuel McCorkle, wrote a letter to the General Assembly in 1794, asking the ruling body to reconsider its stance. Upon this request the ruling body deliberated about "the admission of members into the communion of the church" who believed in "universal redemption," but it reached the same conclusions it had two years earlier. Not only did the General Assembly reject this petition as a violation of orthodoxy but it also referred McCorkle "to their Confession of Faith, and form of Government and Discipline, for a solution of any difficulties which may occur to his mind on the subject of Christian communion."[60]

The ruling body had not heard the last report regarding universal salvation from among the southern churches. This time, however, the story centered on the minister Hezekiah Balch of Greeneville, Tennessee. In 1794, the 53-year-old Balch had no idea that he was on the threshold of a venture that would forever change his life. He waited, unsure of the outcome, for the decision by the Tennessee territory legislature concerning his application for a college charter. That day, the news was good for Reverend Balch. His application was approved, and he was granted a charter to found the first college west of the Allegehny Mountains—Greeneville College. With this bit of news, Balch and the Presbyterian Church were in an excellent position to shape the westward-expanding United States through education; and, in doing so, they could strengthen the universal church. However, unbeknownst to Balch or the Presbyterian General Assembly, their relationship was about to sour.

As the president of Greeneville College, a position he kept until his death in 1810, Balch soon realized that more than a charter was needed to keep the institution open; it also needed money. To solve this problem, Balch journeyed to New England to raise money for his fledgling school.[61]

On his trip he encountered and was swayed by the controversial Congrega-tionalist doctrine known as Hopkinsianism, or New Divinity, which chal-lenged traditional Presbyterian beliefs by stating that Christ's atonement was for all mankind and not the "elect." In essence, according to their oppo-nents, adherents of the New Divinity advocated universal salvation.[62] Upon his return to Tennessee, Balch not only preached his new doctrine but he also published his beliefs in the *Knoxville Gazette.*

Many of Balch's neighbors were unhappy with his new theology, and in 1797 the Presbytery of Abingdon split. The Dissenters formed the In-dependent Abingdon Presbytery. This splinter group made it clear that it would not consider reunion until the Reverend Balch had been disciplined and his theology denounced.[63] When the situation spun out of the control of the local presbytery and synod, it reached the attention of the General Assembly, which then acted. In 1798, Balch was called to stand before the ruling body to receive its decision concerning his controversial and divi-sive actions. Confronted with the General Assembly's condemnation of his "preaching false doctrine," Balch repented and renounced his Hopkinsian creed.[64] Once he convinced the governing body of his regret, he was for-given and "considered in good standing with the Church."[65] However, after Balch returned from his trial and was largely out of the reach of the Gen-eral Assembly, he continued to promote the New Divinity. He was quoted as saying that "he was fifty thousand times stronger in his belief . . . than he was before he went away."[66] His renewed efforts were rewarded with a popular following, and before long he established the largest Presbyterian Church in the Southwest. As the new century dawned, he was brought to trial again and suspended; but again demonstrating the willingness of the ruling body to avoid internal contention, he eventually was restored as min-ister. He continued to be a proponent of the New Divinity movement.[67]

Considered alongside the stories of the Presbytery of Transylvania, the Presbytery of Orange, and the Hampden-Sydney revivals, Balch's tale demonstrates the diverse southern response to the General Assembly's call for interdenominational nationalism. As the Presbyterian leadership was unable to provide its southern members with a consistent cooperative ap-proach, many southerners were willing to openly embrace the doctrines, beliefs, and methodologies they encountered in their local communities, which led to competing understandings of nationalism and interdenomi-nationalism. Determined to regain control, the Presbyterian ruling bodies began issuing pastoral letters to rein in the congregations under their care.

Examples of such exhortations can be found in the pastoral letters and other publications in the late 1790s by the Presbytery of Charleston and Lexington as well as from the General Assembly. In 1797, the General

Assembly wrote, "We perceive with pain, that novel opinions, or at least opinions presented in a novel dress and appearance, have been openly and extensively circulated amongst you, and have excited unusual alarm; whilst at the same time they have given rise to much contention. We are also apprehensive, that in opposing what is thought to be a departure from the plainness and simplicity of our received doctrines, some of our brethren have been precipitate in their conduct."[68] The Presbytery of Lexington, in a similar vein, wrote that the churches under its care would fail as stewards of Christendom "unless proper care be taken to secure our churches from the seductions of erroneous and disorderly teachers." Upholding the General Assembly's vision of interdenominationalism, the presbytery made it clear, however, that it did not forbid its congregations from attending other churches' services when they were "preached in purity and faithfulness, by any regular minister of any regular christian church."[69]

In a unique attempt to inspire, exhort and edify its members, the Presbytery of Charleston moved beyond the traditional boundaries of the psalms and compiled and published hymns for "public and private worship."[70] Once again the Presbyterian leadership relied on music to encourage interdenominationalism, but this time the emphasis was on *proper* cooperation. Through this hymnal, the presbytery was able to reaffirm the necessity of key doctrines and beliefs without the appearance of a reprimand. Among the hundreds of songs were "The Unity of God," "The Immutability of God," "The Divinity of the Son," "The Trinity," "Acceptable Worship," "Christ's Intercession," "The Natural Depravity of Man," "The Necessity of a Saviour," "No Justification by the Law," "The Influences of the Spirit Experienced," and "Submission to Fatherly Chastisements." Yet within their midst were hymns devoted to love, and one in particular revealed the continued Presbyterian pursuit of interdenominationalism—Hymn 151, "Christian Unity":

1. Let party names no more
The Christian world o'erspread;
Gentile and Jew, and bond and free,
Are one in Christ their head.

2. Among the saints on earth
Let mutual love be found;
Heirs of the same inheritance,
With mutual blessings crown'd.

3. Let envy, child of hell,

Be banish'd far away;
Those should in strictest friendship dwell,
Who the same Lord obey.

4. Thus will the church below
Resemble that above;
Where streams of pleasure ever flow,
And ev'ry heart is love.[71]

While the presbytery wished to remind its members of the important doctrines and beliefs of the denomination, it was also determined to sustain the General Assembly's interdenominational vision; these pursuits had to coexist.

Unfortunately for the Presbytery of Charleston, the subtle approach was not as successful as it hoped, and so in 1799, it published a letter of warning to its members. The presbytery still stressed the "high importance of our common Christianity" with other churches because "religion is the cement of society," and, therefore, good relationships with Christians of other denominations needed to be maintained. The presbytery, like Buist and Muir, emphasized the vital importance of this social cement to "national prosperity" and to Christianity. A weak United States, to the ruling body, meant a weaker Christendom. Still, the presbytery warned, interdenominational nationalism was not to be pursued without caution because "Christianity has too many false friends, and too many open enemies, to permit any of its real friends being absent from their post."[72] Despite their efforts, the continued weakness of the Presbyterian ruling bodies in the southern states and territories meant that the General Assembly was largely unsuccessful in controlling the varied and inconsistent responses by southern Presbyterians. This failure of the ruling bodies further stirred doubts within the church concerning intimate cooperation with other denominations. The actions of the Presbyterian leadership also stoked doubts among many Presbyterians about whether the national organization could really represent their interests.

These doubts and concerns were magnified with the arrival of the Cane Ridge revivals. The Cane Ridge revivals, much like the 1801 Plan of Union, represented the realization of Presbyterian interdenominational goals, but they had a decidedly different impact on the denomination than did the union of the Congregationalists and Presbyterians. Starting in early 1797, the charismatic Presbyterian James McGready held Scottish-influenced "communions" in his three Kentucky congregations on the Red, Muddy, and Gasper Rivers.[73] McGready had been inspired by the Hampden-Sydney revivals in Virginia and was determined to see a similar resurgence in his new home of Kentucky. Fully realizing the criticism his work would face, he told his fellow revivalists that "though the world scorn and revile us, call us low preachers and madmen, Methodists—do this we must, or we will be the worst murderers."[74] The Logan County revivals were the catalyst for widespread revivals that followed, including those at Cane Ridge.[75] The links between southern revivals would be extended further when the Reverend Barton W. Stone, a fellow Presbyterian who had attended McGready's revivals, returned to his Cane Ridge church determined to start his own. Between August 6 and August 13, 1801, the Cane Ridge revivals soared in popularity and ultimately thousands joined the experience. Within this great host were Presbyterians, Baptists, Methodists, and black Christians.[76]

As they met both day and night, interdenominationalism became an assumption rather than a concerted effort. The merging of these faiths struck those who attended and made a lasting impression. The scene, as one contemporary historian noted, "at night was one of the wildest grandeur." Accordingly:

> The glare of the blazing camp-fires falling on a dense assemblage of heads simultaneously bowed in adoration, and reflected back from long ranges of tents upon every side; hundreds of candles and lamps suspended among the trees, together with numerous torches flashing to and fro, throwing an uncertain light upon the tremulous foliage, and giving an appearance of dim and indefinite extent to the depth of the forest; the solemn chanting of hymns swelling and falling on the night wind; the impassioned exhortations; the earnest prayers; the sobs, shrieks, or shouts, bursting from persons under intense agitation of mind; the sudden spasms which seized upon scores, and unexpectedly dashed them to the ground;—all conspired to invest the scene with terrific interest, and to work up the feelings to the highest pitch of excitement.[77]

The revivals at Cane Ridge, like those in Logan County and at Hampden-Sydney, were Presbyterian in origin, but they were very much influenced by democratically oriented Christianity. Traditional Calvinism was checked at the door and in its place rose a "badly compromised" Calvinism that "made fairly peaceful accommodation with the ascendancy of Methodist Arminianism. The doctrine preached potential universal redemption, free and full salvation, justification by faith, regeneration by the Holy Spirit, and the joy of a living religion."[78] With this hybrid theology that resembled very little of the orthodox Presbyterian beliefs found in the Westminster

Standards, the southern Presbyterians again broke away from the General Assembly's ideal interdenominational vision. Yet more was still to come, as those who participated in the interdenominational events witnessed the vernacular preaching movements of the Holy Spirit among the laity and sexual activities that came to symbolize the early-nineteenth-century southern revival experience.

The alteration of the approved interdenominational vision at Cane Ridge generated disapproval within the ruling bodies of the Presbyterian Church, just as did the revivals at Hampden-Sydney. With the Cane Ridge revivals, however, the challenge was not confined to individual communities. The spirit of revivalism that spread across the South also spread the compromised doctrine and the enthusiastic excesses the ruling bodies wished to minimize. For many in the Presbyterian Church, those involved in the revivals had taken interdenominationalism too far, and their mistake laid bare the dangers of uncontrolled intimacy. And because the General Assembly and the various southern synods and presbyteries were still ill-equipped to address the situation, the Cane Ridge controversy continued to grow.[79] The Kentucky revivals solidified the final component of the General Assembly's interdenominational approach that had been forming in the postwar period, a destructive fear of complete intimacy with other denominations. The Presbyterians would not have to wait long to witness the effects.

Church leaders' negative responses to the liturgical and theological modifications brought about by the Cane Ridge revivals further contributed to the doubts among many southern Presbyterians that the General Assembly truly represented their local interests. After additional failed attempts to alter various contested policies of the General Assembly, such as its position on slavery, universal salvation, enthusiastic styles of worship, and the ordination of uneducated men, many ministers and members chose to leave. In 1805, several ministers left their churches and the South altogether so as to avoid the policy of silence concerning the sins of slavery. Among these were James Gilliland, Robert G. Wilson, James Hoge, Samuel Davies Hoge, George Bourne, and John Rankin.[80] Close behind them were the Disciples of Christ, composed of Barton W. Stone and thirteen Presbyterian congregations from Kentucky and Ohio, and the Cumberland Presbyterians who, after nine years of debate, formed their own denomination.[81] The General Assembly's interdenominational vision, which appeared to many as a willingness to perpetually compromise for unity's sake, had finally pushed a number of members to the conclusion that their interests would best be served by local organizations. Unfortunately, the church's actions can again be seen strengthening sectional sentiment within the early republic.

With the arrival of the nineteenth century, two important conclusions can be made concerning the Presbyterian Church's search for unity. First, although the General Assembly continued to promote interdenominational nationalism well into the new century, the Plan of Union of 1801 and the Cane Ridge Revivals represented the highs and lows for the approach, religiously. The former demonstrated how far the church had transformed into the purely interdenominational body it hoped to become. The latter symbolized the stumbling block that would forever hinder the Presbyterians in realizing that dream. The second, equally important conclusion is that the methods the Presbyterian ruling body used to pursue interdenominationalism unintentionally fostered sectionalism rather than the desired nationalism. By continuing its pursuit of interdenominational nationalism in the 19th century, the General Assembly was effectively undermining both the integrity of the church and the nation.

Epilogue

In September 1801, Jonathan Freeman came before Hudson Presbytery to defend the use of hymns, especially those by Isaac Watts, in church. Echoing the sentiments of John Todd who made a similar presentation before the Presbytery of Hanover in 1762, Freeman contended that Christians and their churches would only benefit from singing "unto the Lord a *new song*."[1] Writers such as Watts "celebrate the praises of God in Psalms and hymns and spiritual songs which are derived from the gospel of Christ," Freeman commented, and if Christians were to "preach Christ crucified" and "pray in his name" it seemed obvious that "Christ should be the theme of our spiritual songs."[2] Again, like John Todd, he was quick to point out that although he was convinced that his fellow Presbyterians needed to seriously consider adopting both the hymns by Dr. Watts and other psalms that he had reworked, he did not assume the solution would be best for all Christians. Keeping with the Presbyterian interdenominational tradition, which stressed Christian liberty and forbearance, he told the ruling body, "We have no authority to meddle with any church out of our own bounds. They have a right to adopt any version they judge expedient. And if every denomination of Christians would pursue this line of conduct, there would not be so many disputes, and divisions among the professed disciples of Christ."[3] Strikingly similar to the language used by synods and assemblies past, Freeman revealed the continued embodiment of those beliefs. To that end, he hoped that his audience, both reading and listening, would not "be led, by the inchanted chord of implicit faith, to embrace what I have advanced upon this subject." Instead, he called upon them to challenge his opinion and "if other Christians differ, in judgment from me, I have no objection. Let every one act agreeably to scripture, and the dictates of an enlightened, unprejudiced, and good conscience."[4]

The following year the hopes of many Presbyterians living and departed were realized when the Presbyterian General Assembly adopted a system of psalmody and hymnody. Granted, since 1763 the leadership of the re-united Presbyterian Church had been open to individual congregations using such songs in their worship, but this was not tantamount to an official endorsement. The question was not settled, as the numerous cases brought before the ruling bodies testify. As Jonathan Freeman and others would have attested, the situation changed completely with an official, but not mandatory, system of psalmody and hymnody. Not only did this collection help ease tensions between Presbyterians, but as an interdenominational effort it also brought the church further in communion with other Christians. Evidence of the intimacy between the denominations, the man at the helm of this project was the increasingly well-known Congregationalist minister and president of Yale College, Timothy Dwight.[5] In the past Dwight had worked to bring the Presbyterians and Congregationalists closer together, and he used his time as editor for a similar purpose. At the core of his system were the psalms of Dr. Watts and a selection of his own composition, but more than this, Dwight broadened the denominational representation by including hymns and spiritual songs from Christians across the Protestant spectrum. This brought the Presbyterians closer still to the Congregationalists, and gave official endorsement for the spiritual expressions of Christians beyond the Reformed tradition.

Yet, as evidenced by the aftermath of Cane Ridge, the same spirit that fostered cooperation could also lead to divisions. The egalitarian impulses found within the Presbyterian Church that prompted the departure of the Disciples of Christ and the Cumberland Presbyterians were not, however, exclusive to Presbyterians.[6] They were part of a larger "sectarian" movement sweeping through the American religious landscape and shaping society as a whole. Among these influential and democratizing sectarian churches, historians such as Nathan Hatch include the Methodists, Baptists, Mormons, Christian churches, Universalists/Unitarians, and the black churches. Their phenomenal success in the nineteenth century has been attributed primarily to two things. First, the democratic beliefs that the Methodists, Baptists, and other non-Standing Order groups possessed made them very attractive to a populace bent on the liberties and equalities of mankind. These denominations denied the assumption that the clergy were innately better in theological matters than the laymen; they empowered individual members by accepting their spiritual reasoning and impulses, and these churches held a strong passion for equality. Second, the way in which these more egalitarian denominations spread their message made them successful. The "religious newcomers" utilized "vernacular preaching," print culture, and gospel music to attract new members.[7]

It was this same democratic-republican ethos that also inspired Presbyterian splinter groups such as the Barton Stone- and Alexander Campbell-led "Christians" to pursue "a radical simplification of the gospel" as components of a loose network of religious radicals influenced by the self-educated Jeffersonian Elias Smith.[8] For Campbell and Stone, this simplification led to the Restoration movement, which challenged Christians and offered them a way to return to the primitive roots of the early Christian church. The Cumberland Presbyterians, who were also seeking to better represent the wishes and needs of the laity, allowed for greater local control over doctrinal positions. This flexibility provided the congregation with ready means to address the growing democratic demands of the American people, and the approach was partly displayed in the Cumberland Presbyterians' emphasis on the role of individuals in their own salvation and subsequent spiritual life. The extent to which these breakaway groups fulfilled a growing demand within society can be glimpsed by their rapid growth in membership. Upon the merger of Stone's Christians and Campbell's Disciples of Christ in 1832 the church claimed 25,000 members. By 1861 that number had nearly quadrupled to 200,000, and there were nearly as many Disciples of Christ congregations (2,100) as there were Congregational (2,240) and Episcopalian (2,150).[9] Similarly impressive, but less dramatic was the growth of the Cumberland Presbyterian Church. According to Ernest Trice Thompson, by 1835 "it counted nine synods, thirty-five presbyteries, three hundred ordained and one hundred licensed ministers, and 75,000 communicants."[10] And by the 1860s, membership had risen to 100,000.[11]

As striking as these numbers are, they paled when compared with the rise of the Methodist and Baptist churches. Between 1776 and 1860, the success of these "democratic newcomers" was truly amazing.[12] The Baptist churches more than doubled their number of congregations between 1776 and 1797, from approximately 500 to more than 1,100. Additionally, the number of members rose from 30,000 to 40,000 in 1776 to approximately 125,000 in 1800.[13] By 1832 the Baptists boasted 384,920 members, and by 1860 that number had increased to a remarkable 664,556.[14] The Methodists, who were almost nonexistent in 1776 and were tainted by association with a founder who was viewed as pro-British, jumped from 4,921 adherents in 1776 to 65,000 by 1800, with their largest gains occurring between 1780 and 1790.[15] By 1810 Methodist membership had increased to 175,000, and that number would continue to rise in coming decades. Before the denomination's sectional division in 1844, the church had nearly 795,000 members and by 1860, after combining the numbers for the northern and southern branches, it had 1,744,000, making the Methodists the most prevalent Protestant church in the United States.[16]

The Presbyterians and Congregationalists also saw substantial growth, even if it came nowhere near that of the Baptists and Methodists. From 1776 to 1800 the Presbyterian communicant membership fluctuated between 40,000 and 50,000, although, according to some estimates, there were around 410,000 nonmembers who associated with the Presbyterian Church during this period.[17] At the turn of the century the Congregationalists claimed 65,000 members, an increase of approximately 15,000 since 1776.[18] The new century saw the Congregationalist growth diminish—a development that George Marsden connects to the Plan of Union of 1801. Accordingly, the Presbyterian structure was simply more appealing to Congregationalists in New England and elsewhere. "When the union was subsequently elaborated and extended," he wrote, "whole consociations of Congregational churches transformed themselves into Presbyterian presbyteries."[19] Illustrating this point: by 1834, the communicant membership of the Presbyterian Church had risen to 248,000, and some scholars contend that when the number of regularly attending nonmembers is considered, the Presbyterians saw about two million in their pews.[20] By 1850 the Plan of Union had been rejected by both churches, and in 1860 the Congregationalists claimed 2,240 churches and around 250,000 members.[21] The Presbyterian growth continued, but in different directions. In 1840, following the 1837 Old School/New School split, the former claimed 126,585 members and the latter 102,060.[22] The Old School Presbyterians split again in 1861; the splinter group, the Presbyterian Church of the Confederate States of America, claimed 72,000 members. When, in 1869 the remaining Old School and New School Presbyterians reunited, they became the largest Presbyterian Church in America with 446,561 members.[23]

While the Presbyterians lost the numerical advantage they held over the democratic sectarian churches in the mid- to late 18th century, they maintained their influence in American society. The interdenominational nationalism that the Presbyterians developed during the last half of the eighteenth century presented the denomination with ample opportunities to spread the boundaries of Christendom. The 1801 Plan of Union that brought together the Presbyterians and the Connecticut Congregationalists was followed by similar agreements that united the Presbyterians with the other New England Congregational establishments and allowed them to advance the cause of Christ in the western states and territories. In this advance, voluntary societies would play a significant role, as noted in an 1817 pastoral letter from the General Assembly. Specifically, the ruling body encouraged members to "embrace every opportunity, to the extent which God has given you, to form and vigorously support missionary associations, Bible societies, plans for the distribution of religious tracts, and exertions for extending the benefits of knowledge, and especially spiritual knowledge, to all ages and classes of persons around you."[24] It was essential, it reminded members, that as this work continued "to maintain a spirit of harmony with all denominations of Christians. . . . Let all bitterness, and wrath, and evil speaking, be put away from among you, with all malice; and continually look and pray or the happy period when believers of every name shall agree to act together upon the great principle of our common salvation."

While Presbyterians were called to work with all Christians regardless of their beliefs, they were not to stray from orthodoxy. Emphasizing this point, the ruling body wrote in the same letter: "Besides the common bonds of Christian love which unite the great family of believers, the ministers and members of the Presbyterian Church are cemented by a compact which every honest man cannot fail to appreciate. We mean the 'Confession of Faith' of our Church. While we believe the Scriptures of the Old and New Testament to be the only infallible rule of faith and practice, we do also, if we deal faithfully with God and man, sincerely receive and adopt this confession, as containing the system of doctrine taught in the Holy Scriptures."[25] As in the past, this proved to be a difficult requirement for nineteenth-century Presbyterians to meet. Still, as requested, many members embraced interdenominational voluntary societies, and in doing so the church helped form and contribute to several prominent organizations, including the American Board of Commissioners for Foreign Missions (1810), the American Bible Society (1816), the American Tract Society (1825), and the American Home Missionary Society (1826). Within these groups the Presbyterians worked closely with Congregationalists, Baptists, and Methodists throughout the early nineteenth century in what has been called "the Protestant United Front."[26] Yet, as they worked alongside their fellow Christians to redeem and reform, some Presbyterians began adopting questionable orthodox beliefs and taking on controversial social concerns such as slavery. Others worried about the direction these national organizations were taking their fellow Presbyterians and, in turn, they feared for their church. Eventually, theologians such as South Carolina's James Henley Thornwell gave voice to these growing concerns, arguing that Christians should only address issues that were biblically authorized.[27] Fracture lines were increasingly visible, and it was clear that the difficulties the Presbyterian General

Assembly experienced as a result of its interdenominational pursuits also carried over into the new century. Yet voluntary societies were not the only way in which the Presbyterians would grow closer to other churches after the Plan of Union.

The potential danger of cooperation was also present in the Presbyterians' educational pursuits. Nurturing the mind was seen by Presbyterians and Congregationalists as the best foundation for redeeming and reforming America. As Marsden writes, "Evangelicals were convinced that any rational man, properly instructed, could see the superiority of the Christian system. They therefore emphasized the importance of education at all levels."[28] Presbyterians and Congregationalists were especially committed to the mind, so much so that by 1839, as Charles Foster noted, "of the presidents of the fifty-four oldest colleges in the nation, fifty-one were clergymen; and of these fifty-one, forty were Presbyterian or Congregationalists."[29] This position atop the academic world was another reason the churches retained their influence despite losing their numerical advantage in the nineteenth century. Yet, while the Presbyterians were better able to engage Americans through these colleges and seminaries, these same institutions also shaped local Presbyterian beliefs through the outpouring of graduating ministers. Granted, this was only a problem if these ministers were drifting from orthodox theology, and to the chagrin of many Presbyterians it became increasingly clear that many were.

Particularly troublesome was the Congregationalist Andover Seminary, which was founded in 1808 as a joint effort between "Old Calvinists" and Hopkinsians to counteract the rise of Unitarianism. While Unitarianism was growing within Congregationalist circles, it was less of a threat among the Presbyterians, who had concerns about the dangers of working with one heterodox theology to offset another. Doubts were not assuaged when the balance between Old Calvinists and New Divinity men quickly swung toward the latter. What many Presbyterians found troubling was that with the Plan of Union in full effect, many of the ministers graduating from Andover were filling Presbyterian pulpits, especially those in the western territories and states. So while the Presbyterians experienced significant growth by way of the union, the orthodoxy of these "Presbygationalists" came into question.[30]

In 1798, when Hezekiah Balch was charged with teaching Hopkinsianism, the General Assembly had been clear in its admonition that he was "preaching false doctrine." A decade later, however, Presbyterian leadership was slow to act on the growing threat, which prompted New York's Ezra Stiles Ely to denounce the theology in an 1811 book. Ely sparked new debate on Hopkinsianism, one that lasted several years. When the first Presbyterian seminary was founded in Princeton in 1812, it was hoped that it might serve as an orthodox bulwark against, in words of the Synod of Philadelphia, "'the introduction of Arian, Socinian, Arminian, and Hopkinsian heresies, which are some of the means by which the enemy of the soul would, if possible, deceive the very elect.'"[31] While the presence of Archibald Alexander, former president of Hampden-Sydney College and minister of Third Presbyterian Church in Philadelphia, at Princeton provided a sense of doctrinal integrity, that too was questioned when the 1817 General Assembly committee tasked to consider Hopkinsianism did not condemn the theology but rather noted its regret "that zeal on this subject should be manifested in such a manner as to be offensive to other denominations."[32] Princeton's own Dr. Samuel Miller helmed the committee. Concerned Presbyterians found no relief when the church's second seminary, Auburn, was founded in 1819. As one scholar has noted, Auburn Seminary was seen as the first "application of the Andover model to Presbyterian theological education."[33]

Old School and New School Presbyterians, the names that would torment the church for decades to come, were first employed in a debate held at Princeton seminary in 1824. The original point of difference was the Andoverian doctrine of atonement. Yet beleaguered Old School Presbyterians began to see other issues at stake and noted with dismay that by the 1830s, Andover Seminary, with the New School in tow, was moving beyond the relatively tame New Divinity and was quickly embracing the New Haven theology associated with Yale's Nathaniel William Taylor. Taylor was also concerned with the rise of Unitarianism, and he threw aside many orthodox positions in order to better attract those lured by the theology. Among other things, Taylor argued that scripture was not to be interpreted using scripture, but rather with "common-sense" reasoning and that doing so would lead a person to see that there was no original sin, that individuals could save themselves, that the Holy Spirit was a merely a good influence, and that Christ was simply a compelling example. Through the seminaries, New Haven theology made inroads in the Presbyterian Church through the ministry of men such as Albert Barnes, George Duffield, James Wheelock, Lyman Beecher, Edward Beecher, J. M. Sturtevant, and William Kirby. In the early 1830s these men were brought before various presbyteries, many of which were predominately Old School, on charges of doctrinal error. In each case, whether it was settled at the presbytery level or considered on appeal in the General Assembly, the result was either an acquittal or slight reprimand and warning to more carefully phrase their theological beliefs in the future. With each New School victory, the Old School Presbyterians rallied more to their cause.[34]

Charles Grandison Finney experienced first-hand the turmoil that be-set the denomination. A symbol of revivalism and theological innovations within the Presbyterian Church, he often found himself at odds with the Old School. Although his own theology did not always align with Taylor's, Finney left the church in 1835 to distance himself from growing hostilities and the increased orthodox vigilance of the Old School Presbyterians. By this point, the New School theology had prompted an alliance between conservatives such as Ashbel Green, editor of both the *Christian Advocate* and the *Presbyterian*, and moderates such as Charles Hodge and Archibald Alexander. Although the groups disagreed on where and how the New Divinity and New Haven theologies erred, they agreed that the Taylorites "actually subverted the foundations of the Reformed faith."[35] The threat to the faith was such that some Old School men began linking New Haven thought with the phoenixlike Pelagianism. A more concerted effort was needed to stop its advance within the Presbyterian Church. Before the 1835 General Assembly, the Old School party united its forces and with a slight majority it began a serious reconsideration of what it saw as the culprits of the theological faltering within the church, primarily the 1801 Plan of Union and the various voluntary societies of the Protestant United Front. Concerns over interdenominational intimacy were alive and well. Having found success in 1835, the conservatives held high hope for further advance in 1836, especially after the Presbytery of Philadelphia removed Albert Barnes from ministerial duties. Barnes's appeal made it to the General Assembly and was considered in 1836. Yet, despite the new strength of the Old School in the ultimate ruling body, the renowned Taylorite was once more acquitted, prompting many to consider more extremes measures for the following year.[36]

The Old School Presbyterians were beyond debate and even reconcilia-tion. By 1837, it was clear that the interdenominational nationalism rooted in the 1758 Presbyterian reunion had been the door through which the New England errors gained entrance to the church and were threatening to overwhelm it. There were only two possible outcomes for the Old School, and both came in the end to the same result—the Presbyterian Church was to be divided. This would be accomplished either by successfully cutting off the cancerous New School or, in failure, by walking away from the de-nomination. In a 143–110 vote, the Old School Presbyterians struck down "the major source of New School irregularity," the onetime crown jewel of the church's cooperative pursuits—the Plan of Union of 1801. Taking advantage of their strength, they made the decision retroactive and, as baf-fled New School representatives came to understand, that meant a purging of all churches, presbyteries, and synods formed as result of the union. In all, this severed four synods, 28 presbyteries, 509 ministers, and roughly 60,000 members. Yet, the Old School was not finished. They crafted a sixteen-point statement denouncing the doctrinal errors they had seen become commonplace within the church. Shocked, the New School men who survived the onslaught withdrew of their own volition. The following year the exiled Presbyterians briefly attempted to resume their positions within the General Assembly, but they were rebuffed and the desired schism, now accepted by both sides, was complete.[37]

Nearly a century had passed since the Old Light Presbyterians ousted their New Light adversaries when the main body of American Presbyterians embraced schism. Where the first division took nearly two decades and the French and Indian War to mend, the second took more than three decades and the Civil War. However, when reunion finally occurred in 1869, it was not complete. The intermediate period saw both the New School (1857) and Old School (1861) Presbyterian Churches suffer further division, but these were largely sectional in nature pertaining to slavery and loyalty to the Union.[38] The sectionalism fostered through the open-ended definitions of proper national spirit espoused by the Presbyterian Church had finally torn through the veil of national rhetoric. The church's goal in 1758 to bring about a true union in the body of Christ had met with tremendous success in the following years. However, in the end, the Presbyterians only divided their denomination and helped to foster the sectionalism that would tear apart the nation.

Notes

Introduction

1. During the second half of the eighteenth century, the Presbyterian Church was the second-largest denomination in America, and unlike the Congregational or Anglican churches, the Presbyterian Church was not largely confined to one section of the country.

2. By "Christendom," here and elsewhere in the book, I am referring to the informal and voluntary presence of Christianity.

3. Arthur Lyon Cross, *The Anglican Episcopate and the American Colonies* (New York: Longmans, Green, and Co., 1902); Carl Bridenbaugh, *Mitre and Sceptre: Transatlantic Faiths, Ideas, Personalities, and Politics, 1689–1775* (New York: Oxford University Press, 1962); Kenneth R. Elliott, *Anglican Church Policy, Eighteenth Century Conflict, and the American Episcopate* (New York: Peter Lang Academic Publishers, 2011); and James B. Bell, *A War of Religion: Dissenters, Anglicans, and the American Revolution* (New York: Palgrave Macmillan).

4. Alan Heimert, *Religion and the American Mind: From the Great Awakening to the American Revolution* (Cambridge, MA: Harvard University Press, 1966); and Patricia U. Bonomi, *Under the Cope of Heaven: Religion, Society, and Politics in Colonial America* (New York: Oxford University Press, 2003).

5. Nathan O. Hatch, *The Sacred Cause of Liberty: Republican Thought and the Millennium in Revolutionary New England* (New Haven, CT: Yale University Press, 1977); Ruth Bloch, *Visionary Republic: Millennial Themes in American Thought, 1756–1800* (New York: Cambridge University Press, 1989).

6. J. C. D. Clark, *The Language of Liberty, 1660–1832: Political Discourse and Social Dynamics in the Anglo-American World* (New York: Cambridge University Press, 1994). See also Bell, *A War of Religion*.

7. Fred J. Hood, *Reformed America: The Middle and Southern States, 1783–1837*, (Tuscaloosa: University of Alabama Press, 1980); Jon Butler, *Awash in a Sea of Faith; Christianizing the American People* (Cambridge, MA: Harvard University Press, 1990).

8. Nathan O. Hatch, *The Democratization of American Christianity* (New Haven, CT: Yale University Press, 1989); A. Gregory Schneider, "From Democratization to Domestication: The Transitional Orality of the American Methodists Circuit Rider," in *Communication and Change in American Religious History*, ed. Leonard I. Sweet (Grand Rapids, MI: William B. Eerdmans Publishing, 1993), 141–64.

9. My work is indebted to the research of Jonathan Sassi and Robert H. Abzug. Focusing primarily on New England and the Congregationalist churches, Sassi and Abzug have attempted to counteract the reactionary and static view of the "Standing Order" churches. In *A Republic of Righteousness: The Public Christianity of the Post-Revolutionary New England Clergy, 1783–1833* (New York: Oxford University Press, 2001), Sassi contends that after 1800 and the renowned elections of that year, the Congregationalist churches made earnest strides through interdenominational activities to Christianize America. In *Cosmos Crumbling: American Reform and the Religious Imagination* (New York: Oxford University Press, 1994), Abzug reveals how the Standing Order churches in the North, moved by legalized religious pluralism, led the reform and religious voluntary movements of the nineteenth century.

10. Stephen Foster, *The Long Argument: English Puritanism and the Shaping of New England Culture, 1570–1700* (Chapel Hill: University of North Carolina Press, 1991).

11. Gideon Mailer, "Anglo-Scottish Union and John Witherspoon's American Revolution," *William and Mary Quarterly* 67, no. 4 (October 2010): 709–46. For further discussion see Mailer's *Kirk to Congress: John Witherspoon's American Revolution: Enlightenment and Religion from the Creation of Britain to the Founding of the United States* (Chapel Hill: University of North Carolina Press and the Omohundro Institute of Early American History and Culture, 2017).

12. Peter C. Messer, *Stories of Independence: Identity, Ideology, and History in Eighteenth-Century America* (DeKalb: Northern Illinois University Press, 2005), 30–32, 81–82; Clark, *The Language of Liberty*, 154; Mark A. Noll, *The Old Religion in a New World: The History of North American Christianity* (Grand Rapids, MI: William B. Eerdmans Publishing, 2002), 40–41, 45–47; James P. Boyd, *Sacred Scripture, Sacred War: The Bible and the American Revolution* (New York: Oxford University Press, 2013), especially chps. 2, 3, and 4; Ernest Lee Tuveson, *Redeemer Nation: The Idea of America's Millennial Role* (Chicago: University of Chicago Press, 1968), chp. 5; and Keith L. Griffin, *Revolution and Religion: American Revolutionary War and the Reformed Clergy* (New York: Paragon House, 1994).

13. Hatch, *The Sacred Cause of Liberty*, 160, 156.

14. Thomas S. Kidd, *God of Liberty: A Religious History of the American Revolution* (New York: Basic Books, 2010).

15. David Waldstreicher, *In the Midst of Perpetual Fetes: The Making of American Nationalism, 1776–1820* (Chapel Hill: University of North Carolina Press, 1997); Benedict Anderson, *Imagined Communities: Reflections on the Origin and Spread of Nationalism* (New York: Verso, 1991); and Simon P. Newman, *Parades and the Politics of the Street:*

Festive Culture in the Early American Republic (Philadelphia: University of Pennsylvania Press, 1997).

16. See David M. Potter, *The Impending Crisis, 1848–1861* (San Francisco: Harper Perennial, 1976); Michael F. Holt, *The Political Crisis of the 1850s* (New York: W. W. Norton & Company, 1983); William W. Freehling, *The Road to Disunion, Volume I: Secessionists at Bay, 1776–1854* (New York: Oxford University Press, 1990); William J. Cooper Jr., *Liberty and Slavery: Southern Politics to 1860* (New York: Alfred A. Knopf, 1983); J. Mills Thornton III, *Politics and Power in a Slave State: Alabama, 1800–1860* (Baton Rouge: Louisiana State University Press, 1978); and James McPherson, *Battle Cry of Freedom: The Civil War Era* (New York: Oxford University Press, 2003).

17. Donald G. Mathews, *Religion in the Old South* (Chicago: University of Chicago Press, 1977); Rhys Isaac, *The Transformation of Virginia, 1740–1790* (Chapel Hill: University of North Carolina Press, 1999); and Mitchell Snay, *Gospel of Disunion: Religion and Separatism in the Antebellum South* (New York: Cambridge University Press, 1993).

18. Joyce Appleby, *Inheriting the Revolution: The First Generation of Americans* (Cambridge, MA: Harvard University Press, 2000).

19. Waldstreicher, *In the Midst of Perpetual Fetes*, 13.

20. Peter B. Knupfer, *The Union As It Is: Constitutional Unionism and Sectional Compromise, 1787–1861* (Chapel Hill: University of North Carolina Press, 1991).

Chapter 1

1. Matthew 28:18–20 (King James Version).

2. On behalf of the Synod of New York, Robert Treat wrote, "We have been warned and chastised, first more gently, then more terribly; but not returning to him that smites us, his anger is not turned away, but his hand is stretched out still. Judgment yet proceeds, the prospect becomes darker and darker, and all things respecting us are loudly alarming." Presbyterian General Assembly, *Records of the Presbyterian Church in the United States of America, 1706–1788* (Philadelphia: Presbyterian Board of Publication, 1904), 276.

3. Synod of New York and Philadelphia, *The plan of union between the Synods of New-York and Philadelphia. Agreed upon May 29th, 1758* (Philadelphia: W. Dunlap, 1758).

4. The most recent Presbyterian history follows largely in the footsteps of Leonard J. Trinterud, *The Forming of an American Tradition: A Re-examination of Colonial Presbyterianism* (Philadelphia: Westminster Press, 1949). This includes works such as Bradley J. Longfield, *Presbyterians and American Culture: A History* (Louisville, KY: Westminster John Knox Press, 2013); D. G. Hart and John R. Muether, *Seeking a Better Country: 300 Years of American Presbyterianism* (Phillipsburg, NJ: P&R Publishing, 2007), 82–88; Randall Balmer and John R. Fitzmier, *The Presbyterians* (Westport, CT: Praeger, 1994); James Smylie, *A Brief History of the Presbyterians* (Louisville, KY: Geneva Press, 1996); and William G. McLoughlin, *Revivals, Awakenings, and Reform: An Essay on Religion and Social Change in America, 1607–1977* (Chicago: University of Chicago Press, 1978).

5. That conflict has largely defined the eighteenth century can be seen in a sample of general religious histories: Kidd, *God of Liberty*; Bonomi, *Under the Cope of Heaven*;

Mark A. Noll, *America's God: From Jonathan Edwards to Abraham Lincoln* (New York: Oxford University Press, 2002); Philip Goff, "Revivals and Revolution: Historiographic Turns since Alan Heimert's Religion and the American Mind," *Church History* 67, no. 4 (December 1998): 696–721; Gordon S. Wood, "Religion and the American Revolution," in *New Directions in American Religious History*, ed. Harry S. Stout and D. G. Hart (New York: Oxford University Press, 1997), 173–205; Clark, *The Language of Liberty*; Hood, *Reformed America*; Hatch, *The Sacred Cause of Liberty*; Heimert, *Religion and the American Mind*; and Bridenbaugh, *Mitre and Sceptre*.

6. Some historians have investigated cooperative interaction between adherents of different denominations; however, the activity of denominational ruling bodies has received less attention. See Susan O'Brien, "A Transatlantic Community of Saints: The Great Awakening and the First Evangelical Network, 1735–1755," *American Historical Review* 91, no. 4 (October 1986): 811–32; Thomas S. Kidd, *The Great Awakening: The Roots of Evangelical Christianity in Colonial America* (New Haven, CT: Yale University Press, 2007); Mark A. Noll, *The Rise of Evangelicalism: The Age of Edwards, Whitefield, and the Wesleys* (Downers Grove, IL: InterVarsity Press, 2003); and Marilyn J. Westerkamp, *Triumph of the Laity: Scots-Irish Piety and the Great Awakening, 1625–1760* (New York: Oxford University Press, 1987).

7. This is described by the Apostle Paul as working "out your own salvation with fear and trembling." Philippians 2:12 (King James Version). Experimental religion is sometimes called experimental piety or even experiential piety. The renowned Gilbert Tennent required a three-step process: "conviction of sin under the divine law; an experience of spiritual rebirth; and a reformed life that gave evidence of the work of the spirit in practical piety." Whereas this is a specific example, generally the ministerial exam required merely a demonstrable sign of salvation. Balmer and Fitzmier, *The Presbyterians*, 24, 26, 27.

8. General Assembly, *Records of the Presbyterian Church, 1706–1788*, 138.

9. Ibid., 159.

10. Balmer and Fitzmier, *The Presbyterians*, 30; Smylie, *A Brief History of the Presbyterians*, 48–49.

11. By 1776, the Presbyterian Church had roughly 40,000 communicant members, making it second only to the Congregationalists in colonial American membership. Some scholars estimate that Presbyterian adherents numbered 410,000 by 1776. See Roger Finke and Rodney Stark, *The Churching of America, 1776–1990: Winners and Losers in Our Religious Economy* (New Brunswick, NJ: Rutgers University Press, 1992), 26, 55; Edwin Scott Gaustad and Philip L. Barlow, *New Historical Atlas of Religion in America* (Oxford: Oxford University Press, 2001), 374; and Thomas L. Purvis, *Revolutionary America, 1763 to 1800* (New York: Facts on File, 1995), 197.

12. David Hackett Fischer, *Albion's Seed: Four British Folkways in America* (New York: Oxford University Press, 1991), 606–10, 615–17.

13. John E. Ferling, *Struggle for a Continent: The Wars of Early America* (Arlington Heights, IL: Harlan Davidson, Westport, CT: Praeger, 19941993), 165. For another excellent treatment of the French and Indian War, see Fred Anderson, *Crucible of War:*

The Seven Years' War and the Fate of Empire in British North America, 1754–1766 (New York: Vintage Books, 2001).

14. General Assembly, *Records of the Presbyterian Church, 1706–1788*, 276.

15. Balmer and Fitzmier, *The Presbyterians*, 31–32; Smylie, *A Brief History of the Presbyterians*, 54–56.

16. "Peace and union recommended," in *Peace and union recommended; and Self disclaim'd, and Christ exalted: in two sermons, preached at Philadelphia, before the Reverend Synods of New-York and Philadelphia: the first, on the 24th of May, 1758, by Francis Alison, D.D. vice-provost of the college, and rector of the academy, in Philadelphia. And, the second, May 25, 1758, by David Bostwick, A.M. Minister of the Presbyterian-Church, in New-York. Both publish'd at the joint request of the Reverend synods* (Philadelphia: W. Dunlap, 1758), vi.

17. Ibid., vii.

18. Alison, "Peace and union recommended," 11.

19. Ibid.

20. Ibid., 12, 17.

21. Ibid., 39.

22. Gilbert Tennent wrote the preface to the published version of Bostwick's sermon. In the same spirit of interdenominational reunion he wrote, "O! Sirs, should we not either love our poor brethren, with a pure heart, fervently; or disclaim all relation to the God of peace and love! I am, your willing and sincere servant, for Christ's sake." Gilbert Tennent, "Preface," in *Peace and union recommended; and Self disclaim'd, and Christ exalted: in two sermons*, xi.

23. Bostwick, "Self disclaim'd, and Christ exalted," in *Peace and union recommended; and Self disclaim'd, and Christ exalted: in two sermons*, 15, 18, 31.

24. Ibid., 43.

25. General Assembly, *Records of the Presbyterian Church, 1706–1788*, 276; Synod, *The plan of union*, 3.

26. General Assembly, *Records of the Presbyterian Church, 1706–1788*, 288.

27. Synod, *The plan of union*, 3, 4.

28. Ibid., 4, 12.

29. For more on Subordinate Standards, see John MacPherson, *The Westminster Confession of Faith. With Introduction and Notes by the Reverend John MacPherson, MA* (Edinburgh: T & T Clark, 1881), 1–3.

30. Westminster Divines, *The Humble Advice of the Assembly of Divines, Now by Authority of Parliament sitting at Westminster, Concerning A Confession of Faith: With Quotations and Texts of Scripture annexed. Presented by them lately to both Houses of Parliament* (Repr., Edinburgh: Evan Tyler, 1647): 3, 5; available at Princeton Theological Seminary Internet Archive: http://ia700301.us.archive.org/28/items/humbleadviceofas00west/humbleadviceofas00west.pdf, accessed July 16, 2013.

31. General Assembly, *Records of the Presbyterian Church, 1706–1788*, 286–88.

32. Synod, *The plan of union*, 4, 12, 13.

33. Ibid., 13.

34. General Assembly, *Records of the Presbyterian Church, 1706–1788*, 290.

35. By Reformed churches, I mean churches that stemmed from John Calvin and his interpretation of Christianity. Although the synod did not specify what it meant by the term, it probably was referring to the Dutch Reformed Church, English Congregationalists, and Calvinistic Methodists, Scottish Presbyterians, Irish Presbyterians, and their colonial counterparts.

36. For more on these men, see Mark A. Noll, *A History of Christianity in the United States and Canada* (Grand Rapids, MI: William B. Eerdmans Publishing, 1992), 111; Milton J. Coalter, *Gilbert Tennent, Son of Thunder: A Case Study of Continental Pietism's Impact on the First Great Awakening in the Middle Colonies* (Westport, CT: Greenwood Publishing Group, 1986); Whitfield Jenks Bell, *Patriot-improvers: Biographical Sketches of Members of the American Philosophical Society* (Darby, PA: Diane Publishing, 1997), 149–58; Elizabeth I. Nybakken, *The Centinel: Warnings of a Revolution* (Newark: University of Delaware Press, 1979), 19–23; Jon Butler, *Becoming America: The Revolution Before 1776* (Cambridge, MA: Harvard University Press, 2001), 201; Edward D. Neill, "Matthew Wilson, D. D., of Lewes, Delaware," *Pennsylvania Magazine of History and Biography* 8 (1884): 45. Treat and Cross are overshadowed by the scholarship on Tennent and Alison, but their activities within the synod are indicative of their importance to the church.

37. Smylie, *A Brief History of the Presbyterians*, 50–51.

38. Ernest Trice Thompson, *Presbyterians in the South, Volume One: 1607–1861* (Richmond, VA: John Knox Press, 1963), 1:189–91; Smylie, *A Brief History of the Presbyterians*, 51.

39. I have chosen the spelling "Occom" instead of "Occum" or "Occam," as it is sometimes written, as that is the preference of recent historians. See Joanna Brooks, ed., *The Collected Writings of Samson Occom, Mohegan: Leadership and Literature in Eighteenth-Century Native America* (New York: Oxford University Press, 2006).

40. Ready to depart for the Cherokee, Occom would be thwarted by the same hostilities that prevented William Richardson from making inroads. Occom was instead sent to the Mohawk.

41. Smylie, *A Brief History of the Presbyterians*, 50–51; Brooks, *The Collected Writings of Samson Occom*, xxi.

42. William DeLoss Love, *Samson Occom and the Christian Indians of New England* (Cleveland: Pilgrim Press, 1899), 52.

43. Interestingly, Occum was ordained in 1759 but John Chavis, the first black minister, was not licensed until 1800. The considerable gap suggests much concerning Americans' perceptions of the Native Americans and Africans in their midst.

44. Samuel Buell, *The excellence and importance of the saving knowledge of the Lord Jesus Christ in the Gospel-preacher, plainly and seriously represented and enforced: and Christ preached to the gentiles in obedience to the call of God. A sermon, preached at East-Hampton, August 29, 1759; at the ordination of Mr. Samson Occum, a missionary among the Indians. By Samuel Buell, M.A. Pastor of the Church of Christ, at East-Hampton, Long-Island. To which is prefixed, a letter to the Rev. Mr. David Bostwick, Minister of the Presbyterian*

Church, in New-York, giving some account of Mr. Occum's education, character, &c. (New York: James Parker and Company, 1761), xiv-v.

45. Ibid., xv.

46. Ibid.

47. For more on the ethnocentric views (whether based on doubt or fear) of Presbyterians and Congregationalists, see Francis Whiting Halsey, *The Old New York Frontier: Its Wars with Indians and Tories; Its Missionary Schools, Pioneers and Land Titles, 1614–1800* (New York: Charles Scribner's Sons, 1901), 71; Smylie, *A Brief History of the Presbyterians*, 50–51, 66; and Thompson, *Presbyterians in the South*, 1:113, 1:189–203.

48. Another example of this cooperative missionary spirit among the Presbyterians can be seen when Charles Jeffry Smith consulted his Congregationalist friend Ezra Stiles concerning his upcoming mission trip to the Mohawks. Knowing "of none more likely to answer these Querys," Smith asked Stiles's advice on "Indian Affairs, and the great design of diffusing the light of the glorious Gospel among them." Charles Jeffry Smith to Ezra Stiles, April 9, 1763, in *Ezra Stiles Papers, Correspondence, Reel 1*, ed. Harold Selesky (New Haven, CT: Yale University, 1976).

49. Jonathan Clark notes that colonial Dissenters "kept fully briefed about its history and its origin in Anglican persecution" through works like "Daniel Neal's *The History of the Puritans or Protestant Non-Conformists, from the Reformation* (4 vols., London, 1732–38) and in pocket compendia like Samuel Palmer's *The Protestant-Dissenter's Catechism* (London, 1774)." See Clark, *The Language of Liberty*, 161–62.

50. John Brown, *The Pilgrim Fathers of New England and their Puritan Successors* (Pasadena, TX: Pilgrim Publications, 1970), 30–34, 96–97.

51. Elizabeth I. Nybakken, "A New Light on the Old Side: Irish Influences on Colonial Presbyterianism," *Journal of American History* 68, no. 4 (March 1982): 817–18; Kerby A. Miller, ed., *Irish Immigrants in the Land of Canaan; Letters and Memoirs from Colonial and Revolutionary America, 1675–1815* (Oxford: Oxford University Press, 2003), 518; and William Warren Sweet, *Religion in the Development of American Culture, 1765–1840* (New York: Charles Scribner's Sons, 1952), 9.

52. Sweet, *Religion in the Development of American Culture*, 10; Smylie, *A Brief History of the Presbyterians*, 58.

53. Trinterud, *The Forming of an American Tradition*, 228.

54. The original letter was not published by the Presbyterians, and so the emphasis of certain words is not their doing but that of their critic "An old covenanting and true Presbyterian layman." *A True copy of a genuine letter, sent to the Archbishop of Canterbury, by eighteen Presbyterian ministers, in America: with some remarks thereon; in another letter to the congregations of the said ministers. By an old covenanting, and true Presbyterian layman* (Philadelphia: Andrew Steuart, 1761), 2–3.

55. General Assembly, *Records of the Presbyterian Church, 1706–1788*, 306.

56. Ibid. It seems plausible that the synod was sincere in its statement of general ignorance concerning the petition, as only eighteen of the one hundred and six ministers on record are shown to have any knowledge of it.

57. General Assembly, *Records of the Presbyterian Church, 1706–1788*, 311.

58. Ibid., 312.

59. Additionally, the Presbyterians and Congregationalists perpetually feared that the colonial Church of England would try to claim for itself power equal to that of its English counterpart. This aspect will be discussed more fully in the next chapter. For more information, see Bridenbaugh, *Mitre and Sceptre.*

60. Ibid., 4. For more on the Covenanters, especially those in America, see Joseph S. Moore, *Founding Sins: How a Group of Antislavery Radicals Fought to Put Christ into the Constituion* (New York: Oxford University Press, 2016). Covenanters were, as Moore writes, "an assortment of radical Scotch-Irish Presbyterian sects sharing the conviction that all nations must be in an explicit covenant with God." These individuals, Moore states, were found in all branches of the Presbyterian faith that professed "the 1638 National Covenant and the 1643 Solemn League and Covenant as models of Christian statehood." *Founding Sins,* 2, 5.

61. Ibid., 6.

62. Ibid., 15.

63. *The conduct of the Presbyterian-ministers, who sent the letter to the Archbishop of Canterbury, the year 1760, considered, and set in true light: in answer to some remarks thereon. In a letter to a friend. By an elder of the Presbyterian Church. [Three lines from Isaiah]* (Philadelphia: Andrew Steuart, 1761), 4.

64. Ibid., 7.

65. Ibid., 5.

66. Ibid., 17.

67. Ibid., 18.

68. Ibid., 19.

69. Mechanick, *The mechanick's address to the farmer: being a short reply to some of the layman's Remarks on the eighteen Presbyterian ministers letter to the arch-bishop* (Philadelphia: Andrew Steuart, 1761), 12.

70. General Assembly, *Records of the Presbyterian Church, 1706–1788,* 297. The members of the committee were John Pierson, Caleb Smith, Jacob Green, Timothy Jones, Azariah Horton, Samuel Kennedy, and Jonathan Elmore.

71. Ibid., 283–84.

72. Ibid., 308.

73. Ibid., 301.

74. Divines, *The Humble Advice,* 7.

75. Alistair E. McGrath, *Iustitia Dei: A History of the Christian Doctrine of Justification* (Cambridge, UK: Cambridge University Press, 1986), 1:128–45; Alistair E. McGrath, *Reformation Thought: An Introduction* (Oxford: Basil Blackwell, 1988), 55–61.

76. General Assembly, *Records of the Presbyterian Church, 1706–1788,* 302.

77. Ibid., 308, 315.

78. Ibid., 329, 330.

79. Francis Alison to Ezra Stiles, June 2, 1761, *Ezra Stiles Papers, Correspondence, Reel 1.*

80. General Assembly, *Records of the Presbyterian Church, 1706–1788,* 319.

81. Ibid., 319, 320.

82. Of the committee members at least one had prepared for such a situation. A year earlier, Alison had consulted his friend Ezra Stiles because his "churches have long been in this practice of demanding some satisfaction by a Declaration of experiences," and he continued, "You would greatly oblige me by giving me [your] sentiments on this subject." Francis Alison to Ezra Stiles, June 2, 1761, *Ezra Stiles Papers, Correspondence, Reel 1.*

83. General Assembly, *Records of the Presbyterian Church, 1706–1788*, 321.

84. Ibid., 319; Divines, *Humble Advice*, 35. According to the Divines, "God alone is Lord of the Conscience, and hath left it free from the Doctrines and Commandments of men, which are in any thing contrary to his Word; or beside it, if matters of Faith, or Worship. So that, to believe such Doctrines, or to obey such Commands out of conscience, is to betray true Liberty of Conscience."

85. Divines, *Humble Advice*, 36.

86. General Assembly, *Records of the Presbyterian Church, 1706–1788*, 324.

87. For more information regarding the importance of religion to the pan-Indian alliance, see Gregory Evans Dowd, *A Spirited Resistance: The North American Indian Struggle for Unity, 1745–1815* (Baltimore, MD: Johns Hopkins University Press, 1992).

88. Kevin Kenny, *Peaceable Kingdom Lost: The Paxton Boys and the Destruction of William Penn's Holy Experiment* (New York: Oxford University Press: 2009), 130–59; Alan Taylor, *American Colonies: The Settling of North America*, (New York: Penguin Books, 2002), 435–36; Melvin H. Baxbaum, *Benjamin Franklin and the Zealous Presbyterians* (University Park: Penn State University Press, 1975), 185–93; John R. Dunbar, "Introduction," in *The Paxton Papers*, ed. John R. Dunbar (The Hague, Netherlands: Martinus Nijhoff, 1957), 3; and Thomas Fleming, ed., *Benjamin Franklin: A Biography in His Own Words* (New York: *Newsweek*, 1972), 1:181.

89. James H. Hutson, *Pennsylvania Politics 1746–1770: The Movement for Royal Government and Its Consequences* (Princeton, NJ: Princeton University Press, 1972), 84–180; Dietmar Rothermund, *The Layman's Progress: Religious and Political Experience in Colonial Pennsylvania, 1740–1770* (Philadelphia: University of Pennsylvania Press, 1961), 82; Baxbaum, *Benjamin Franklin and the Zealous Presbyterians*, 194–219; and Dunbar, "Introduction," in *The Paxton Papers*, 50–51.

90. *A Dialogue, containing some reflections on the late declaration and remonstrance, of the back-inhabitants of the province of Pennsylvania. With a serious and short address, to those Presbyterians, who (to their dishonor) have too much abetted, and conniv'd at the late insurrection. By a member of that community* (Philadelphia: Andrew Steuart, 1764), 1.

91. Ibid., 4.

92. Ibid., 11–12.

93. Ibid., 14.

94. Ibid., 16.

95. Another good example of Quaker writers attacking Presbyterian churchmen is the satire *The Substance, of a council held at Lancaster August the 28th 1764. By a committee of Presbyterian ministers and elders deputed from all parts of Pennsylvania, in order to settle the ensuing election of members for the Assembly* (Philadelphia: Anthony Armbruster, 1764).

96. David James Dove escalated the war with his *The Quaker unmask'd; or, Plain*

truth: humbly address'd to the consideration of all the freemen of Pennsylvania (Philadelphia: Andrew Steuart, 1764); *A Conference between the D——l and Doctor D——e. Together with the doctor's epitaph on himself* (Philadelphia: Andrew Steuart, 1764); *The addition to the epitaph, without the copper-plate* (Philadelphia: Anthony Armbruster, 1764); and *The counter-medly, being a proper answer to all the dunces of the medly and their abettors* (Philadelphia: Anthony Armbruster, 1764). Not to be outdone, his opponents countered with Thomas Wigwagg, *The author of Quaker unmask'd strip'd start [sic] naked, or The delineated Presbyterian play'd hob with* (Philadelphia: Anthony Armbruster, 1764); Philalethes, *The Quaker vindicated; or, Observations on a late pamphlet, entituled, The Quaker unmask'd, or, Plain truth* (Philadelphia: Andrew Steuart, 1764). Interestingly, the Presbyterian Isaac Hunt did his best to denounce and decry the Paxton Boys and their supporters by publishing *A looking-glass for Presbyterians. Or A brief examination of their loyalty, merit, and other qualifications for government. With some animadversions on the Quaker unmask'd. Humbly addres'd to the consideration of the loyal freemen of Pennsylvania* (Philadelphia: Anthony Armbruster, 1764); and *A humble attempt at scurrility: in imitation of those great masters of the art, the Rev. Dr. S——th; the Rev. Dr. Al———n; the Rev. Mr. Ew-n; the irreverend D.J. D-ve, and the heroic J—n D————n, Esq; being a full answer to the observations on Mr. H——s's advertisement* (Philadelphia: Anthony Armbruster, 1765).

97. Gilbert Tennent, Francis Alison, and John Ewing, "Circular Letter" (Philadelphia, March 30, 1764), in *The Paxton Papers*, 311.

98. Tennent, Alison, and Ewing, "Circular Letter," 312.

99. Hutson, *Pennsylvania Politics 1746–1770*, 84–180; Rothermund, *The Layman's Progress*, 82; Baxbaum, *Benjamin Franklin and the Zealous Presbyterians*, 211; and Dunbar, "Introduction," in *The Paxton Papers*, 50–51.

100. Robert M. Calhoon, *Evangelicals and Conservatives in the Early South, 1740–1861* (Columbia: University of South Carolina Press, 1988), 62. See also Thomas E. Buckley, *Church and State in Revolutionary Virginia, 1776–1787* (Charlottesville: University of Virginia Press, 1977), 13–14; and Philip N. Mulder, *A Controversial Spirit: Evangelical Awakenings in the South* (New York: Oxford University Press, 2002), 35–36.

101. Thompson, *Presbyterians in the South*, 1:59. See also Mathews, *Religion in the Old South*, 17–18.

102. Samuel Davies, "Brotherly Love. (annext to a Sermon on 1 John iii. 14. Dec. 9, 1750," in *Collected Poems of Samuel Davies, 1723–1761*, ed. Richard Beale Davis (Gainesville, FL: Scholars' Facsimiles & Reprints, 1968), 101–2.

103. For an excellent study that not only addresses Davies's disciples in Virginia but also discusses his many connections and supporters in Great Britain, see Jeffrey H. Richards, "Samuel Davies and the Transatlantic Campaign for Slave literacy in Virginia," *Virginia Magazine of History and Biography* 111, no. 4 (2003): 333–78.

104. John Todd, *An Humble Attempt towards the Improvement of Psalmody: The Propriety Necessity and Use of Evangelical Psalms, in Christian Worship. Delivered at a Meeting of the Presbytery of Hanover in Virginia, October 6th, 1762* (Philadelphia: Andrew Steuart, 1763), 3.

105. Ibid., 4.

106. Ibid., 15. The psalmbooks represent, respectively, those favored by Presbyterians, Congregationalist, and Anglicans.

107. Ibid., 12, 15, 17.

108. Ibid., 18, 20, 22.

109. Ibid., 29, 24, 27.

110. Ibid., 28, 31.

111. Ibid., 33.

112. Demonstrative of his potential, David Rice was licensed to preach in Virginia and North Carolina by the Presbytery of Hanover in 1762, which was three years prior to his ordination, according to most sources. By 1764 he had already established a successful home church in Bedford County, Virginia, at the Peaks of the Otter and a thriving missionary circuit to other churches in Virginia and North Carolina. For more information, see Thompson, *Presbyterians in the South*, 1:115.

113. Philanthropos, *The Universal Peace-Maker, or Modern Author's Instructor* (Philadelphia, 1764), 2, 3, 5, 8.

114. Philanthropos, *The Universal Peace-Maker*, 9, 10, 13, 14.

115. James Smylie, "Samuel Davies: Preacher, Teacher, and Pastor," in *Colonial Presbyterianism: Old Faith in a New Land*, ed. Donald Fortson III (Eugene, OR: Pickwick Publications, 2007), 190–91.

116. Samuel Davies, *Sermons on the most useful and important subjects, adapted to the family and closet. By the Rev. Samuel Davies, A.M. late President of the College at Princeton in New-Jersey. In three volumes. . . . To which are prefixed, A sermon on the death of Mr Davies, By Samuel Finley, D.D. and another discourse on the same occasion, together with an elegiac poem to the memory of Mr Davies, by Thomas Gibbons, D.D.* (London: J. Buckland and J. Payne, 1766), 317.

117. Ibid., 318–19.

118. Charles Jeffrey Smith, *The nature and necessity of regeneration, considered in a discourse delivered at Williamsburg, in Virginia: with a dedication to the Episcopal Church in that city: containing, an apology for Presbyterians* (Woodbridge, NJ: Samuel Parker, 1765), vi.

119. Ibid., viii.

120. Ibid., xv.

Chapter 2

1. Peter D. G. Thomas, "The Stamp Act crisis and its repercussions, including the Quartering Act controversy," in *A Companion to the American Revolution*, eds. Jack P. Greene and J. R. Pole (Malden, MA: Blackwell Publishing, 2004), 124. See also Edmund S. Morgan and Helen M. Morgan, *The Stamp Act Crisis: Prologue to Revolution* (New York: Collier Books, 1963).

2. Clark, *The Language of Liberty*; Griffin, *Revolution and Religion*.

3. Gilbert Tennent, *The Blessedness of Peace-makers represented; and the Danger of Persecution considered; in Two Sermons, On Mat. v. 9. Preach'd at Philadelphia, the 3d*

Wednesday in May, 1759, before the Reverend the Synod, of New-York and Philadelphia, (Philadelphia: William Bradford, 1765).

4. Ibid., 3, 4.

5. Ibid., 5, 9–10.

6. Ibid., 11, 12.

7. Ibid., 9.

8. Ibid., 4, 5.

9. Ibid., 17.

10. Ibid., 19–20.

11. Ibid., 38.

12. Ibid., 20, 21.

13. Ibid., 44.

14. Ibid., 48, 49, 50.

15. Trinterud, *The Forming of an American Tradition*, 158.

16. General Assembly, *Records of the Presbyterian Church, 1706–1788*, 355.

17. Trinterud, *The Forming of an American Tradition*, 165.

18. General Assembly, *Records of the Presbyterian Church, 1706–1788*, 358.

19. Seven Old Lights formed the Donegal Presbytery and seceded from the synod. They were John Steel, Joseph Tate, Samuel Thomson, Sampson Smith, Robert McMordie, John Elder, and John Beard.

20. J. David Hoeveler, *Creating the American Mind: Intellect and Politics in the Colonial* Colleges (New York: Rowman & Littlefield Publishers, 2002), 113; Bryan F. Le Beau, *Jonathan Dickinson and the Formative Years of American Presbyterianism* (Lexington: University Press of Kentucky, 1997), 177–84; and Trinterud, *The Forming of an American Tradition*, 216.

21. John Rodgers to Witherspoon, Dec. 24, 1766, in *John Witherspoon Comes to America: A Documentary Account Based Largely on New Materials*, ed. L. H. Butterfield (Princeton, NJ: Princeton University Press, 1953), 22.

22. William Warren Sweet, *Religion on the American Frontier, 1783–1840, Volume II: The Presbyterians, A Collection of Source Materials* (New York: Cooper Square Publishers, 1964), 2:7. See also Mark A. Noll, *Princeton and the Republic, 1768–1822: The Search for a Christian Enlightenment in the Era of Samuel Stanhope Smith* (Princeton, NJ: Princeton University Press, 1989), 16–17.

23. "Introduction," *John Witherspoon Comes to America*, 3; Trinterud, *The Forming of an American Tradition*, 213–16.

24. Trinterud, *The Forming of an American Tradition*, 216.

25. Samuel Purviance Jr. to Ezra Stiles, Nov. 1, 1766, in *John Witherspoon Comes to America*, 4.

26. Ibid., 4–5.

27. Trinterud, *The Forming of an American Tradition*, 218–20.

28. Witherspoon rejected the first offer because his wife did not want to leave Scotland; however, after persistent negotiations, primarily by Benjamin Rush, Witherspoon accepted the offer in 1767.

29. Francis Alison to Ezra Stiles, Dec. 4, 1766, in *John Witherspoon Comes to America*, 14.

30. Ibid., 15.

31. Trinterud, *The Forming of an American Tradition*, 220.

32. Ibid., 221–22.

33. Rush to Witherspoon, Oct. 23, 1767, in *John Witherspoon Comes to America*, 58.

34. Gordon L. Tait, "John Witherspoon's Prescription for a Nation Strong, Free, and Virtuous," in *Colonial Presbyterianism: Old Faith in a New Land*, ed. Donald Fortson III (Eugene, OR: Pickwick Publications, 2007), 203; Trinterud, *The Forming of an American Tradition*, 221–22.

35. For additional information on the importance of the College of New Jersey to the New Lights/Old Lights, see Howard Miller, *The Revolutionary College: American Presbyterian Higher Education 1707–1837* (New York: New York University Press, 1976), 75–79; Hoeveler, *Creating the American Mind*, 117–27; and John R. Thelin, *A History of American Higher Education* (Baltimore, MD: Johns Hopkins University Press, 2004), 29.

36. General Assembly, *Records of the Presbyterian Church, 1706–1788*, 383.

37. Ibid., 384.

38. For instance, if one of the Old Light churches in question was located in New York City but it did not wish to belong to the local New Light presbytery, it could join the Old Light Presbytery of Philadelphia even though it was not in that presbytery's jurisdiction.

39. General Assembly, *Records of the Presbyterian Church, 1706–1788*, 384–86; Trinterud, *The Forming of an American Tradition*, 165.

40. Trinterud, *The Forming of an American Tradition*, 222–23.

41. General Assembly, *Records of the Presbyterian Church, 1706–1788*, 414.

42. Trinterud, *The Forming of an American Tradition*, 222–23.

43. General Assembly, *Records of the Presbyterian Church, 1706–1788*, 431.

44. Ibid., 430.

45. Ibid., 449. Pine Street Church was another name for the Third Presbyterian Church Philadelphia.

46. Trinterud, *The Forming of an American Tradition*, 222–23; General Assembly, *Records of the Presbyterian Church, 1706–1788*, 448–49.

47. Joseph Rhea to Francis Alison, in Joseph Rhea's papers, box 1, folder 1, Presbyterian Historical Society, Philadelphia.

48. General Assembly, *Records of the Presbyterian Church, 1706–1788*, 360.

49. Ibid., 362.

50. Ibid., 363.

51. Ibid., 364.

52. For more information on the intermittent conflict over a colonial bishopric, see Kenneth R. Elliott, *Anglican Church Policy, Eighteenth Century Conflict, and the American Episcopate* (New York: Peter Lang Academic Publishers, 2011); Bridenbaugh, *Mitre and Sceptre*; and Stephen Taylor, "Whigs, Bishops, and America: The Politics of Church

Reform in Mid-Eighteenth-Century England," *Historical Journal* 36, no. 2 (June 1993): 331–56.

53. *Minutes of the Convention of Delegates from the Synod of New York and Philadelphia, and from the Association of Connecticut; held annually from 1766 to 1775, Inclusive* (Hartford, CT: E. Gleason, 1843), 6.

54. Ezra Stiles, *A Discourse on the Christian Union* (Boston: Edes & Gill, 1761).

55. *Minutes of the Convention, 1766 to 1775*, 6.

56. Ibid., 8.

57. Ibid., 7.

58. Complementing the efforts of the synod, Francis Alison pleaded with Ezra Stiles in August 1766 to promote the convention among his friends in various denominations. He wrote, "I think ye union of all, or most of the antiprelatical churches necessary to prevent such encroachments on our liberty, & promote the Kingdom of Christ both in our churches, & among the Indians. All may be admitted as members of this Assembly, who belong to ye Congregational; Consociated; or Presbyterian Churches." Francis Alison to Ezra Stiles, Aug. 20, 1766, in *Ezra Stiles Papers, Correspondence, Reel 2*.

59. *Minutes of the Convention, 1766 to 1775*, 10–14.

60. Although Rohrer's primary focus is on the Presbyterian minister Jacob Green, S. Scott Rohrer, *Jacob Green's Revolution: Radical Religion and Reform in a Revolutionary Age* (University Park: Penn State University Press, 2014) is also an insightful dual biography of both Green and Thomas Bradbury Chandler.

61. Bridenbaugh, *Mitre and Sceptre*, 291.

62. For a good discussion of the bishopric crisis in newspapers, see Cross, *The Anglican Episcopate*, 195–214.

63. Nybakken, *The Centinel: Warnings of a Revolution*, 71–72. This chapter owes a great debt to Nybakken's argument that the "Centinel" afforded Presbyterians the ability to help colonists understand the constitutional crisis. I augment Nybakken's argument that the "Centinel's" audience was composed of three groups—king/parliament, Pennsylvanians, and southern Anglicans—by tying the "Centinel" into a greater Presbyterian interdenominational plan (which included the "American Whig") to use print to reach most colonists and not just a select few.

64. For more on this journal and the careers of these men, see Dorothy Rita Dillon, *The New York Triumvirate: A Study of the Legal and Political Careers of William Livingstone, John Morin Scott, and William Smith Jr.* (New York: Columbia University Press, 1949).

65. Bridenbaugh, *Mitre and Sceptre*, 298; Cross, *The Anglican Episcopate*, 195–200.

66. "American Whig [No. I]," in *A Collection of tracts from the late news papers, &c. Containing particularly The American Whig, A whip for the American Whig, with some other pieces, on the subject of the residence of Protestant bishops in the American colonies, and in answer to the writers who opposed it, &c.*, (New York: John Holt, 1768), 4–5.

67. "American Whig [No. II]," in *A Collection of tracts*, 6.

68. Francis Alison represented the Old Light, George Bryan the New Light, and Jonathan Dickinson the Quakers.

69. "Centinel [V]," April 21, 1768, in Nybakken, *The Centinel*, 113. In this edition,

the "Centinel" posed a blunt question: "Did not almost all the Bishops in Parliament Vote against the Repeal of the Stamp-Act and use their Influence to rivet the Shackles on the Colonies which our Enemies had formed."

70. "Centinel [VI]," April 28, 1768, in Nybakken, *The Centinel*, 118.

71. For more information on the various colonial Anglican positions on the proposed bishop, see John Frederick Woolverton, *Colonial Anglicanism in North America* (Detroit, MI: Wayne State University Press, 1984), 231–32.

72. "Centinel [VIII]," May 12, 1768, in Nybakken, *The Centinel*, 127.

73. "Centinel [XIII]," June 16, 1768, in Nybakken, *The Centinel*, 154.

74. *Minutes of the Convention, 1766 to 1775*, 23.

75. Ibid., 68.

76. Bridenbaugh, *Mitre and Sceptre*, 287.

77. The founders of the Society of Dissenters were Peter Van Brugh Livingstone, Henry Williams, Samuel Broome, Thomas Smith, Alexander McDougall, Samuel Loudon, William Goforth, Joseph Hallett, John Morin Scott, William Livingston, William McKinley, Robert Boyd, Francis Van Dycke, Samuel Edmonds, Jonathan Blake, William Neilson, John Broome, and John McKesson.

78. Bridenbaugh, *Mitre and Sceptre*, 278; Herbert L. Osgood, "Preface," in "The Society of Dissenters founded at New York in 1769," *American Historical Review* 6, no. 3 (April 1901): 498–99.

79. "The Society of Dissenters founded at New York in 1769," 499.

80. Ibid., 500.

81. Ibid., 501.

82. Ibid., 503.

83. Ibid., 505.

84. Ibid., 506.

85. Ibid., 498–99.

86. Ibid., 506.

87. The annual convention of the Presbyterians and Congregationalists last met in 1775. They planned to meet in 1776, but the Declaration of Independence ended the threat of an Anglican bishop in America, so the convention came to an end.

88. Bridenbaugh, *Mitre and Sceptre*, 312.

89. John Rodgers, *The Case of the Scotch Presbyterians, of the city of New-York*, published in 1773, alongside the work of the annual Convention of Presbyterians and Congregationalists, served as a lone reminder to the colonists of the constitutional threat posed by an Anglican bishop in the colonies. Interestingly, Rodgers's work was probably the result of the convention's attempt to write a history of religious freedom and persecution throughout the colonies. For more information, see *Minutes of the Convention, 1766 to 1775*, 31–32, 37–38, 40–41, 44–48.

90. *Considerations on the nature and the extent of the legislative authority of the British Parliament* (Philadelphia: William and Thomas Bradford, 1774), 1.

91. Ibid., 2.

92. Ibid., 3.

93. Ibid., 5.

94. Ibid., 24.

95. Francis Alison to Ezra Stiles, June 19, 1767, in *Ezra Stiles Papers, Correspondence, Reel 2.*

96. James Sproat, *A discourse, occasioned by the death of the Reverend George Whitefield, A.M. late chaplain to the Right Honourable the countess of Huntingdon; delivered October 14, 1770, in the Second Presbyterian Church, in the city of Philadelphia* (Philadelphia: William and Thomas Bradford, 1771), 4–5.

97. Sproat, *A discourse,* 15.

98. Ibid., 18.

99. Ibid., 22.

100. Ibid., 23. Also published in 1771 was another posthumous work of Samuel Davies, *A touch stone for the clergy. To which is added, a poem, wrote by a clergyman in Virginia, in a storm of wind and rain,* in which the Virginian promoted interdenominationalism.

101. General Assembly, *Records of the Presbyterian Church, 1706–1788,* 456; Trinterud, *The Forming of an American Tradition,* 208.

102. General Assembly, *Records of the Presbyterian Church, 1706–1788,* 458–59.

103. Samson Occom, *A Choice Collection of Hymns and Spiritual Songs; Intended for the Edification of Sincere Christians, of All Denominations* (New London: Timothy Green, 1774), 3.

104. Occom, *A Choice Collection of Hymns,* 4.

105. Ibid., 93.

106. Ibid., 8–9.

107. Ibid., 106.

108. Hugh Knox, *The moral and religious miscellany; or, Sixty-one aphoretical essays, on some of the most important Christian doctrines and virtues* (New York: Hodge and Shober, 1775), v.

109. Ibid., 84.

110. Ibid., 178.

111. Ibid., 189.

112. Elmer T. Clark, J. Manning Potts, and Jacob S. Payton, eds., *The Journal and Letters of Francis Asbury* (Nashville, TN: Abingdon Press, 1958), 1:455.

Chapter 3

1. John Witherspoon is given credit for penning this letter by John Rodgers in *The works of the Rev. John Witherspoon, D.D. L.L.D. late president of the college, at Princeton New-Jersey. To which is prefixed an account of the author's life, in a sermon occasioned by his death, by the Rev. Dr. John Rodgers, of New York. In three volumes.* (Philadelphia: Woodward, 1800): 3:599–605.

2. General Assembly, *Records of the Presbyterian Church, 1706–1788,* 466.

3. Ibid., 467.

4. Ibid., 468.

5. John Carmichael, *A self-defensive war lawful, proved in a sermon, preached at Lancaster, before Captain Ross's company of militia, in the Presbyterian Church on Sabbath morning, June 4th, 1775* (Lancaster, PA: Francis Bailey, 1775), 5.

6. Carmichael, *A self-defensive war*, 20.

7. Ibid., 22.

8. Ibid., 18.

9. Ibid., 22.

10. Ibid., 25.

11. For further evidence of this unified Presbyterian approach, see Francis Alison, James Sproat, George Duffield, and Robert Davidson, *An Address of the Presbyterian ministers, of the city of Philadelphia, to the ministers and Presbyterian congregations, in the county of [blank] in North-Carolina* (Philadelphia, 1775).

12. General Assembly, *Records of the Presbyterian Church, 1706–1788*, 467–68. For more information on the general support of Presbyterians for American independence, see Longfield, *Presbyterians and American Culture*, 41–42; Smylie, *A Brief History of the Presbyterians*, 59–61; Balmer and Fitzmier, *The Presbyterians*, 34–37; and Leonard J. Kramer, "Muskets in the Pulpit: 1776–1783," *Journal of Presbyterian History* 31, no. 4 (December 1953): 230.

13. James Smylie, ed., "Presbyterians and the American Revolution: A Documentary Account," *Journal of Presbyterian History* 52, no. 4 (Winter 1974): 400.

14. William Warren Sweet, *The Story of Religion in America* (New York: Harper & Brothers Publishers, 1939), 258–59; Balmer and Fitzmier, *The Presbyterians*, 37.

15. Not only was Jacob Green influential in New Jersey Presbyterian circles, he was also important politically. Among other things, he helped to craft the state's 1776 constitution. For more on Green, see Rohrer, *Jacob Green's Revolution*; and Trinterud, *The Forming of an American Tradition*, 253.

16. Jacob Green, *Observations, on the reconciliation of Great-Britain and the colonies. By a friend of American liberty* (New York: John Holt, 1776), 3.

17. Ibid., 6, 7.

18. Ibid., 9, 10.

19. Ibid., 15.

20. Noll, *The Old Religion in a New World*, 37–41; and Griffin, *Revolution and Religion*, 76–85.

21. For more on Mount Independence, Ticonderoga, and Saratoga, see Richard M. Ketchum, *Saratoga: Turning Point of America's Revolutionary War* (New York: Macmillan, 1999.)

22. Joel Tyler Headley, *The Forgotten Heroes of Liberty: Chaplains and Clergy of the American Revolution* (Birmingham, AL: Solid Ground Christian Books, 2005), 366–67.

23. Headley, *The Forgotten Heroes of Liberty*, 377, 378.

24. W. C. Ford, ed., *Journals of the Continental Congress, 1774–1789*, June 5—October 8, 1776 (Washington, DC: Government Printing Office, 1906), 5:640.

25. Ibid., 5: 653, 654.

26. Benjamin Rush to Richard Henry Lee, January 1777, in *Letters of Benjamin Rush, Volume I: 1761–1792*, ed. L. H. Butterfield (Princeton, NJ: Princeton University Press, 1951), 1:126.

27. Headley, *Forgotten Heroes of Liberty*, 108–9.

28. Smylie, "Presbyterians and the American Revolution," 412.

29. General Assembly, *Records of the Presbyterian Church, 1706–1788*, 477.

30. Headley, *Forgotten Heroes of Liberty*, 158–62.

31. Ibid., 224–30; Smylie, "Presbyterians and the American Revolution," 408; Maude Glascow, *The Scotch-Irish in Northern Ireland and in the American Colonies* (New York: G. P. Putnam's Sons, 1936), 274; and J. J. Boudinot, ed., *The Life, Public Services, Addresses, and Letters of Elias Boudinot* (New York: Capo Press, 1971), 1:188.

32. General Assembly, *Records of the Presbyterian Church, 1706–1788*, 478.

33. Abraham Keteltas, *God arising and pleading his people's cause; or The American war in favor of liberty, against the measures and arms of Great Britain, shewn to be the cause of God: in a sermon preached October 5th, 1777 at an evening lecture, in the Presbyterian church in Newbury-Port* (Newbury, MA: John Mycall, 1777), 3.

34. Ibid., 9, 19, 21–22.

35. Ibid., 26.

36. Ibid., 31, 32.

37. General Assembly, *Records of the Presbyterian Church, 1706–1788*, 481.

38. In many ways Benjamin Rush embodied the spirit of Christian unity discussed here. In 1787 he ended his membership with First Presbyterian Church in Philadelphia, but he would still regularly attend Presbyterian services. He also frequented Episcopal churches even after his brief formal relationship with that church ended in 1789. For a short while, Rush even attended a Universalist Baptist Church. However, that relationship seems to be largely due to his friend and minister Elhanan Winchester, as Rush never joined the church; after the minister died in 1797 his visits ceased. Even if Rush was formally detached from churches, he maintained cordial relationships with Christians across the denominational spectrum. And Rush had an intimate relationship throughout his life with the Presbyterian Church, as he regularly attended its services and saw all of his children baptized by Presbyterian ministers. See Abzug, *Cosmos Crumbling*, 11–29; and Donald J. D'Elia, "Benjamin Rush: Philosopher of the American Revolution," *Transactions of the American Philosophical Society* 64, no. 5 (Philadelphia: American Philosophical Society, 1974).

39. Benjamin Rush, *An Address to the Inhabitants of the British Settlements in America, upon Slave-Keeping* (Philadelphia: Dunlap, 1773), 1.

40. Ibid., 30.

41. Divines, *Humble Advice*, 5.

42. Rush, *An Address*, 4, 9.

43. Ibid., 12, 13, 14.

44. Ibid., 16, 17, 18.

45. Ibid., 20–21.

46. Ibid., 26, 27.

47. Ibid., 29, 30.

48. Other notable Presbyterians, including George Bryan, Elias Boudinot, David Rice, Ebenezer Hazard, and Daniel Roberdeau, were influential in both church and society and opposed the "sin" of slavery in addition to men discussed in this chapter. For more information see Trinterud, *The Forming of an American Tradition*, 272–74.

49. General Assembly, *Records of the Presbyterian Church, 1706–1788*, 478.

50. James F. Armstrong, "Righteousness Exalteth A Nation," in *Light to My Path: Sermons by the Rev. James F. Armstrong Revolutionary Chaplain*, ed. Marian B. McLeod (Trenton, NJ: First Presbyterian Church, 1976), 10, 11.

51. Ibid., 12, 15.

52. Ibid., 17, 16.

53. Ibid., 17, 18.

54. For more on antislavery efforts in New Jersey, see James J. Gigantino, *The Ragged Road to Abolition: Slavery and Freedom in New Jersey* (Philadelphia: University of Pennsylvania Press, 2015). Governor Livingston was not alone in his efforts to use public office against slavery. There is also the well-documented story of George Bryan who, while serving as president of the Supreme Executive Council of the Pennsylvania legislature, began fighting in 1778 for the abolition of slavery. See Douglas R. Egerton, *Death or Liberty: African Americans and Revolutionary America* (New York: Oxford University Press, 2009), 99–101; Gary B. Nash, *Unknown American Revolution: The Unruly Birth of Democracy and the Struggle to Create America* (New York: Viking, 2005), 322–23; and Arthur Zilversmit, *First Emancipation: The Abolition of Slavery in the North* (Chicago: University of Chicago Press, 1967), 128–29.

55. The political contest over slavery in New York would continue until 1799, when a gradual emancipation law was finally passed. See David Brion Davis, *Inhuman Bondage: The Rise and Fall of Slavery in the New World* (New York: Oxford University Press, 2006), 145–56.

56. William Livingston to Samuel Allinson, July 25, 1778, in *The Papers of William Livingston*, eds. Carl E. Prince and Dennis P. Ryan (Trenton, NJ: New Jersey Historical Commission, 1980), 2:403.

57. Smylie, "Presbyterians and the American Revolution," 451.

58. Ibid., 452, 453.

59. Ibid., 453, 454. In 1779 Jacob Green, who believed the Presbyterian structure was undemocratic, quietly seceded from the Synod of New York and Philadelphia in order to form a better Presbyterian Church. For more, see Rohrer, *Jacob Green's Revolution*, 222–39.

60. John Murray, *Nehemiah, or The struggle for liberty never in vain, when managed with virtue and perseverance. A discourse delivered at the Presbyterian Church in Newbury-Port, Nov. 4th, 1779. Being the day appointed by government to be observed as a day of solemn fasting and prayer throughout the state of Massachusetts-Bay. Published in compliance with the request of some hearers* (Newbury, MA: John Mycall, 1779), 5.

61. Ibid., 17–18.

62. Ibid., 49.

63. Ibid., 9.

64. Ibid., 9, 11.

65. Ibid., 56.

66. General Assembly, *Records of the Presbyterian Church, 1706–1788*, 456, 458–59.

67. Ibid., 487, 488.

68. Benjamin Rush to Nathanial Greene, September 1782, in *Letters of Benjamin Rush*, 1:286.

69. George Duffield, *A Sermon Preached in the Third Presbyterian Church in the City of Philadelphia, On Thursday December 11, 1783* (Boston: T. & J. Fleet, 1784), 5.

70. Duffield, *A Sermon*, 19, 26.

71. Ibid., 25.

72. Samuel Stanhope Smith to Thomas Jefferson, March 1779, in *The Papers of Thomas Jefferson*, ed. Julian P. Boyd (Princeton, NJ: Princeton University Press, 1950), 2:247.

73. Ibid.

74. Ibid., 248.

75. William Livingston to Samuel Allinson, March 1780, in *The Papers of William Livingston*, eds. Carl E. Prince et al. (Trenton: New Jersey Historical Commission), 3:339.

76. William Livingston to Samuel Allinson, July 1780, in ibid., 3:409.

77. Ewing was so fond of this sermon that he had already presented it five times before June 1780, and he would go on to give it five times after. For more, see Smylie, "Presbyterians and the American Revolution," 478.

78. Ibid.

79. Ibid., 479.

80. John Murray, *Bath-Kol. A voice from the wilderness. Being an humble attempt to support the sinking truths of God, against some of the principal errors, raging at this time. Or, a joint testimony to some of the grand articles of the Christian religion, judicially delivered to the churches under their care. By the first presbytery of the eastward* (Boston: N. Coverly, 1783), 5.

81. Ibid., 6.

82. Ibid., 14.

83. Ibid., 19.

84. Robert Smith, *The Obligations of the Confederate States of North America to Praise God* (Baltimore, MD: John Hayes, 1783), 1–2.

85. Smylie, "Presbyterians and the American Revolution," 458–59.

86. Synod, *The plan of union*, 4, 12, 13.

87. General Assembly, *Records of the Presbyterian Church, 1706–1788*, 499.

88. Benjamin Rush to John King, April 2, 1783, in Butterfield, *Letters of Benjamin Rush*, 1:300.

Chapter 4

1. This argument is greatly indebted to that of Foster, *The Long Argument*. In this book, Foster argues that the internal divisions initiated by promising external forces—the Long Parliament during the English Civil War and the Great Awakening in colonial America—led to the demise of Puritanism. The American Revolution—or individually, the constitutional crisis, the War for Independence, and the government of the Articles of Confederation—served a similar function for the Presbyterian Church; it afforded the church the opportunity to better realize long-held interdenominational goals. However, where Puritanism was done in by internal divisions, the Presbyterian

ruling bodies' interdenominationalism was thwarted by fears of divisions and the precautions taken to avoid them, which eventually resulted in schisms.

2. Gerald F. De Jong, *The Dutch Reformed Church in the American Colonies* (Grand Rapids, MI: William B. Eerdmans Publishing, 1978), 200–2; and Randall Balmer, *A Perfect Babel of Confusion: Dutch Religion and English Culture in the Middle Colonies* (New York: Oxford University Press, 1989), 152. De Jong states that the problems between the Presbyterians and the Dutch were partly due to the division of the Dutch church into Old Light and New Light factions known as the Conferentie and the Coetus. The conservative Conferentie supported the Anglican institution with the hope of securing a Dutch professor of theology in the school, and the evangelical Coetus supported the anti-Anglican group, which consisted largely of Presbyterians. The subsequent hostilities resulted in the division of the Dutch church, but by the time independence had been secured the Dutch had reunited with the New Lights in charge. Both De Jong and Balmer state that the union talks in 1784 were the culmination of the longstanding New Light hopes within each church for unity.

3. General Assembly, *Records of the Presbyterian Church, 1706–1788*, 505. The committee members were Rodgers, McWhorter, Spencer, and Smith, along with Alexander Miller, J. Woodhull, and Israel Reed.

4. The Associate Reformed Synod was the result of the union in 1782 between the Scottish-based Reformed Presbytery and the Associate Presbytery (the Seceders). There were only two congregations that did not join this union, and by 1798 they had reestablished a separate Reformed Presbyterian Church. See Smylie, *A Brief History of the Presbyterians*, 62; and W. Melancthon Glasgow, *History of the Reformed Presbyterian Church in America* (Baltimore, MD: Hill & Harvey Publishers, 1888), 398.

5. General Assembly, *Records of the Presbyterian Church, 1706–1788*, 508.

6. Ibid., 520.

7. The reunited Dutch church still suffered internal divisions, and these were roused by the possible union with the Presbyterians. The conservatives believed the Presbyterians were too relaxed in their doctrine and that this would in turn affect their churches. The very existence of the Associate Reformed Synod was, by 1787, being challenged by the Supreme Judicatory of the Scottish Reformed Presbytery. See Trinterud, *The Forming of an American Tradition*, 277.

8. Noll, *Princeton and the Republic*, 89.

9. For more on the divisive issues at play, see Hart and Muether, *Seeking a Better Country*, 82–84.

10. At the base of this new system were the 419 local churches that were led by their elected sessions. Each session sent delegates to the 16 local presbyteries. According to the proposed plan, the presbyteries then sent representatives to the four regional synods, which were responsible for overseeing the actions of the presbyteries. Those presbyteries also sent delegates to the General Assembly itself, but instead of representatives from each church there was one minister and elder sent for every six congregations. This was a considerable change from the previous system that required every church to send delegates to the annual synod.

11. General Assembly, *Records of the Presbyterian Church, 1706–1788,* 522–24; Balmer and Fitzmier, *The Presbyterians,* 38; and Trinterud, *The Forming of an American Tradition,* 298–302.

12. General Assembly, *Records of the Presbyterian Church, 1706–1788,* 547. This task of combining and publishing this material was given to George Duffield, James Armstrong, and Jacob Green.

13. Ibid., 545–47. See also Hart and Muether, *Seeking a Better Country,* 84–87.

14. As Gideon Mailer has summarized, "Witherspoon taught one president (James Madison, B.A. 1771) and one vice president (Aaron Burr, B.A. 1772), forty-nine U.S. representatives, twenty-eight U.S. senators, three Supreme Court justices, one secretary of state, three attorneys general, and two foreign ministers. More than 11 percent of his graduates became college presidents, in eight different American states." Mailer, "Anglo-Scottish Union and John Witherspoon's American Revolution," 710. Among Witherspoon's Americanist students was the Presbyterian David Ramsay whose work as a historian fostered "republicanism and national unity" in the early republic. For the quote, see Peter C. Messer, *Stories of Independence: Identity, Ideology, and History in Eighteenth-Century America* (DeKalb: Northern Illinois University Press, 2005), 197. For a more in-depth discussion, see chps. 4 and 5, as well as the epilogue of the same book. On the broader impact of Witherspoon, see Robert M. Calhoon, "The religious consequences of the Revolution," in *A Companion to the American Revolution,* eds. Jack P. Greene and J. R. Pole (Malden, MA: Blackwell Publishing, 2004), 581; Miller, *The Revolutionary College*; Jeffry H. Morrison, *John Witherspoon and the Founding of the American Republic* (Notre Dame, IN: University of Notre Dame Press, 2005); David. W. Robson, *Educating Republicans: The College in the Era of the American Revolution, 1750–1800* (Westport, CT: Greenwood Press, 1985); and James W. Alexander, *The Life of Archibald Alexander, D. D. First Professor in the Theological Seminary, at Princeton, New Jersey* (Harrisonburg, VA: Sprinkle Publications, 1991), 15–16.

15. Smylie, *A Brief History of the Presbyterians,* 61. Concerning those Presbyterians who supported the Constitution, Smylie pays particular attention to the ten or eleven Presbyterians who helped shape "the document at the Constitutional Convention."

16. Stephen A. Marini, "Religion, Politics, and Ratification," in *Religion in a Revolutionary Age,* eds. Ronald Hoffman and Peter J. Albert (Charlottesville: University of Virginia Press, 1994), 192.

17. Prominent Federalists included Benjamin Rush, James Wilson, John Witherspoon, Samuel Stanhope Smith, and David Ramsay. Prominent anti-Federalist Presbyterians were George Bryan, Robert Whitehill, and William Findley. For more on religious divisions over the Constitution, see Owen S. Ireland, *Religion, Ethnicity, and Politics: Ratifying the Constitution in Pennsylvania* (University Park: Penn State University Press, 1995); Stephen A. Marini, "Religion, Politics, and Ratification" in *Religion in a Revolutionary Age,* 184–217; Miller, *The Revolutionary College,* 128–38; and Gordon S. Wood, *The Radicalism of the American Revolution* (New York: Vintage Books, 1993), 255. Marini sees at the heart of this disagreement a persistent Old/New Light contest. Howard Miller contends (and Gordon Wood agrees) that the disagreement was based on the fears of western settlers regarding an eastern centralized aristocracy.

18. Robert Davidson, *An oration, on the independence of the United States of America. Delivered on the 4th of July, 1787. By the Rev. Robert Davidson, D.D. Pastor of the Presbyterian congregation in Carlisle, and professor of history and belles lettres, in Dickinson College* (Carlisle, PA, 1787), 5.

19. Ibid., 14.

20. Ibid., 15.

21. Ibid.

22. Benjamin Rush to the Ministers of the Gospel of All Denominations, June 21, 1788, in Butterfield, *Letters of Benjamin Rush*, 1:466.

23. Rush to the Ministers of the Gospel of All Denominations, June 21, 1788, in Butterfield, *Letters of Benjamin Rush*, 1:467.

24. Elias Boudinot was another Presbyterian nationalist who would also play a significant role in shaping the Federalist Party. For more, see Jonathan J. Den Hartog, *Patriotism & Piety: Federalist Politics and Religious Struggle in the New American Nation* (Charlottesville: University of Virginia Press), 93–115.

25. Benjamin Rush to Elias Boudinot, July 9, 1788, in Butterfield, *Letters of Benjamin Rush*, 474.

26. Ibid., 473, 475.

27. James Wilson, *Oration Delivered on the Fourth of July 1788, at the Procession formed at Philadelphia: To Celebrate the Adoption of the Constitution of the United States,* in *The Works of James Wilson*, ed. Robert Green McCloskey (Cambridge, MA: Belknap Press, 1967), 2:780.

28. Presbyterian General Assembly, *Minutes of the General Assembly of the Presbyterian Church in the United States of America from its Organization, A.D. 1789 to A.D. 1820 Inclusive* (Philadelphia: Presbyterian Board of Publication, n.d.), 6.

29. Ibid., 10.

30. Ibid., 12.

31. Ibid.

32. John Woodhull, *A sermon, for the day of publick thanksgiving, appointed by the president, on account of the establishment of the new Constitution, &c. November 26, 1789. By the Rev. John Woodhull, A.M. Pastor of the First Presbyterian Church in Freehold* (Trenton, NJ: Isaac Collins, 1790), 7.

33. Samuel J. Baird, *A Collection of the Acts, Deliverances, and Testimonies of the Supreme Judicatory of the Presbyterian Church, From its Origins in America to the Present Time. With Notes and Documents Explanatory and Historical: Constituting a Complete Illustration of Her Polity, Faith, and History* (Philadelphia: Presbyterian Board of Publication, 1856), 497.

34. General Assembly, *Minutes of the General Assembly of the Presbyterian Church, 1789 to 1820,* 52.

35. It was also in 1794 that the Presbyterian General Assembly and the Massachusetts Congregationalists begin discussing a plan of cooperation similar to that the Presbyterians had with the Connecticut Congregationalists. See General Assembly, *Minutes of the General Assembly of the Presbyterian Church, 1789 to 1820,* 91–92.

36. Samuel Langdon, *A Discourse on the Unity of the Church as a Monumental Pillar of*

the Truth; Designed to Reconcile Christians of all Parties and Denominations in Charity and Fellowship, as One Body in Christ (Exeter, NH: Henry Ranlet, 1792), 12–13.

37. David Austin, ed., *The American preacher; or, A collection of sermons from some of the most eminent preachers, now living, in the United States, of different denominations in the Christian Church. Never before published. Volume I [–IV]* (Elizabethtown, NJ: Shepard Kollock, 1791).

38. Austin, *The American Preacher*, vi.

39. David Austin, Jonathan Edwards II, and Walter King, *Circular Letters, Containing, An Invitation to the Ministers and Churches of Every Christian Denomination in the United States, to Unite in Their Endeavours to carry into Execution the "Humble Attempt" of President Edwards, To promote explicit Agreement and visible Union of God's People, in Extraordinary Prayer, for the revival of Religion and advancement of Christ's Kingdom on Earth* (Concord, MA: George Hough, 1798), 3, 5, 6.

40. Although the published history of this call to prayer only included the responses of northern Presbyterians, several prominent southerners also gave their support, including the Reverend William Graham of Lexington, Virginia, and Reverend Thomas Reese of Salem, South Carolina.

41. Austin, *Circular Letters*, 12, 16.

42. There are several instances of strictly Congregationalist-Presbyterian print culture ventures found within the records of both ruling bodies. Two examples would be the "religiously improved" history of the Revolutionary War and the rewriting of Isaac Watts's psalms. For more, see General Association, *The Records of the General Association of Ye Colony of Connecticut, Begun June 20th, 1738, Ending June 19th, 1799* (Hartford, CT: Press of the Case, Lockwood & Brainard, 1888), 118, 147, 172.

43. For examples of eighteenth-century communication networks, see Frank Luther Mott, *American Journalism; A History, 1690–1960* (New York: Macmillan, 1962), 111–64.

44. *The Christian's, Scholar's, and Farmer's Magazine* (Ann Arbor, MI: University Microfilms, 1979) APS I, Microfilm Reel 10; *The Theological Magazine* (Ann Arbor, MI: University Microfilms, 1979) APS I, Microfilm Reel 28; *The United States Christian Magazine* (Ann Arbor, MI: University Microfilms, 1979) APS I, Microfilm Reel 30; *The Religious Monitor* (Ann Arbor, MI: University Microfilms, 1979) APS I, Microfilm Reel 26; and *Connecticut Evangelical Magazine* (Ann Arbor, MI: University Microfilms, 1979) APS II, Microfilm Reel 14.

45. Baird, *A Collection*, 301.

46. Occom, *A Choice Collection of Hymns and Spiritual Songs*, 4.

47. General Assembly, *Records of the Presbyterian Church, 1706–1788*, 513–14.

48. Ibid., 535.

49. George Duffield, *Psalms Carefully Suited to the Christian Worship in the United States of America. Being An Improvement of the Old Versions of the Psalms of David. Allowed by the reverend Synod of New-York and Philadelphia, to be used in churches and private families* (Philadelphia: Francis Bailey, 1787).

50. Duffield, *Psalms carefully suited*, iii.

51. Ibid., 30.

52. Ibid., 242.

53. Ibid.

54. Ibid., 197.

55. Ibid., 87.

56. General Assembly, *Minutes of the General Assembly of the Presbyterian Church, 1789 to 1820*, 124.

57. Ibid.

58. For more information on the support of the American clergy, including Presbyterian, for the French Revolution see Ruth Bloch, *Visionary Republic: Millennial Themes in American Thought, 1756–1800* (New York: Cambridge University Press, 1989), 150–86; and Miller, *The Revolutionary College*, 198.

59. Strong is one of the few ministers most aptly described as a "Presbygationalist." His base was within the Connecticut Congregationalist ruling body, but he served as one of the early representatives with increasing authority in the Presbyterian General Assembly. His influence was felt in both churches intimately.

60. Nathan Strong, *A Sermon, Preached at the Annual Thanksgiving, November 16th, 1797* (Hartford, CT: Hudson and Goodwin, 1797), 10.

61. Nathan Strong, *A Thanksgiving Sermon, Delivered November 27th, 1800* (Hartford, CT: Hudson and Goodwin, 1800), 24.

62. Nathan Strong, *Political Instruction from the Prophecies of God's Word. A Sermon Preached on the State Thanksgiving, November 29, 1799* (New York: G. Forman, 1799), 3.

63. Strong, *A Thanksgiving Sermon, 1800*, 11.

64. Ibid.

65. Strong, *A Sermon, 1797*, 15.

66. Strong, *A Thanksgiving Sermon, 1800*, 17, 18.

67. Jonathan Freeman, *A Sermon Delivered at New-Windsor and Bethlehem. August 30. 1798. Being the Day Appointed by the General Assembly of the Presbyterian Church in the United States of America: To be Observed as a Day of Solemn Humiliation, Fasting and Prayer, in all the Churches under their Care* (New Windsor, NY: Jacob Schultz, 1799), 12.

68. Freeman, *A Sermon Delivered at New-Windsor and Bethlehem*, 49.

69. Ibid., 49, 50.

70. General Assembly, *Minutes of the General Assembly of the Presbyterian Church, 1789 to 1820*, 152.

71. Ibid., 153.

72. Ibid., 153–54.

73. Presbyterian General Assembly, *The Plan for correspondence and friendly intercourse proposed by a convention of delegates appointed by the General Assembly of the Presbyterian Church, the General Synod of the Reformed Dutch Church, and the Synod of the Associate Reformed Church, when met in New York, on the 3d Tuesday of June, 1798, and agreed to be reported to these respective judicatories; which plan has been unanimously approved by the General Assembly of the Presbyterian Church, in May 1799; has been adopted in part, by the Associate Reformed Synod, at their last meeting; and is to come under the consideration of the General Synod of the Reformed Dutch Church, at their next meeting at Albany, on the first Tuesday of June, 1800* (New York: 1800), 4, 1.

74. General Assembly, *The Plan for correspondence*, 1–4.

75. Williston Walker, *The Creeds and Platforms of Congregationalism* (Philadelphia: Pilgrim Press, 1969), 529.

76. Robert L. Ferm, *A Colonial Pastor: Jonathan Edwards the Younger, 1745–1801* (Grand Rapids, MI: William B. Eerdmans Publishing, 1976), 167–69; Sweet, *The Story of Religion in America*, 307.

77. General Assembly, *Minutes of the General Assembly of the Presbyterian Church, 1789 to 1820*, 224.

78. Ibid., 12.

Chapter 5

1. William B. Sprague, *Annals of the American Pulpit: Or, Commemorative Notices of Distinguished American Clergymen of Various Denominations: from the Early Settlement of the Country to the Close of the Year Eighteen Hundred and Fifty-five: with Historical Introductions* (New York: Robert Carter & Brothers, 1858), 71–74.

2. George Buist, *A sermon, preached in the Presbyterian Church, of Charleston; before the incorporated Grand Lodge of South-Carolina, Ancient York Masons. And the brethren of that fraternity assembled in general communication, on the festival of Saint John the Evangelist, December 27, 1793* (Charleston, SC: Harrison and Bowen, 1794), 1.

3. Ibid., 5.

4. Ibid., 10.

5. Ibid., 13.

6. Ibid., 17.

7. Ibid., 26–27.

8. This refers to the Presbyterian contribution to Christian journals noted in the last chapter.

9. George Buist, *Oration delivered at the Orphan-House of Charleston, South Carolina, October 18th, 1795, Being the Sixth Anniversary of the Institution* (Charleston, SC: Markland & M'Iver, 1795), 13.

10. Ibid., 13.

11. This position is similar to those of John Witherspoon, Samuel Stanhope Smith, and Benjamin Rush mentioned in chps. 3 and 4.

12. Buist, *Oration delivered at the Orphan-House*, 10.

13. Ibid., 21.

14. For more information on orations and print culture in the public sphere, see Waldstreicher, *In the Midst of Perpetual Fetes*, 217–21, and David D. Hall, *Cultures of Print: Essays in the History of the Book* (Amherst: University of Massachusetts Press, 1996), 159–62.

15. Buist, *Oration delivered at the Orphan-House*, 10.

16. Ibid., 24.

17. Samuel Porter, *An Address to the Rev. John Jamison, by Samuel Porter, V.D.M.* (Hagerstown: Stewart Herbert, 1794), 17.

18. Ibid., 17, 16.

19. Ibid., 3–4.

20. Ibid., 4.

21. Ibid., 2.

22. James Muir, *A Funeral Sermon* (Alexandria, VA: Hanson and Bond, 1793), 6.

23. Ibid., 11.

24. Ibid.

25. General Assembly, *Minutes of the General Assembly of the Presbyterian Church, 1789 to 1820*, 14–21.

26. For yearly accounts through 1802, see ibid., 21, 47–48, 63, 77, 93, 106, 117, 132, 159, 186, 210, 234, 262.

27. Forrest McDonald wrote that "the safest generalization about the South was one that nobody ever made: that each state in it differed more from the others than did states elsewhere differ from their neighbors." McDonald, *E Pluribus Unum: The Formation of the American Republic, 1776–1790* (Indianapolis, IN: Liberty Fund, 1979), 117.

28. For more on this view of nationalism to which the Presbyterian Church contributed, see Walter A. McDougall, *Throes of Democracy: The American Civil War Era, 1829–1877* (New York: HarperCollins Publishers, 2008), 40; and David Brion Davis, *The Problem of Slavery in the Age of Revolution, 1770–1823* (Ithaca, NY: Cornell University Press, 1975), 100–6.

29. Henry Patillo, *The plain planter's family assistant; containing an address to husbands and wives, children and servants. With some helps for instruction by catechisms; and examples of devotion for families: with a brief paraphrase on the Lord's prayer* (Wilmington, NC: James Adams, 1787), 23, 22.

30. Kidd, *God of Liberty*, 161. For more on the development of American proslavery Christianity, see Charles F. Irons, *The Origins of Proslavery Christianity: White and Black Evangelicals in Colonial and Antebellum Virginia.* (Chapel Hill: University of North Carolina Press, 2008); Christine Leigh Heyrman, *The Southern Cross: The Beginnings of the Bible Belt* (Chapel Hill: University of North Carolina Press, 1998); Douglas Ambrose, "Of Stations and Relations: Proslavery Christianity in Early National Virginia," in *Religion and the Antebellum Debate over Slavery*, eds. John R. McKivigan and Mitchell Snay (Athens: University of Georgia Press, 1998), 35–67. For more on slave-owning Presbyterian churches, see Jennifer Oast, "'The Worst Kind of Slavery': Slave-Owning Presbyterian Churches in Prince Edward County, Virginia," *Journal of Southern History* 76, no. 4 (November 2010): 867–900.

31. The synod meetings of 1781, 1782, 1783, and 1784 largely consisted of individual presbytery reports of finances, membership, and deaths. After the reports the synod during those years addressed what it considered immediate needs, such as securing more Bibles, but nothing else. These brief meetings represented the ruling body's determination to operate in spite of the war, but it was nothing close to a fully operational synod.

32. Instead of a matter of orthodoxy, historians have traditionally argued the synod's position in 1787 reflected the prevalent American conflict between the desires to end an apparent evil and the racist fears over a divided and strained society teeming with newly freed slaves. The church's leadership was faced with the difficult question of "which was more important, the building of a church in a slaveholding society or the wrecking of

a denomination in an effort to free the blacks." Accordingly, the Presbyterians chose the former and then crafted "numerous arguments . . . to explain or to justify why the ideals of the Declaration of Independence were not applicable to blacks." Yet, "despite the arguments and the rhetoric," the synod's position on slavery "was a policy based mainly upon fear and racism." Quotes are from W. Harrison Daniel, "Southern Presbyterians and the Negro in the Early National Period," *Journal of Negro History* 58, no. 3 (July 1973): 305, 312. This interpretation did not originate with Daniel but rather with Andrew E. Murray, *Presbyterians and the Negro: A History* (Philadelphia: Presbyterian Historical Society, 1966). Since the work of Murray and Daniel, this argument has been consistently supported by the histories of the Presbyterian Church, including: Longfield, *Presbyterians and American Culture*; Hart and Muether, *Seeking a Better Country*; and Smylie, *A Brief History of the Presbyterians*.

33. General Assembly, *Records of the Presbyterian Church, 1706–1788*, 532, 537.

34. Often these committees consisted of most, if not all, the available ruling elders to ensure lay representation.

35. This committee consisted of John Davenport (Dutchess County Presbytery), John McDonald (New York Presbytery), William Boyd (New Brunswick Presbytery), Nathaniel Irwin (Philadelphia Presbytery), John Burton (Newcastle Presbytery), Samuel McMasters (Lewes Presbytery), John McKnight (Carlisle Presbytery), Isaac Keith (Baltimore Presbytery), James Power (Redstone Presbytery), John Montgomery (Lexington Presbytery), John Blair Smith (Hanover Presbytery), John Simonton (Philadelphia Presbytery), and Hezekiah Balch (Abingdon Presbytery) for the ministers. The ruling elders were Abraham Vangelder, John Bayard, John Pinkerton, Robert Taggart, Benjamin Snodgrass, and William Boyd. The presbyteries of the elders are not specified in the minutes; however, this list represents every ruling elder except one, who attended the 1787 meeting.

36. In *Slavery and Sin: The Fight Against Slavery and the Rise of Liberal Protestantism* (New York: Oxford University Press, 2012), Molly Oshatz argues that early nineteenth century Protestant reformers addressed the problem of biblical support for and against slavery by historicizing its truths. Unintentionally, she argues, this activity laid the foundation for the liberal Christian theology that would challenge traditional Protestant thought later in the century.

37. Ibid., 538.

38. Ibid., 539.

39. In the more general studies addressing slavery in eighteenth-century America, this view, noted in an earlier note, is extended to most Christians of the period. For more, see David Brion Davis, *Inhuman Bondage: The Rise and Fall of Slavery in the New World* (New York: Oxford University Press, 2006); Kidd, *God of Liberty*; Douglas R. Egerton, *Death or Liberty: African Americans and Revolutionary America* (New York: Oxford University Press, 2009); Noll, *The Rise of Evangelicalism*; Ira Berlin, *Many Thousands Gone: The First Two Centuries of Slavery in North America* (Louisville, KY: Belknap Press, 2000); and Peter Kolchin, *American Slavery, 1619–1877* (New York: Hill and Wang, 1993).

40. Between 1758 and 1787 there were numerous recorded protests to synodal decisions. From 1762 through 1768, and in 1770, 1772, 1773, 1774, 1782, 1783, and 1784,

the synod recorded at least one formal protest by members of the ruling body during the session.

41. For more information on the international component of slavery in the American interior, see John Craig Hammond, "Slavery, Settlement, and Empire: The Expansion and Growth of Slavery in the Interior of the North American Continent, 1770–1820," *Journal of the Early Republic* 32, no. 2 (2012): 175–206; Stephen Aron, *How the West Was Lost: The Transformation of Kentucky from Daniel Boone to Henry Clay* (Baltimore, MD: Johns Hopkins University Press, 1996); and Andrew R. L. Cayton, "'When Shall We Cease to Have Judases?': The Blount Conspiracy and the Limits of the Extended Republic,'" in *Launching the "Extended Republic": The Federalist Era*, eds. Ronald J. Hoffman and Peter J. Albert (Charlottesville: University of Virginia Press, 1996).

42. Hammond, "Slavery, Settlement, and Empire," 201.

43. David Rice, *Slavery Inconsistent with Justice and Good Policy Proved By a Speech Delivered in the Convention, Held at Danville, Kentucky* (Philadelphia, 1792), 3. Like his earlier work, *The Universal Peace-Maker*, Rice had this published in Philadelphia in order to reach as broad an American audience as possible.

44. Ibid., 6, 22.

45. Ibid., 21, 24, 26, 27.

46. Ibid., 33, 34.

47. Lowell Hayes Harrison and James C. Clotter, *A New History of Kentucky* (Lexington: University of Kentucky Press, 1997), 61-63; General Assembly, *Minutes of the General Assembly of the Presbyterian Church, 1789 to 1820*, 103.

48. Louis B. Weeks, *Kentucky Presbyterians* (Atlanta: John Knox Press, 1983), 14–20; Davis, *The Problem of Slavery in the Age of Revolution*, 201.

49. General Assembly, *Minutes of the General Assembly of the Presbyterian Church, 1789 to 1820*, 104.

50. Ibid., 104, 105. Other good examples of individual Presbyterian efforts to stress charity concerning slavery is the previously mentioned work by Patillo, *The plain planter's family assistant*; and Elias Boudinot, *An oration, delivered at Elizabeth-Town, New-Jersey, agreeable to a resolution of the state Society of Cincinnati, on the Fourth of July, M.DCC. XCIII. Being the seventeenth anniversary of the independence of America* (Elizabeth-Town: Shepard Kollock, 1793). For good recent scholarly studies, see Irons, *The Origins of Proslavery Christianity*; and Adam Rothman, *Slave Country: American Expansion and the Origins of the Deep South* (Cambridge, MA: Harvard University Press, 2005).

51. General Assembly, *Minutes of the General Assembly of the Presbyterian Church, 1789 to 1820*, 105.

52. Thompson, *Presbyterians in the South*, 1:325.

53. General Assembly, *Minutes of the General Assembly of the Presbyterian Church, 1789 to 1820*, 229; Baird, *A Collection of the Acts, Deliverances, and Testimonies of . . . the Presbyterian Church*, 816; Helen Chavis Othow, *John Chavis: African American Patriot, Preacher, Teacher, and Mentor, 1763–1838* (Jefferson, NC: McFarland and Company, 2001), 53–54; and Daniel, "Southern Presbyterians and the Negro," 309–10.

54. William Henry Foote, ed., *Sketches of Virginia, Historical and Biographical* (Richmond, VA: John Knox Press, 1966), 396.

55. Robert Davidson, *History of the Presbyterian Church in the State of Kentucky; with a Preliminary Sketch of the Churches in the Valley of Virginia* (New York: Robert Carter, 1847), 42. Davidson also notes that the group consisted of "William Calhoun, Clement Reed, Cary Allen, and William Hill, with James Blythe."

56. Foote, *Sketches of Virginia*, 417 and 418.

57. Kidd, *God of Liberty*, 200.

58. Ibid., 424.

59. General Assembly, *Minutes of the General Assembly of the Presbyterian Church, 1789 to 1820*, 60.

60. Ibid., 86, 87.

61. Herman A. Norton, *Religion in Tennessee 1777–1945* (Knoxville: University of Tennessee Press, 1981), 8; Stephen Haynes and Franklin H. Littell, *Holocaust Education and the Church-Related College: Restoring Ruptured Traditions* (West Port, CT: Greenwood Press, 1997), xx.

62. The New Divinity movement, also known as Hopkinsianism, consisted of friends and followers of Jonathan Edwards the Elder, who decided to make their Calvinist theology more compatible with Enlightenment ideology. Samuel Hopkins and nearly all those who embraced his teaching denied that "universal atonement" was equivalent to "universal salvation." For further information, see William Breitenbach, "The Consistent Calvinism of the New Divinity Movement," *William and Mary Quarterly* 41, no. 2 (1984): 241–64; Joseph A. Conforti, *Samuel Hopkins and the New Divinity Movement: Calvinism, the Congregational Ministry, and Reform in New England between the Great Awakenings* (Grand Rapids, MI: Christian University Press, 1981); and Mark Valeri, *Law and Providence in Joseph Bellamy's New England: The Origins of the New Divinity in Revolutionary America* (New York: Oxford University Press, 1994).

63. Baird, *A Collection of the Acts, Deliverances, and Testimonies of . . . the Presbyterian Church*, 614–15.

64. General Assembly, *Minutes of the General Assembly of the Presbyterian Church, 1789 to 1820*, 155.

65. Ibid., 158.

66. Baird, *A Collection of the Acts, Deliverances, and Testimonies of . . . the Presbyterian Church*, 618.

67. Norton, *Religion in Tennessee 1777–1945*, 8; Baird, *A Collection of the Acts, Deliverances, and Testimonies of . . . the Presbyterian Church*, 618; Haynes and Littell, *Holocaust Education and the Church-Related College: Restoring Ruptured Traditions*, xx; and James H. Moorehead, "The 'Restless Spirit of Radicalism': Old School Fears and the Schism of 1837," *Journal of Presbyterian History* 78, no. 1 (Spring 2000): 23.

68. General Assembly, *Minutes of the General Assembly of the Presbyterian Church, 1789 to 1820*, 129.

69. Presbytery of Lexington, *A pastoral letter, from the Presbytery of Lexington, to the people under their care* (Lexington, VA: Presbyterian Church in the USA, 1790), 1, 6.

70. Presbytery of Charleston, *A Collection of hymns for public and private worship, approved of by the Presbytery of Charleston* (Charleston, SC: J. M'Iver, 1796), 1.

71. Ibid., 123.

72. Presbytery of Charleston, *Pastoral letter, of the Presbytery of Charleston, to the churches of the Presbyterian denomination, within their bounds* (Charleston, SC: Benjamin Timothy, 1799), 1, 7, 3, 10.

73. For more on these Scottish-influenced communion services, see Leigh Eric Schmidt, *Holy Fairs: Scotland and the Making of American Revivalism* (Grand Rapids, MI: William B. Eerdmans Publishing, 2001).

74. James McGready is quoted in John B. Boles, *The Great Revival: Beginnings of the Bible Belt* (Lexington: University Press of Kentucky, 1996), 41.

75. Paul Conkin, *Cane Ridge: America's Pentecost* (Madison: University of Wisconsin Press, 1990), 60; Kidd, *God of Liberty*, 201–2; Philip N. Mulder, *A Controversial Spirit: Evangelical Awakenings in the South* (New York: Oxford University Press, 2002), 125; Weeks, *Kentucky Presbyterians*, 35; and Norton, *Religion in Tennessee 1777–1945*, 22–25.

76. Boles, *The Great Revival*, 63–64. Thomas Kidd notes that since Lexington, the nearest city, consisted of 2,000 people it is unlikely that there were any more than 10,000 people there at one time. However, it was possible that upwards of 20,000 people attended the revivals at various times throughout a day. Kidd, *God of Liberty*, 206.

77. Davidson, *History of the Presbyterian Church in the State of Kentucky*, 138.

78. Norton, *Religion in Tennessee 1777–1945*, 25. See also Boles, *The Great Revival*, 66.

79. The controversy over the Cane Ridge revivals in the Presbyterian Church eventually led to the creation of the Cumberland Presbyterians and the Church of Christ. See Boles, *The Great Revival*, 100; Weeks, *Kentucky Presbyterians*, 35, 44–50; Mulder, *A Controversial Spirit*, 128; and Davis, *The Problem of Slavery in the Age of Revolution*, 205.

80. Thompson, *Presbyterians in the South*, 1:336–38; Daniel, "Southern Presbyterians and the Negro," 299. For a study that examines the Presbyterians' attitudes toward the institution of chattel slavery in areas ranging from the New Hebrides, Scotland, the United States, to East Central Africa, see William Harrison Taylor and Peter C. Messer, eds., *Faith and Slavery in the Presbyterian Diaspora* (Bethlehem, PA: Lehigh University Press, 2016).

81. Thompson, *Presbyterians in the South*, 155–65 and 144–53; Boles, *The Great Revival*, 100; Weeks, *Kentucky Presbyterians*, 35, 44–50; Mulder, *A Controversial Spirit*, 128; and Davis, *The Problem of Slavery in the Age of Revolution*, 205.

Epilogue

1. Jonathan Freeman, *A Discourse on Psalmody. Delivered at Newburgh, Before the Presbytery of Hudson, September, 1801* (Newburgh: Dennis Coles, 1801), 9.

2. Ibid., 5, 16.

3. Ibid., 26.

4. Ibid., 30.

5. Baird, *A Collection of the Acts, Deliverances, and Testimonies of . . . the Presbyterian Church*, 182.

6. For more on these impulses that resonated throughout American Christianity, see Hatch, *The Democratization of American Christianity*.

7. Ibid., 9–11, 133, 141, 146.

8. Ibid., 68.

9. Mark G. Toulouse, Gary Holloway, and Douglas A. Foster, *Renewing Christian Unity: A Concise History of the Christian Church (Disciples of Christ)* (Abilene, TX: Abilene Christian University Press, 2010), 67; and Mark A. Noll, *The Old Religion in the New World: The History of North American Christianity* (Grand Rapids, MI: William B. Eerdmans Publishing, 2002), 66–67.

10. Thompson, *Presbyterians in the South*, 1:153.

11. Sydney E. Ahlstrom, *A Religious History of the American People* (Garden City, NY: Image Books, 1975), 2:160–61.

12. For more information on the rise of the Baptists and Methodists during the early republic, see Thomas S. Kidd and Barry Hankins, *The Baptists in America: A History* (New York: Oxford University Press, 2015), 76–148; John H. Wigger, *Taking Heaven by Storm: Methodism and the Rise of Popular Christianity in America* (New York: Oxford University Press, 1998); Hatch, *The Democratization of American Christianity*; John B. Boles, *The Great Revival, 1787–1805: The Origins of the Southern Evangelical Mind* (Lexington: University Press of Kentucky, 1972); and Louis Weeks, *A New Christian Nation* (College Park, MD: McGrath Publishing, 1977), 27–35.

13. Finke and Stark, *The Churching of America, 1776–1990*, 26, 55; Gaustad and Barlow, *New Historical Atlas of Religion in America*, 79.

14. Noll, *America's God*, 181.

15. Bret E. Carroll, *The Routledge Historical Atlas of Religion in America* (New York: Routledge Press, 2000), 45, 64. One reason for the less-than-impressive membership gains by the Methodist Church in the 1790s as compared with 1780s was the separation of James O'Kelly's Republican Methodist Church in 1794, which took several thousand from the Methodists's membership rolls.

16. Noll, *America's God*, 169.

17. Purvis, *Revolutionary America, 1763 to 1800*, 197.

18. Finke and Stark, *The Churching of America*, 26, 55; Gaustad and Barlow, *New Historical Atlas of Religion in America*, 374.

19. George M. Marsden, *The Evangelical Mind and the New School Presbyterian Experience: A Case Study of Thought and Theology in Nineteenth-Century America* (New Haven, CT: Yale University Press, 1970), 11.

20. Ahlstrom, *A Religious History of the American People*, 1:555; Marsden, *The Evangelical Mind*, 12.

21. J. William T. Youngs, *The Congregationalists* (Westport, CT: Greenwood Publishing Group, 1998), 7.

22. Thompson, *Presbyterians in the South*, 1:411.

23. Hart and Muether, *Seeking a Better Country*, 150; Smylie, *A Brief History of the Presbyterians*, 91–92.

24. General Assembly, *Minutes of the General Assembly of the Presbyterian Church*, 662–63.

25. Ibid., 663–64.

26. Ahlstrom, *A Religious History*, 1:553–55, 561–62. Concerning the significance of Elias Boudinot on voluntary societies, including his election as the first president of

the American Bible Society, see Den Hartog, *Patriotism & Piety*), 107–15, 188–96. For good in-depth studies on voluntary societies, see Charles I. Foster, *An Errand of Mercy: The Evangelical United Front, 1790–1837* (Chapel Hill: University of North Carolina Press, 1960); Abzug, *Cosmos Crumbling*; and Hood, *Reformed America*.

27. Thompson, *Presbyterians in the South*, 1:511–13. Thompson connects Thornwell's thought to the broader Reformed tradition in Ernest Trice Thompson, *The Spirituality of the Church: A Distinctive Doctrine of the Presbyterian Church in the United States* (Richmond, VA: John Knox Press, 1961). Also see Noll, *The Old Religion in the New World*, 69–70; and James O. Farmer Jr., *The Metaphysical Confederacy: James Henley Thornwell and the Synthesis of Southern Values* (Macon, GA: Mercer University Press, 1986).

28. Marsden, *The Evangelical Mind*, 30.

29. Foster, *An Errand of Mercy*, 241.

30. Marsden, *The Evangelical Mind*, 42–43.

31. Ibid., 41–42.

32. General Assembly, *Minutes of the General Assembly of the Presbyterian Church, 1789 to 1820*, 653.

33. Elwyn A. Smith, *The Presbyterian Ministry in American Culture: A Study in Changing Concepts* (Philadelphia: Westminster Press, 1962), 164.

34. Marsden, *The Evangelical Mind*, 43–58; Hart and Muether, *Seeking a Better Country*, 116–21.

35. Marsden, *The Evangelical Mind*, 58.

36. Hart and Muether, *Seeking a Better Country*, 124–25.

37. Marsden, *The Evangelical Mind*, 62, 63. Marsden contends on p. 67 that there were six underlying and interconnected issues at the root of the schism: "(1) the meaning of confessionalism, (2) Presbyterian polity, (3) the relation of the church to the voluntary societies of the 'Evangelical united front,' (4) methods of revivalism, (5) theology itself, and (6) slavery."

38. Longfield, *Presbyterians and American Culture*, 91–115; Hart and Muether, *Seeking a Better Country*, 109–27.

Bibliography

Primary Sources

Alison, Francis, and David Bostwick. *Peace and union recommended; and Self disclaim'd, and Christ exalted: in two sermons, preached at Philadelphia, before the Reverend Synods of New-York and Philadelphia: the first, on the 24th of May, 1758, by Francis Alison, D.D. vice-provost of the college, and rector of the academy, in Philadelphia. And, the second, May 25, 1758, by David Bostwick, A.M. Minister of the Presbyterian-Church, in New-York. Both publish'd at the joint request of the Reverend synods.* Philadelphia: W. Dunlap, 1758.

Alison, Francis, James Sproat, George Duffield, and Robert Davidson. *An Address of the Presbyterian ministers, of the city of Philadelphia, to the ministers and Presbyterian congregations, in the county of [blank] in North-Carolina.* Philadelphia: 1775.

Armstrong, James F. "Righteousness Exalteth A Nation." In *Light to My Path: Sermons by the Rev. James F. Armstrong Revolutionary Chaplain,* edited by Marian B. McLeod, 10-18. Trenton, NJ: First Presbyterian Church, 1976.

Austin, David, Jonathan Edwards II, and Walter King. *Circular Letters, Containing, An Invitation to the Ministers and Churches of Every Christian Denomination in the United States, to Unite in Their Endeavours to carry into Execution the "Humble Attempt" of President Edwards, To promote explicit Agreement and visible Union of God's People, in Extraordinary Prayer, for the revival of Religion and advancement of Christ's Kingdom on Earth.* Concord, MA: George Hough, 1798.

Austin, David, ed. *The American Preacher; or, A collection of sermons from some of the most eminent preachers, now living, in the United States, of different denominations in the Christian Church. Never before published.* 4 vols. Elizabethtown, NJ: Shepard Kollock, 1791.

Baird, Samuel J., ed. *A Collection of the Acts, Deliverances, and Testimonies of the Supreme Judicatory of the Presbyterian Church, From its Origins in America to the Present Time. With Notes and Documents Explanatory and Historical: Constituting a Complete Illustration of Her Polity, Faith, and History.* Philadelphia: Presbyterian Board of Publication, 1856.

Boudinot, J. J., ed. *The Life, Public Services, Addresses, and Letters of Elias Boudinot.* Vol 1. New York: Capo Press, 1971.

Boyd, Julian P., ed. *The Papers of Thomas Jefferson.* Vol. 2. Princeton, NJ: Princeton University Press, 1950.

Brooks, Joanna, ed. *The Collected Writings of Samson Occom, Mohegan: Leadership and Literature in Eighteenth-Century Native America.* New York: Oxford University Press, 2006.

Buell, Samuel. *The excellence and importance of the saving knowledge of the Lord Jesus Christ in the Gospel-preacher, plainly and seriously represented and enforced: and Christ preached to the gentiles in obedience to the call of God. A sermon, preached at East-Hampton, August 29, 1759; at the ordination of Mr. Samson Occum, a missionary among the Indians. By Samuel Buell, M.A. Pastor of the Church of Christ, at East-Hampton, Long-Island. To which is prefixed, a letter to the Rev. Mr. David Bostwick, Minister of the Presbyterian Church, in New-York, giving some account of Mr. Occum's education, character, &c.* New York: James Parker and Company, 1761.

Buist, George. *Oration delivered at the Orphan-House of Charleston, South Carolina, October 18th, 1795, Being the Sixth Anniversary of the Institution.* Charleston, SC: Markland & M'Iver, 1795.

————. *A sermon, preached in the Presbyterian Church, of Charleston; before the incorporated Grand Lodge of South-Carolina, Ancient York Masons. And the brethren of that fraternity assembled in general communication, on the festival of Saint John the Evangelist, December 27, 1793.* Charleston, SC: Harrison and Bowen, 1794.

Butterfield, L. H., ed., *John Witherspoon Comes to America: A Documentary Account Based Largely on New Materials.* Princeton, NJ: Princeton University Press, 1953.

————, ed. *Letters of Benjamin Rush.* Vol. 1, 1761–1792. Princeton, NJ: Princeton University Press, 1951.

Carmichael, John. *A self-defensive war lawful, proved in a sermon, preached at Lancaster, before Captain Ross's company of militia, in the Presbyterian Church on Sabbath morning, June 4th, 1775.* Lancaster, PA: Francis Bailey, 1775.

The Christian's, Scholar's, and Farmer's Magazine. Ann Arbor, MI: University Microfilms, 1979.

Clark, Elmer, T. J. Manning Potts, and Jacob S. Payton, eds. *The Journal and Letters of Francis Asbury.* Vol. 1, Nashville, TN: Abingdon Press, 1958.

A Collection of tracts from the late news papers, &c. Containing particularly The American Whig, A whip for the American Whig, with some other pieces, on the subject of the residence of Protestant bishops in the American colonies, and in answer to the writers who opposed it, &c. New York: John Holt, 1768.

The conduct of the Presbyterian-ministers, who sent the letter to the Archbishop of Canterbury, the year 1760, considered, and set in true light: in answer to some remarks thereon. In a letter to a friend. By an elder of the Presbyterian Church. [Three lines from Isaiah]. Philadelphia: Andrew Steuart, 1761.

Connecticut Congregationalist General Association. *The Records of the General Association of Ye Colony of Connecticut, Begun June 20th, 1738, Ending June 19th, 1799*. Hartford, CT: Press of the Case, Lockwood & Brainard, 1888.

Connecticut Evangelical Magazine. Ann Arbor, MI: University Microfilms, 1979.

Considerations on the nature and the extent of the legislative authority of the British Parliament. Philadelphia: William and Thomas Bradford, 1774.

Davidson, Robert. *An oration, on the independence of the United States of America. Delivered on the 4th of July, 1787. By the Rev. Robert Davidson, D.D. Pastor of the Presbyterian congregation in Carlisle, and professor of history and belles lettres, in Dickinson College*. Carlisle, PA: Kline and Reynolds, 1787.

Davies, Samuel. "Brotherly Love. (annext to a Sermon on 1 John iii. 14. Dec. 9, 1750." In *Collected Poems of Samuel Davies, 1723–1761*, edited by Richard Beale. Gainesville, FL: Scholars' Facsimiles & Reprints, 1968.

———. *A touch stone for the clergy. To which is added, a poem, wrote by a clergyman in Virginia, in a storm of wind and rain*. 1771.

———. *Sermons on the most useful and important subjects, adapted to the family and closet. By the Rev. Samuel Davies, A.M. late President of the College at Princeton in New-Jersey. In three volumes. . . . To which are prefixed, A sermon on the death of Mr Davies, By Samuel Finley, D.D. and another discourse on the same occasion, together with an elegiac poem to the memory of Mr Davies, by Thomas Gibbons, D.D.* London: J. Buckland and J. Payne, 1766.

A Dialogue, containing some reflections on the late declaration and remonstrance, of the back-inhabitants of the province of Pennsylvania. With a serious and short address, to those Presbyterians, who (to their dishonor) have too much abetted, and conniv'd at the late insurrection. By a member of that community. Philadelphia: Andrew Steuart, 1764.

Dove, David James. *The addition to the epitaph, without the copper-plate*. Philadelphia: Anthony Armbruster, 1764.

———. *A Conference between the D——l and Doctor D——e. Together with the doctor's epitaph on himself*. Philadelphia: Andrew Steuart, 1764.

———. *The counter-medly, being a proper answer to all the dunces of the medly and their abettors*. Philadelphia: Anthony Armbruster, 1764.

———. *The Quaker unmask'd; or, Plain truth: humbly address'd to the consideration of all the freemen of Pennsylvania*. Philadelphia: Andrew Steuart, 1764.

Duffield, George. *Psalms Carefully Suited to the Christian Worship in the United States of America. Being An Improvement of the Old Versions of the Psalms of David. Allowed by the reverend Synod of New-York and Philadelphia, to be used in churches and private families*. Philadelphia: Francis Bailey, 1787.

———. *A Sermon Preached in the Third Presbyterian Church in the City of Philadelphia, On Thursday December 11, 1783*. Boston: Reprinted and Sold by T. & J. Fleet, 1784.

Dunbar, John R., ed. *The Paxton Papers*. The Hague, Netherlands: Martinus Nijhoff, 1957.

Foote, William Henry, ed. *Sketches of Virginia, Historical 1789*. Vol. 5. Washington, DC: Government Printing Office, 1906.

Ford, W. C., ed., *Journals of the Continental Congress, 1774–Presbytery of Hudson, September, 1801*. Newburgh: Dennis Coles, 1801.

———. *A Sermon Delivered at New-Windsor and Bethlehem. August 30 1798. Being the Day Appointed by the General Assembly of the Presbyterian Church in the United States of America: To be Observed as a Day of Solemn Humiliation, Fasting and Prayer, in all the Churches under their Care*. New Windsor, NY: Jacob Schultz, 1799.

Freeman, Jonathan. *A Discourse on Psalmody. Delivered at Newburgh, Before the and Biographical*. Richmond, VA: John Knox Press, 1966.

Green, Jacob. *Observations, on the reconciliation of Great-Britain and the colonies. By a friend of American liberty*. New York: John Holt, 1776.

Harker, Samuel. *An appeal from the Synod of New-York and Philadelphia, to the Christian world, relating to the censure and sentence of the said Synod, in their last session at Philadelphia, against the Rev. Mr. Samuel Harker, Pastor of the church at Black-River, in East-Jersey. Written by himself*. Philadelphia: William Dunlap, 1763.

Hunt, Isaac. *A humble attempt at scurrility: in imitation of those great masters of the art, the Rev. Dr. S—th; the Rev. Dr. Al——n; the Rev. Mr. Ew-n; the irreverend D.J. D–ve, and the heroic J—n D———n, Esq; being a full answer to the observations on Mr. H——s's advertisement*. Philadelphia: Anthony Armbruster, 1765.

———. *A looking-glass for Presbyterians. Or A brief examination of their loyalty, merit, and other qualifications for government. With some animadversions on the Quaker unmask'd. Humbly addres'd to the consideration of the loyal freemen of Pennsylvania*. Philadelphia: Anthony Armbruster, 1764.

Keteltas, Abraham. *God arising and pleading his people's cause; or The American war in favor of liberty, against the measures and arms of Great Britain, shewn to be the cause of God: in a sermon preached October 5th, 1777 at an evening lecture, in the Presbyterian church in Newbury-Port*. Newbury, MA: John Mycall, 1777.

Knox, Hugh. *The moral and religious miscellany; or, Sixty-one aphoretical essays, on some of the most important Christian doctrines and virtues*. New York: Hodge and Shober, 1775.

Langdon, Samuel. *A Discourse on the Unity of the Church as a Monumental Pillar of the Truth; Designed to Reconcile Christians of all Parties and Denominations in Charity and Fellowship, as One Body in Christ*. Exeter, NH: Henry Ranlet, 1792.

McCloskey, Robert Green, ed. *The Works of James Wilson*. 2 vols. Cambridge, MA: Belknap Press, 1967.

The mechanick's address to the farmer: being a short reply to some of the layman's Remarks on the eighteen Presbyterian ministers letter to the arch-bishop. Philadelphia: Andrew Steuart, 1761.

Miller, Kerby A., ed. *Irish Immigrants in the Land of Canaan; Letters and Memoirs from Colonial and Revolutionary America, 1675–1815*. Oxford: Oxford University Press, 2003.

Minutes of the Convention of Delegates from the Synod of New York and Philadelphia, and from the Association of Connecticut; held annually from 1766 to 1775, Inclusive. Hartford, CT: E. Gleason, 1843.

Muir, James. *An Examination of the Principles Contained in the Age of Reason. In Ten Discourses. By James Muir, D.D. Minister of the Presbyterian Church, Alexandria.* Baltimore, MD: S. & J. Adams, 1795.

———. *A Funeral Sermon.* Alexandria, VA: Hanson and Bond, 1793.

Murray, John. *Bath-Kol. A voice from the wilderness. Being an humble attempt to support the sinking truths of God, against some of the principal errors, raging at this time. Or, a joint testimony to some of the grand articles of the Christian religion, judicially delivered to the churches under their care. By the first presbytery of the eastward.* Boston: N. Coverly, 1783.

———. *Nehemiah, or The struggle for liberty never in vain, when managed with virtue and perseverance. A discourse delivered at the Presbyterian Church in Newbury-Port, Nov. 4th, 1779. Being the day appointed by government to be observed as a day of solemn fasting and prayer throughout the state of Massachusetts-Bay. Published in compliance with the request of some hearers.* Newbury, MA: John Mycall, 1779.

Nybakken, Elizabeth I., ed. *The Centinel: Warnings of a Revolution.* Newark: University of Delaware Press, 1980.

Occom, Samson. *A Choice collection of hymns and spiritual songs; intended for the edification of sincere Christians, of all denominations.* New London, CT: Timothy Green, 1774.

Osgood, Herbert L., ed. "The Society of Dissenters founded at New York in 1769." *American Historical Review* 6, no. 1 (April 1901): 498–507.

Patillo, Henry. *The plain planter's family assistant; containing an address to husbands and wives, children and servants. With some helps for instruction by catechisms; and examples of devotion for families: with a brief paraphrase on the Lord's prayer.* Wilmington, NC: James Adams, 1787.

Philalethes, *The Quaker vindicated; or, Observations on a late pamphlet, entituled, The Quaker unmask'd, or, Plain truth.* Philadelphia: Andrew Steuart, 1764.

Porter, Samuel. *An Address to the Rev. John Jamison, by Samuel Porter, V.D.M.* Hagerstown, MD: Stewart Herbert, 1794.

Presbyterian General Assembly. *Minutes of the General Assembly of the Presbyterian Church in the United States of America from its Organization, A.D. 1789 to A.D. 1820 Inclusive.* Philadelphia: Presbyterian Board of Publication, n.d.

———. *The Plan for correspondence and friendly intercourse proposed by a convention of delegates appointed by the General Assembly of the Presbyterian Church, the General Synod of the Reformed Dutch Church, and the Synod of the Associate Reformed Church, when met in New York, on the 3d Tuesday of June, 1798, and agreed to be reported to these respective judicatories; which plan has been unanimously approved by the General Assembly of the Presbyterian Church, in May 1799; has been adopted in part, by the Associate Reformed Synod, at their last meeting; and is to come under the consideration of the General Synod of the Reformed Dutch Church, at their next meeting at Albany, on the first Tuesday of June, 1800.* New York, 1800.

———. *Records of the Presbyterian Church in the United States of America, 1706–1788.* Philadelphia: Presbyterian Board of Publication, 1904.

Presbytery of Charleston. *A Collection of hymns for public and private worship, approved of by the Presbytery of Charleston.* Charleston, SC: J. M'Iver, 1796.

———. *Pastoral letter, of the Presbytery of Charleston, to the churches of the Presbyterian denomination, within their bounds.* Charleston, SC: Benjamin Timothy, 1799.

Presbytery of Lexington. *A pastoral letter, from the Presbytery of Lexington, to the people under their care.* Lexington, VA: Presbyterian Church in the USA, 1790.

Prince, Carl E., and Dennis P. Ryan, eds. *The Papers of William Livingston.* 3 vols. Trenton: New Jersey Historical Commission, 1980.

The Religious Monitor. Ann Arbor, MI: University Microfilms, 1979.

Rodgers, John. *The Case of the Scotch Presbyterians, of the city of New-York.* New York, 1773.

———, ed. *The works of the Rev. John Witherspoon, D.D. L.L.D. late president of the college, at Princeton New-Jersey. To which is prefixed an account of the author's life, in a sermon occasioned by his death, by the Rev. Dr. John Rodgers, of New York. In three volumes.* Vol. 3. Philadelphia: Woodward, 1800.

Rhea, Joseph. Joseph Rhea to Ezra Stiles. In Joseph Rhea's Papers, box 1, folder 1, Presbyterian Historical Society, Philadelphia.

Rice, David. *Slavery Inconsistent with Justice and Good Policy Proved By a Speech Delivered in the Convention, Held at Danville, Kentucky.* Philadelphia, 1792.

Philanthropos, (David Rice). *The Universal Peace-Maker, or Modern Author's Instructor.* Philadelphia: Anthony Armbruster, 1764.

Rush, Benjamin. *An Address to the Inhabitants of the British Settlements in America, upon Slave-Keeping.* Philadelphia: Dunlap, 1773.

Selesky, Harold, ed. Ezra Stiles Papers, Correspondence. Yale University, New Haven, CT: National Historical Publications Commission, Microfilm Publication Program, 1976.

Smith, Charles Jeffrey. *The nature and necessity of regeneration, considered in a discourse delivered at Williamsburg, in Virginia: with a dedication to the Episcopal Church in that city: containing, an apology for Presbyterians.* Woodbridge, NJ: Samuel Parker, 1765.

Smith, Robert. *The Obligations of the Confederate States of North America to Praise God.* Baltimore, MD: John Hayes, 1783.

Smylie, James, ed. "Presbyterians and the American Revolution: A Documentary Account." *Journal of Presbyterian History* 52, no. 4 (Winter 1974): 296–487.

Sproat, James. *A discourse, occasioned by the death of the Reverend George Whitefield, A.M. late chaplain to the Right Honourable the countess of Huntingdon; delivered October 14, 1770, in the Second Presbyterian Church, in the city of Philadelphia.* Philadelphia: William and Thomas Bradford, 1771.

Stiles, Ezra. *A Discourse on the Christian Union.* Boston: Edes & Gill, 1761.

Strong, Nathan. *Political Instruction from the Prophecies of God's Word. A Sermon Preached on the State Thanksgiving, November 29, 1799.* New York: G. Forman, 1799.

———. *A Sermon, Preached at the Annual Thanksgiving, November 16th, 1797.* Hartford, CT: Hudson and Goodwin, 1797.

———. *A Thanksgiving Sermon, Delivered November 27th, 1800.* Hartford, CT: Hudson and Goodwin, 1800.

The Substance, of a council held at Lancaster August the 28th 1764. By a committee of Presbyterian ministers and elders deputed from all parts of Pennsylvania, in order to settle the ensuing election of members for the Assembly. Philadelphia: Anthony Armbruster, 1764.

Sweet, William Warren, ed. *Religion on the American Frontier, 1783–1840, Volume II: The Presbyterians, A Collection of Source Materials.* New York: Cooper Square Publishers, 1964.

Synod of New York and Philadelphia. *The plan of union between the Synods of New-York and Philadelphia. Agreed upon May 29th, 1758.* Philadelphia: W. Dunlap, 1758.

Tennent, Gilbert. *The Blessedness of Peace-makers represented; and the Danger of Persecution considered; in Two Sermons, On Mat. v. 9. Preach'd at Philadelphia, the 3d Wednesday in May, 1759, before the Reverend the Synod, of New-York and Philadelphia.* Philadelphia: William Bradford, 1765.

The Theological Magazine. Ann Arbor, MI: University Microfilms, 1979.

Todd, John. *An Humble Attempt towards the Improvement of Psalmody: The Propriety Necessity and Use of Evangelical Psalms, in Christian Worship. Delivered at a Meeting of the Presbytery of Hanover in Virginia, October 6th, 1762.* Philadelphia: Andrew Steuart, 1763.

A True copy of a genuine letter, sent to the Archbishop of Canterbury, by eighteen Presbyterian ministers, in America: with some remarks thereon; in another letter to the congregations of the said ministers. By an old covenanting, and true Presbyterian layman. Philadelphia: Andrew Steuart, 1761.

The United States Christian Magazine. Ann Arbor, MI: University Microfilms, 1979.

Westminster Divines. *The Humble Advice of the Assembly of Divines, Now by Authority of Parliament sitting at Westminster, Concerning A Confession of Faith: With Quotations and Texts of Scripture annexed. Presented by them lately to both Houses of Parliament.* Edinburgh: Reprinted by Evan Tyler, 1647). Available at Princeton Theological Seminary Internet Archive: http://ia700301.us.archive.org/28/items/humbleadviceofas00west/humbleadviceofas00west.pdf.

Wigwagg, Thomas. *The author of Quaker unmask'd strip'd start [sic] naked, or The delineated Presbyterian play'd hob with.* Philadelphia: Anthony Armbruster, 1764.

Woodhull, John. *A sermon, for the day of publick thanksgiving, appointed by the president, on account of the establishment of the new Constitution, &c. November 26, 1789. By the Rev. John Woodhull, A.M. Pastor of the First Presbyterian Church in Freehold.* Trenton, NJ: Isaac Collins, 1790.

Secondary Sources

Abzug, Robert. *Cosmos Crumbling: American Reform and the Religious Imagination.* New York: Oxford University Press, 1994.

Ahlstrom, Sydney E. *A Religious History of the American People.* 2 vols. Garden City, NY: Image Books, 1975.

Alexander, James W. *The Life of Archibald Alexander, D. D. First Professor in the Theological Seminary, at Princeton, New Jersey.* Harrisonburg, VA: Sprinkle Publications, 1991.

Ambrose, Douglas. "Of Stations and Relations: Proslavery Christianity in Early National Virginia," in John R. McKivigan and Mitchell Snay, eds. *Religion and the Antebellum Debate over Slavery.* Athens: University of Georgia Press, 1998.

Anderson, Benedict. *Imagined Communities: Reflections on the Origin and Spread of Nationalism*. New York: Verso, 1991.

Anderson, Fred. *Crucible of War: The Seven Years' War and the Fate of Empire in British North America, 1754–1766*. New York: Vintage Books, 2001.

Appleby, Joyce. *Inheriting the Revolution: The First Generation of Americans*. Cambridge, MA: Harvard University Press, 2000.

Aron, Stephen. *How the West Was Lost: The Transformation of Kentucky from Daniel Boone to Henry Clay*. Baltimore, MD: Johns Hopkins University Press, 1996.

Bailyn, Bernard. *The Ideological Origins of the American Revolution*. Cambridge, MA: Harvard University Press, 1967.

Baird, Robert. *Religion in America, Or, An Account of the Origin, Progress, Relation to the State, and Present Condition of the Evangelical Churches in the United States*. Philadelphia: Harper, 1844.

Baldwin, Alice. "Sowers of Sedition: The Political Theories of Some of the New Light Presbyterian Clergy of Virginia and North Carolina." *William and Mary Quarterly* 3, no. 5 (1948): 52–76.

Balmer, Randall. *A Perfect Babel of Confusion: Dutch Religion and English Culture in the Middle Colonies*. New York: Oxford University Press, 1989.

Balmer, Randall, and John R. Fitzmier. *The Presbyterians*. Westport, CT: Praeger, 1994.

Baxbaum, Melvin H. *Benjamin Franklin and the Zealous Presbyterians*. University Park: Penn State University Press, 1975.

Bell, Whitfield Jenks. *Patriot-improvers: Biographical Sketches of Members of the American Philosophical Society*. Darby, PA: Diane Publishing, 1997.

Bell, James B. *A War of Religion: Dissenters, Anglicans, and the American Revolution*. New York: Palgrave Macmillan, 2008.

Berlin, Ira. *Many Thousands Gone: The First Two Centuries of Slavery in North America*. Cambridge, MA: Belknap Press, 2000.

Bloch, Ruth. *Visionary Republic: Millennial Themes in American Thought, 1756–1800*. New York: Cambridge University Press, 1989.

Boles, John B. *The Great Revival: Beginnings of the Bible Belt*. Lexington: University Press of Kentucky, 1996.

Bonomi, Patricia U. *Under the Cope of Heaven: Religion, Society, and Politics in Colonial America*. New York: Oxford University Press, 2003.

Boyd, James P. *Sacred Scripture, Sacred War: The Bible and the American Revolution*. New York: Oxford University Press, 2013.

Breed, W. P. *Presbyterians and the Revolution*. Decatur, MS: Issacharian Press, 1993.

Breitenbach, William. "The Consistent Calvinism of the New Divinity Movement." *William and Mary Quarterly* 41, no. 2 (1984): 241–64.

Bridenbaugh, Carl. *Mitre and Sceptre: Transatlantic Faiths, Ideas, Personalities, and Politics, 1689–1775*. New York: Oxford University Press, 1962.

Brown, John. *The Pilgrim Fathers of New England and their Puritan Successors*. Pasadena, TX: Pilgrim Publications, 1970.

Buckley, Thomas E. *Church and State in Revolutionary Virginia, 1776–1787*. Charlottesville: University of Virginia Press, 1977.

Butler, Jon. *Awash in a Sea of Faith; Christianizing the American People.* Cambridge, MA: Harvard University Press, 1990.

———. *Becoming America: The Revolution Before 1776.* Cambridge, MA: Harvard University Press, 2001.

Calhoon, Robert M. *Evangelicals and Conservatives in the Early South, 1740–1861.* Columbia: University of South Carolina Press, 1988.

———. *Religion and the American Revolution in North Carolina.* Raleigh: North Carolina Department of Cultural Resources, 1976.

———. "Religion, Moderation, and Regime-Building in Post-Revolutionary America." In *Empire and Nation: The American Revolution in the Atlantic World*, edited by Eliga H. Gould and Peter S. Onuf, 217–36. Baltimore, MD: Johns Hopkins University Press, 2005.

———. "The religious consequences of the Revolution." In *A Companion to the American Revolution*, edited by Jack P. Greene and J. R. Pole, 579–85. Malden, MA: Blackwell Publishing, 2004.

Carroll, Bret E. *The Routledge Historical Atlas of Religion in America.* New York: Routledge Press, 2000.

Cayton, Andrew R. L. "'When Shall We Cease to Have Judases?': The Blount Conspiracy and the Limits of the Extended Republic." In *Launching the "Extended Republic": The Federalist Era*, edited by Ronald J. Hoffman and Peter J. Albert, 156–89. Charlottesville: University of Virginia Press, 1996.

Clark, J. C. D. *The Language of Liberty, 1660–1832: Political Discourse and Social Dynamics in the Anglo-American World.* New York: Cambridge University Press, 1994.

Coalter, Milton J. *Gilbert Tennent, Son of Thunder: A Case Study of Continental Pietism's Impact on the First Great Awakening in the Middle Colonies.* Westport, CT: Greenwood Publishing Group, 1986.

Conforti, Joseph A. *Samuel Hopkins and the New Divinity Movement: Calvinism, the Congregational Ministry, and Reform in New England between the Great Awakenings.* Grand Rapids, MI: Christian University Press, 1981.

Conkin, Paul. *Cane Ridge: America's Pentecost.* Madison: University of Wisconsin Press, 1990.

Cooper, William J. *Liberty and Slavery: Southern Politics to 1860.* New York: Alfred A. Knopf, 1983.

Cross, Arthur Lyon. *The Anglican Episcopate and the American Colonies.* New York: Longmans, Green, and Co., 1902.

Countryman, Edward. *The American Revolution.* New York: Hill and Wang, 2003.

Daniel, W. Harrison. "Southern Presbyterians and the Negro in the Early National Period." *Journal of Negro History* 58, no. 3 (July 1973): 291–312.

Davidson, Robert. *History of the Presbyterian Church in the State of Kentucky; with a Preliminary Sketch of the Churches in the Valley of Virginia.* New York: Robert Carter, 1847.

Davis, David Brion. *Inhuman Bondage: The Rise and Fall of Slavery in the New World.* New York: Oxford University Press, 2006.

———. *The Problem of Slavery in the Age of Revolution, 1770–1823.* Ithaca, NY: Cornell University Press, 1975.

De Jong, Gerald F. *The Dutch Reformed Church in the American Colonies.* Grand Rapids, MI: William B. Eerdmans Publishing, 1978.

D'Elia, Donald J. *Benjamin Rush: Philosopher of the American Revolution.* Transactions of the American Philosophical Society. Vol. 64, no. 5. Philadelphia: American Philosophical Society, 1974.

Den Hartog, Jonathan J. *Patriotism & Piety: Federalist Politics and Religious Struggle in the New American Nation.* Charlottesville: University of Virginia Press, 2015.

Dillon, Dorothy Rita. *The New York Triumvirate: A Study of the Legal and Political Careers of William Livingstone, John Morin Scott, and William Smith, Jr.* New York: Columbia University Press, 1949.

Dowd, Gregory Evans. *A Spirited Resistance: The North American Indian Struggle for Unity, 1745–1815.* Baltimore, MD: John Hopkins University Press, 1992.

Egerton, Douglas R. *Death or Liberty: African Americans and Revolutionary America.* New York: Oxford University Press, 2009.

Elliott, Kenneth R. *Anglican Church Policy, Eighteenth Century Conflict, and the American Episcopate.* New York: Peter Lang Academic Publishers, 2011.

Farmer, James O. Jr. *The Metaphysical Confederacy: James Henley Thornwell and the Synthesis of Southern Values.* Macon, GA: Mercer University Press, 1986.

Ferling, John E. *Struggle for a Continent: The Wars of Early America.* Arlington Heights, IL: Harlan Davidson, 1993.

Ferm, Robert L. *A Colonial Pastor: Jonathan Edwards the Younger, 1745–1801.* Grand Rapids, MI: William B. Eerdmans Publishing, 1976.

Finke, Roger, and Rodney Stark. *The Churching of America, 1776–1990: Winners and Losers in Our Religious Economy.* New Brunswick, NJ: Rutgers University Press, 1992.

Fischer, David Hackett. *Albion's Seed: Four British Folkways in America.* New York: Oxford University Press, 1991.

Fleming, Thomas, ed, *Benjamin Franklin: A Biography in His Own Words.* Vol. 1. New York: *Newsweek*, 1972.

Foster, Charles I. *An Errand of Mercy: The Evangelical United Front, 1790–1837.* Chapel Hill: University of North Carolina Press, 1960.

Foster, Stephen. *The Long Argument: English Puritanism and the Shaping of New England Culture, 1570–1700.* Chapel Hill: University of North Carolina Press, 1991.

Freehling, William W. *The Road to Disunion, Volume I: Secessionists at Bay, 1776–1854.* New York: Oxford University Press, 1990.

Gaustad, Edwin Scott, and Philip L. Barlow. *New Historical Atlas of Religion in America.* Oxford: Oxford University Press, 2001.

Gigantino, James J. *The Ragged Road to Abolition: Slavery and Freedom in New Jersey.* Philadelphia: University of Pennsylvania Press, 2015.

Glascow, Maude. *The Scotch-Irish in Northern Ireland and in the American Colonies.* New York: G. P. Putnam's Sons, 1936.

Glasgow, W. Melancthon. *History of the Reformed Presbyterian Church in America.* Baltimore, MD: Hill & Harvey Publishers, 1888.

Goff, Philip. "Revivals and Revolution: Historiographic Turns since Alan Heimert's Religion and the American Mind." *Church History* 67, no. 4 (December 1998): 696–721.

Griffin, Keith L. *Revolution and Religion: American Revolutionary War and the Reformed Clergy*. New York: Paragon House, 1994.

Hall, David D. *Cultures of Print: Essays in the History of the Book*. Amherst: University of Massachusetts Press, 1996.

Halsey, Francis Whiting. *The Old New York Frontier: Its Wars with Indians and Tories; Its Missionary Schools, Pioneers and Land Titles, 1614–1800*. New York: Charles Scribner's Sons, 1901.

Hammond, John Craig. "Slavery, Settlement, and Empire: The Expansion and Growth of Slavery in the Interior of the North American Continent, 1770–1820." *Journal of the Early Republic* 32, no. 2 (2012): 175–206.

Harrison, Lowell Hayes and James C. Clotter, *A New History of Kentucky*. Lexington: University of Kentucky Press, 1997.

Hart, D. G., and John R. Muether. *Seeking a Better Country: 300 Years of American Presbyterianism*. Phillipsburg, NJ: P&R Publishing, 2007.

Hatch, Nathan O. *The Democratization of American Christianity*. New Haven, CT: Yale University Press, 1989.

———. *The Sacred Cause of Liberty: Republican Thought and the Millennium in Revolutionary New England*. New Haven, CT: Yale University Press, 1977.

Haynes, Stephen, and Franklin H. Littell. *Holocaust Education and the Church-Related College: Restoring Ruptured Traditions*. Westport, CT: Greenwood Press, 1997.

Headley, Joel Tyler. *The Forgotten Heroes of Liberty: Chaplains and Clergy of the American Revolution*. Birmingham, AL: Solid Ground Christian Books, 2005.

Heimert, Alan. *Religion and the American Mind: From the Great Awakening to the American Revolution*. Cambridge, MA: Harvard University Press, 1966.

Heyrman, Christine Leigh. *The Southern Cross: The Beginnings of the Bible Belt*. Chapel Hill: University of North Carolina Press, 1998.

Hobsbawm, E. J. *Nations and Nationalism since 1780: Programme, Myth, Reality*. New York: Cambridge University Press, 1992.

Hoeveler, J. David. *Creating the American Mind: Intellect and Politics in the Colonial Colleges*. New York: Rowman & Littlefield Publishers, 2002.

Holt, Michael F. *The Political Crisis of the 1850s*. New York: W. W. Norton & Company, 1983.

Hood, Fred J. *Reformed America: The Middle and Southern States, 1783–1837*. Tuscaloosa: University of Alabama Press, 1980.

Humphrey, Edward Frank. *Nationalism and Religion in America, 1774–1789*. New York: Russell & Russell, 1965.

Hutson, James H. *Pennsylvania Politics 1746–1770: The Movement for Royal Government and Its Consequences*. Princeton, NJ: Princeton University Press, 1972.

Ireland, Owen S. *Religion, Ethnicity, and Politics: Ratifying the Constitution in Pennsylvania*. University Park: Penn State University Press, 1995.

Irons, Charles F. *The Origins of Proslavery Christianity: White and Black Evangelicals in Colonial and Antebellum Virginia*. Chapel Hill: University of North Carolina Press, 2008.

Isaac, Rhys. *The Transformation of Virginia, 1740–1790*. Chapel Hill: University of North Carolina Press, 1999.

Jackson, Joseph. "A Philadelphia Schoolmaster of the Eighteenth Century." *Pennsylvania Magazine of History and Biography* 35 (1911): 315–322.

Johnson, Paul E. *A Shopkeeper's Millennium: Society and Revivals in Rochester, New York, 1815–1837*. New York: Hill and Wang, 2004.

Kenny, Kevin. *Peaceable Kingdom Lost: The Paxton Boys and the Destruction of William Penn's Holy Experiment*. New York: Oxford University Press: 2009.

Ketchum, Richard M. *Saratoga: Turning Point of America's Revolutionary War*. New York: Macmillan, 1999.

Kidd, Thomas S. *God of Liberty: A Religious History of the American Revolution*. New York: Basic Books, 2010).

———. *The Great Awakening: The Roots of Evangelical Christianity in Colonial America* . New Haven, CT: Yale University Press, 2007.

Kidd, Thomas S., and Barry Hankins. *The Baptists in America: A History*. New York: Oxford University Press, 2015.

Knupfer, Peter B. *The Union As It Is: Constitutional Unionism and Sectional Compromise, 1787–1861*. Chapel Hill: University of North Carolina Press, 1991.

Kolchin, Peter. *American Slavery, 1619–1877*. New York: Hill and Wang, 1993.

Kramer, Leonard J. "Muskets in the Pulpit: 1776–1783." *Journal of Presbyterian History* 31, no. 4 (December 1953): 229–44.

Le Beau, Bryan F. *Jonathan Dickinson and the Formative Years of American Presbyterianism*. Lexington: University Press of Kentucky, 1997.

Liensch, Michael. "The Role of Political Millennialism in Early American Nationalism." *Western Political Quarterly* 36, no. 3 (September 1983): 445–65.

Longfield, Bradley J. *Presbyterians and American Culture: A History*. Louisville, KY: Westminster John Knox Press, 2013.

Love, William DeLoss. *Samson Occom and the Christian Indians of New England*. Cleveland: Pilgrim Press, 1899.

MacPherson, John. *The Westminster Confession of Faith. With Introduction and Notes by the Reverend John MacPherson, MA*. Edinburgh: T & T Clark, 1881.

Mailer, Gideon. "Anglo-Scottish Union and John Witherspoon's American Revolution." *William and Mary Quarterly* 67, no. 4 (October 2010): 709–46.

Marini, Stephen. "Religion, Politics, and Ratification." In *Religion in a Revolutionary Age*, edited by Ronald Hoffman and Peter J. Albert, 184–217. Charlottesville: University of Virginia Press, 1994.

Marsden, George M. *The Evangelical Mind and the New School Presbyterian Experience: A Case Study of Thought and Theology in Nineteenth-Century America*. New Haven, CT: Yale University Press, 1970.

———. *Religion and American Culture*. New York: Harcourt Brace Jovanovich College Publishers, 1990.

Mathews, Donald G. *Religion in the Old South*. Chicago: University of Chicago Press, 1977.

McDonald, Forrest. *E Pluribus Unum: The Formation of the American Republic, 1776–1790*. Indianapolis, IN: Liberty Fund, 1979.

McDougall, Walter A. *Throes of Democracy: The American Civil War Era, 1829–1877*. New York: HarperCollins Publishers, 2008.

McGrath, Alistair E. *Iustitia Dei: A History of the Christian Doctrine of Justification*. 2 vols. Cambridge, UK: Cambridge University Press, 1986,

———. *Reformation Thought: An Introduction*. Oxford, UK: Basil Blackwell, 1988.

McLoughlin, William G. *Revivals, Awakenings, and Reform: An Essay on Religion and Social Change in America, 1607–1977*. Chicago: University of Chicago Press, 1978.

McPherson, James. *Battle Cry of Freedom: The Civil War Era*. New York: Oxford University Press, 2003.

Messer, Peter C. *Stories of Independence: Identity, Ideology, and History in Eighteenth-Century America*. DeKalb: Northern Illinois University Press, 2005.

Miller, Howard. *The Revolutionary College: American Presbyterian Higher Education 1707–1837*. New York: New York University Press, 1976.

Moore, Joseph S. *Founding Sins: How a Group of Antislavery Radicals Fought to Put Christ into the Constitution*. New York: Oxford University Press, 2016.

Moorehead, James H. "The 'Restless Spirit of Radicalism': Old School Fears and the Schism of 1837." *Journal of Presbyterian History* 78, no. 1 (Spring 2000): 19–33.

Morgan, Edmund S., and Helen M. Morgan. *The Stamp Act Crisis: Prologue to Revolution*. New York: Collier Books, 1963.

Morrison, Jeffry H. *John Witherspoon and the Founding of the American Republic*. Notre Dame, IN: University of Notre Dame Press, 2005.

Mott, Frank Luther. *American Journalism: A History, 1690–1960*. New York: Macmillan, 1962.

Mulder, Philip N. *A Controversial Spirit: Evangelical Awakenings in the South*. New York: Oxford University Press, 2002.

Murray, Andrew E. *Presbyterians and the Negro: A History*. Philadelphia: Presbyterian Historical Society, 1966.

Nash, Gary B. *Unknown American Revolution: The Unruly Birth of Democracy and the Struggle to Create America*. New York: Viking, 2005.

Neill, Edward D. "Matthew Wilson, D. D., of Lewes, Delaware." *Pennsylvania Magazine of History and Biography* 8 (1884): 45–56.

Newman, Simon P. *Parades and the Politics of the Street: Festive Culture in the Early American Republic*. Philadelphia: University of Pennsylvania Press, 1997.

Noll, Mark A. *America's God: From Jonathan Edwards to Abraham Lincoln*. New York: Oxford University Press, 2002.

———. *A History of Christianity in the United States and Canada*. Grand Rapids, MI: William. B. Eerdmans Publishing, 1992.

———. *The Old Religion in a New World: The History of North American Christianity*. Grand Rapids, MI: William B. Eerdmans Publishing, 2002.

———. *Princeton and the Republic, 1768–1822: The Search for a Christian Enlightenment in the Era of Samuel Stanhope Smith*. Princeton, NJ: Princeton University Press, 1989.

———. *The Rise of Evangelicalism: The Age of Edwards, Whitefield, and the Wesleys*. Downers Grove, IL: InterVarsity Press, 2003.

Nord, David Paul. *Communities of Journalism: A History of American Newspapers and Their Readers.* Chicago: University of Illinois Press, 2001.

Norton, Herman A. *Religion in Tennessee 1777–1945.* Knoxville: University of Tennessee Press, 1981.

Nybakken, Elizabeth I. *The Centinel, Warnings of a Revolution.* Newark: University of Delaware Press, 1979.

———. "A New Light on the Old Side: Irish Influences on Colonial Presbyterianism." *Journal of American History* 68, no. 4 (March 1982): 813–32.

Oast, Jennifer. "'The Worst Kind of Slavery': Slave-Owning Presbyterian Churches in Prince Edward County, Virginia." *Journal of Southern History* 76, no. 4 (November 2010): 867–900.

O'Brien, Susan. "A Transatlantic Community of Saints: The Great Awakening and the First Evangelical Network, 1735–1755." *American Historical Review* 91, no. 4 (October 1986): 811–32.

Oshatz, Molly. *Slavery and Sin: The Fight Against Slavery and the Rise of Liberal Protestantism.* New York: Oxford University Press, 2012.

Othow, Helen Chavis. *John Chavis: African American Patriot, Preacher, Teacher, and Mentor, 1763–1838.* Jefferson, NC: McFarland and Company, 2001.

Pocock, J. G. A. *The Machiavellian Moment: Florentine Political Thought and the Atlantic Republican Tradition.* Princeton, NJ: Princeton University Press, 1975.

Potter, David M. *The Impending Crisis, 1848–1861.* San Francisco: Harper Perennial, 1976.

Purvis, Thomas L. *Revolutionary America, 1763 to 1800.* New York: Facts on File, 1995.

Richards, Jeffrey H. "Samuel Davies and the Transatlantic Campaign for Slave literacy in Virginia." *Virginia Magazine of History and Biography* 111, no. 4 (2003): 333–78.

Robbins, Caroline. *The Eighteenth-Century Commonwealthman: Studies in the Transmission, Development, and Circumstance of English Liberal Thought from the Restoration of Charles II until the War with the Thirteen Colonies.* Cambridge, MA: Harvard University Press, 1959.

Robson, David. W. *Educating Republicans: The College in the Era of the American Revolution, 1750–1800.* Westport, CT: Greenwood Press, 1985.

Rohrer, S. Scott. *Jacob Green's Revolution: Radical Religion and Reform in a Revolutionary Age.* University Park: Penn State University Press, 2014.

Rothermund, Dietmar. *The Layman's Progress: Religious and Political Experience in Colonial Pennsylvania, 1740–1770.* Philadelphia: University of Pennsylvania Press, 1961.

Rothman, Adam. *Slave Country: American Expansion and the Origins of the Deep South.* Cambridge, MA: Harvard University Press, 2005.

Sandoz, Ellis. *Republicanism, Religion, and the Soul of America.* Columbia: University of Missouri Press, 2006.

Sassi, Jonathan. *A Republic of Righteousness: The Public Christianity of the Post-Revolutionary New England Clergy.* New York: Oxford University Press, 2001.

Schmidt, Leigh Eric. *Holy Fairs: Scotland and the Making of American Revivalism.* Grand Rapids, MI: William B. Eerdmans Publishing, 2001.

Schneider, A. Gregory. "From Democratization to Domestication: The Transitional

Orality of the American Methodists Circuit Rider." In *Communication and Change in American Religious History*, edited by Leonard I. Sweet, 141–64. Grand Rapids, MI: William B. Eerdmans Publishing, 1993.

Smith, Elwyn A. *The Presbyterian Ministry in American Culture: A Study in Changing Concepts*. Philadelphia: Westminster Press, 1962.

Smylie, James. *A Brief History of the Presbyterians*. Louisville, KY: Geneva Press, 1996.

———. "Samuel Davies: Preacher, Teacher, and Pastor." In *Colonial Presbyterianism: Old Faith in a New Land*, edited by Donald Fortson III, 181–98. Eugene, OR: Pickwick Publications, 2007.

Snay, Mitchell. *Gospel of Disunion Religion and Separatism in the Antebellum South*. New York: Cambridge University Press, 1993.

Sprague, William B. *Annals of the American Pulpit: Or, Commemorative Notices of Distinguished American Clergymen of Various Denominations: from the Early Settlement of the Country to the Close of the Year Eighteen Hundred and Fifty-five: with Historical Introductions*. New York: Robert Carter & Brothers, 1858.

Sweet, William Warren. *Religion in the Development of American Culture, 1765–1840*. New York: Charles Scribner's Sons, 1952.

———. *The Story of Religion in America*. New York: Harper & Brothers Publishers, 1939.

Tait, Gordon L. "John Witherspoon's Prescription for a Nation Strong, Free, and Virtuous." In *Colonial Presbyterianism: Old Faith in a New Land*, edited by Donald Fortson III, 199–218. Eugene, OR: Pickwick Publications, 2007.

Taylor, Alan. *American Colonies: The Settling of North America*. New York: Penguin Books, 2002.

Taylor, Stephen. "Whigs, Bishops and America: The Politics of Church Reform in Mid-Eighteenth-Century England." In *Historical Journal* 36, no. 2 (June 1993): 331–56.

Taylor, William Harrison, and Peter C. Messer, eds. *Faith and Slavery in the Presbyterian Diaspora*. Bethlehem, PA: Lehigh University Press, 2016.

Thelin, John R. *A History of American Higher Education*. Baltimore, MD: Johns Hopkins University Press, 2004.

Thomas, Peter D. G. "The Stamp Act crisis and its repercussions, including the Quartering Act controversy." In *A Companion to the American Revolution*, edited by Jack P. Greene and J. R. Pole, 123–33. Malden, MA: Blackwell Publishing, 2004.

Thompson, Ernest Trice. *Presbyterians in the South, Volume One: 1607–1861*. Richmond, VA: John Knox Press, 1963.

———. *The Spirituality of the Church: A Distinctive Doctrine of the Presbyterian Church in the United States*. Richmond, VA: John Knox Press, 1961.

Thornton, J. Mills III. *Politics and Power in a Slave State: Alabama, 1800–1860*. Baton Rouge: Louisiana State University Press, 1978.

Toulouse, Mark G., Gary Holloway, and Douglas A. Foster. *Renewing Christian Unity: A Concise History of the Christian Church (Disciples of Christ)*. Abilene, TX: Abilene Christian University Press, 2010.

Trinterud, Leonard J. *The Forming of an American Tradition: A Re-examination of Colonial Presbyterianism*. Philadelphia: Westminster Press, 1949.

Tuveson, Ernest Lee. *Redeemer Nation: The Idea of America's Millennial Role*. Chicago: University of Chicago Press, 1968.

Valeri, Mark. *Law and Providence in Joseph Bellamy's New England: The Origins of the New Divinity in Revolutionary America*. New York: Oxford University Press, 1994.

Waldstreicher, David. *In the Midst of Perpetual Fetes: The Making of American Nationalism, 1776–1820*. Chapel Hill: University of North Carolina Press, 1997.

Walker, Williston. *The Creeds and Platforms of Congregationalism*. Philadelphia: Pilgrim Press, 1969.

Weeks, Louis B. *Kentucky Presbyterians*. Atlanta: John Knox Press, 1983.

———. *A New Christian Nation*. College Park, MD: McGrath Publishing, 1977.

Westerkamp, Marilyn J. *Triumph of the Laity: Scots-Irish Piety and the Great Awakening, 1625–1760*. New York: Oxford University Press, 1987.

Wigger, John H. *Taking Heaven by Storm: Methodism and the Rise of Popular Christianity in America*. New York: Oxford University Press, 1998.

Wood, Gordon S. *The Radicalism of the American Revolution*. New York: Vintage Books, 1993.

———. "Religion and the American Revolution." In *New Directions in American Religious History*, edited by Harry S. Stout and D. G. Hart, 173–205. New York: Oxford University Press, 1997.

Woolverton, John Frederick. *Colonial Anglicanism in North America*. Detroit, MI: Wayne State University Press, 1984.

Youngs, J. William T. *The Congregationalists*. Westport, CT: Greenwood Publishing Group, 1998.

Zilversmit, Arthur. *First Emancipation: The Abolition of Slavery in the North*. Chicago: University of Chicago Press, 1967.

Index

127, 157n31; Old Testament, 67, 72;
New Testament, 85, 111, 125
bishopric crisis, 2, 6, 45–52, 143n52,
144n62
Black, John, 87
Blair, John, 39, 42
Blair, Samuel, 42–43, 89
Bostwick, David, 12–13, 135n22
Boudinot, Elias, 85, 148n48, 153n24,
159n50, 162n26
Bourne, George, 119
Brainerd, David, 16, 18
Brainerd, John, 16, 18
Bryan, George, 44, 48, 144n68, 148n48,
149n54, 152n17
Buell, Samuel, 17–18
Buist, George, 99–101, 117

Caldwell, James, 60, 64, 73
Calvin, John (Calvinism), 24, 118, 126,
136n35, 160n62
Campbell, Alexander, 123
Cane Ridge. *See* revivals (revivalism)
Carmichael, John, 59–60
"Centinel," 48–50, 144n63, 144n69
Chandler, Thomas Bradbury, 47–49,
144n60
Chauncey, Charles, 48
Chavis, John, 112, 136n43
Cherokee, 17, 136n40
Christendom (Christian Church, "catholic
spirit of Christianity"), 1, 7, 10, 13,
15–18, 20, 25, 28–30, 32–34, 36, 37,
40, 51, 53–55, 58, 69, 75–79, 80, 82,
84, 86–88, 93–94, 96, 100–102, 104,
116, 117, 123, 124, 131n2
Christian Churches (Christian Movement),
2, 122
Christian liberty ("xtian liberty," liberty of
conscience), 15, 26, 32, 37, 40, 52, 68,
82, 89, 99, 105–6, 121, 139n84
Church of Christ, 8, 161n79
Civil War, 1, 129
Clarendon Code, 19
College of Charleston, 99

College of New Jersey (Princeton), 19, 30,
40–43, 47, 54, 63, 75, 83, 127, 143n35
College of Philadelphia, 40, 44
Conestoga, 27
Congregationalists, 2, 7–8, 17, 25, 41,
46–47, 48–49, 52, 54, 73, 80, 81,
87–89, 95, 98, 112, 115, 117, 122,
124–25, 132n9, 134n11, 136n35,
137n8, 138n59, 141n106, 145n87,
145n89, 153n35, 154n42, 155n59;
of Connecticut, 7, 45, 88, 95–97, 98;
of Massachusetts, 47, 88; of New
Hampshire, 47, 88; of Rhode Island, 47
Constitution, UK, 6, 35, 36, 47–53, 58,
60–61, 62, 68, 75, 144n63, 145n89,
150n1
Constitution, US, 4–5, 7, 83–85, 92,
152n15, 152n17
Continental Congress, 59–60, 63
Covenanters, 138n60; "Old Covenanter,"
20–22
covenant of grace, 22–24
Cross, Robert, 16, 136n36
Cumberland Presbyterians, 8, 119, 122,
123, 161n79
Curse of Cain, 66–67

David, 31, 74
Davidson, Robert, 83–84, 89
Davies, Samuel, 17–18, 19, 29–30, 33–34,
140n103, 146n100
Declaration of Independence, 60–61,
145n87, 150n1, 157n32
Dickinson College, 83
Dickinson, Jonathan, 48, 144n68
Disciples of Christ, 119, 122, 123
Dissenters (colonial), 2, 22, 29, 34, 46–47,
49, 137n49, 145n77
Dove, David James, 28, 139n96
Duffield, George, 43–44, 73–74, 78,
89–90; son of (also named George
Duffield), 127, 147n11, 152n12
Dwight, Timothy, 87, 122

Eakin, Samuel, 44

Presbytery of Donegal, 39–40, 43–45, 142n19

Presbytery of Hanover, 30–32, 112–13, 121–22, 141n112, 158n35

Presbytery of Lexington, 112, 115–16, 158n35

Presbytery of Long Island, 17

Presbytery of New Brunswick, 10–11, 23, 30, 64, 158n35

Presbytery of New York, 11, 88, 158n35

Presbytery of Orange, 114–15

Presbytery of Philadelphia, 39–40, 44, 128

Presbytery of Philadelphia (Second), 39–40, 44

Presbytery of Redstone, 101, 158n35

Presbytery of Suffolk County, 105

Presbytery of Transylvania, 111–12

Prime, Ebenezer, 64

Princeton. *See* College of New Jersey (Princeton)

Princeton Seminary, 126–27

proprietary party, 27–29

Protestation, 11

"Protestant United Front," 125, 128

psalmody (psalms): controversy over, 30–32, 105, 106, 121–22; of Isaac Watts or Watts and Barlow, 30–32, 89–91, 121–22, 154n42; the *New-England* or *Sternhold and Hopkins*, 30–31; *Rouse's* or the *Scotch Version*, 30–31; related to Samson Occom, 54–55

Puritans, 18, 150n1

Purviance Jr., Samuel, 41–42

Quaker party, 27–29

Quakers, 48, 60, 71, 76, 139n95, 139–40n96, 144n68

Rankin, John, 119

Real Whig ideology, 3

Reformed faith: Reformed churches, 3, 16, 47, 51, 80–81, 88–89, 95, 98, 136n35, 151n2, 151n4, 151n7; Reformed tradition, 6, 122, 128, 163n27

"religious newcomers," 2–3, 123

republicanism, 4, 93–94, 100–101, 123, 152n14, 162n15

Restoration movement, 123

revivals (revivalism), 10, 88, 89, 128, 163n37; Cane Ridge, 117–20, 161n76, 161n79; Hampden-Sydney, 112–14, 115, 117–18, 119; Logan County, 117–18

Rhea, Joseph, 44–45

Rice, David (Philanthropos), 32–33, 56, 108–12, 141n112, 148n48, 159n43

Richardson, William, 17, 30, 136n40

Robinson, William ("One-Eyed"), 29

Rodgers, John, 40, 48, 73, 81, 145n89, 146n1, 151n3

Rosborough, John, 64

Ruggles, Thomas, 46

Rush, Benjamin, 42–43, 63, 66–69, 71, 73, 79, 84–85, 104, 106, 142n28, 148n38, 152n17, 156n11

Scott, John Morin, 48, 50–51, 145n77

scriptures. *See* Bible (scriptures)

Second Presbyterian Church in Philadelphia, 53, 88, 105

"sectarian" movement, 122–24

slavery, 4, 5, 7, 17, 33, 66, 73–74, 79, 104–8, 109–11, 112, 119, 125, 129, 149n55, 157n32, 158n39, 159n41, 159n50, 161n80, 163n37; proslavery ideology, 66–67, 104, 107–8, 111, 157n30

Smith, Charles Jeffrey, 33–34, 137n48

Smith, Elias, 123

Smith, John Blair, 113–14, 158n35

Smith, Robert, 24, 78

Smith, Samuel Stanhope, 75–76, 82, 152n17, 156n11

Smith, William (Anglican), 40

Smith Jr., William (Presbyterian), 48

Society for Managing the Mission and School Society for the Propagation of the Gospel, 17

Society for the Propagation of the Gospel in Foreign Parts, 17, 19